P9-AGH-501

Global Environmental Governance
Options & Opportunities

Daniel C. Esty and Maria H. Ivanova, EDITORS

YALE SCHOOL OF FORESTRY & ENVIRONMENTAL STUDIES

2002

Volume editors	Daniel C. Esty and Maria H. Ivanova
Series editor	Jane Coppock
Editorial assistants	Pierre-Luc Arsenault, Melissa Goodall, Emily Noah
Graphic design	Peter W. Johnson and Maura Gianakos
Page layout	Dottie Scott, Tupos Type House
Printing	Yale Reprographics and Imaging Services (RIS)
Paper	Mohawk Crème Satin, recycled
Cover image	*New Light 2: Self Portrait 3*, a quilt by David Walker, Artist, Teacher, and Quiltmaker, Cincinnati, Ohio, www.davidwalker.us Original piece reproduced courtesy of the collection of Kathy and Dennis Bryant, Winters, CA.

The editors gratefully acknowledge generous support from the following in the production of this volume:

Heinrich Böll Foundation
http://www.boell.de

The Yale Center for the Study of Globalization
http://www.ycsg.yale.edu

Yale School of Forestry & Environmental Studies
http://www.yale.edu/environment

YCELP

Yale Center for Environmental Law & Policy
http://www.yale.edu/envirocenter

The opinions, findings, and interpretations of research contained in this volume are those of the individual authors and do not necessarily reflect positions of their institutions or the Yale School of Forestry & Environmental Studies.

ISBN 0-9707882-2-3

© 2002 Yale School of Forestry & Environmental Studies.
Permission is granted to reproduce articles in this volume without prior written consent so long as proper attribution is made. Downloadable PDFs of individual chapters are available at no charge at www.yale.edu/environment/publications. Order forms for hard copies of the volume are available at the same website.

Table of Contents

Note from the Editors   5
Daniel C. Esty and Maria H. Ivanova

Foreword   9
Strobe Talbott

The Global Environmental Agenda: Origins and Prospects   11
James Gustave Speth

Flying Blind: Assessing Progress Toward Sustainability   31
David Hales and Robert Prescott-Allen

The North-South Knowledge Divide: 53
Consequences for Global Environmental Governance
Sylvia Karlsson

The Role of NGOs and Civil Society in Global   77
Environmental Governance
Barbara Gemmill and Abimbola Bamidele-Izu

Regional Environmental Governance: Examining the   101
Association of Southeast Asian Nations (ASEAN) Model
Koh Kheng Lian and Nicholas A. Robinson

Global Public Policy Networks as Coalitions for Change   121
Charlotte Streck

Sustaining Global Environmental Governance: 141
Innovation in Environment and
Development Finance
Maritta R.v.B. Koch-Weser

Making Environmental Deals: The Economic Case   163
for a World Environmental Organization
John Whalley and Ben Zissimos

Revitalizing Global Environmental Governance: 181
A Function-Driven Approach
Daniel C. Esty and Maria H. Ivanova

Climate Change: National Interests or a Global Regime?   205
Christiana Figueres and Maria H. Ivanova

The Road Ahead: Conclusions and Action Agenda   225
Daniel C. Esty and Maria H. Ivanova

Contributors   241

Index   249

A Note from the Editors

Daniel C. Esty and Maria H. Ivanova

This book grew out of the Global Environmental Governance Project sponsored by the Yale Center for Environmental Law and Policy. The project began in 1998 as a dialogue among environmental professionals, government officials, business people, non-governmental organization leaders, and scholars from around the world keenly aware of the magnitude of modern environmental challenges, the inability of existing institutions to respond effectively, and the need for fundamental reforms in the way we manage our global ecological interdependence. A diverse group has continued to gather over the years to push the boundaries of the current debate and to delineate options and opportunities for strengthened global environmental governance.

The World Summit on Sustainable Development to be held in Johannesburg in August 2002 provided the impetus for assembling the accumulated collective knowledge into a concise volume aiming to contribute to the policy dialogue with a thoughtful yet rigorous reform agenda. What seemed like an impossible timeframe for a publication became a feasible project with editorial and publicity support from the Yale School of Forestry & Environmental Studies (F&ES). Dean James Gustave Speth contributed visionary leadership, policy guidance, and financial support. Jane Coppock, Assistant Dean and Editor of the Yale F&ES Book Series, ingeniously pulled all the pieces together and made this volume a vibrant part of the School's book series on environmental subjects of current interest.

We owe a great debt of gratitude to the extraordinary group of authors that gave life to this book. The fifteen contributors brought to the project a depth and breadth of expertise, invaluable experience from all social sectors, and a range of national perspectives from Africa, Asia, Latin America, Western and Eastern Europe, and North America. Above all, they offered energy, enthusiasm, and commitment. The authors submitted drafts and revisions under pressing deadlines, quickly and thoughtfully responded to comments, and traveled great distances to enliven the dialogue that this volume reflects.

The truly collaborative nature of this project was manifested in a two-day workshop in New Haven in April 2002 that allowed us to discuss the draft chapters, elaborate the overall analytical framework of the volume, and test preliminary findings. A grant from the Yale Center for the Study of Globalization made this event possible. The broad support, active engagement, and insightful advice of its Director Strobe Talbott helped immeasurably. We are also grateful for the encouragement and assistance of Associate Director Haynie Wheeler.

The commentaries and critiques of two reviewers, Peter Haas of the University of Massachusetts and David Driesen of University of Syracuse Law School, strengthened the book considerably. The valuable comments of Mehjabeen Habidi-Abib of UNDP in Pakistan also helped to bolster several of the chapters.

The analytical framework for this book has greatly benefited from our extensive discussions over a number of years with the participants in the Yale Center for Environmental Law and Policy's Global Environmental Governance Project (and the recently constituted Global Environmental Mechanism Policy Action Group that grew out of that project). We wish to thank all those who have been part of this process: Mehjabeen Abidi-Habib (Pakistan), Adnan Amin (Kenya), Ali Azimi (Afghanistan), Abimbola Bamidele-Izu (Nigeria), Alicia Bàrcena (Mexico), Johannah Bernstein (Canada), Frank Biermann (Germany), Al Binger (Jamaica), Zbigniew Bochniarz (Poland), Laurence Boisson de Chazournes (Switzerland), Delphine Borione (France), Tom Burke (United Kingdom), James Cameron (United Kingdom), Paulo Henrique Cardoso (Brazil), Daniele Cesano (Italy), Anilla Cherian (India), Nazli Choucri (Egypt), Angela Cropper (Trinidad and Tobago), Carolyn Deere (Australia), Bharat H. Desai (India), Neno Dimov (Bulgaria), Rudolf Dolzer (Germany), Elizabeth Dowdeswell (Canada), Saliem Fakir (South Africa), Janine Ferretti (Canada), Christiana Figueres (Costa Rica), Dan Fleshler (United States), Claude Fussler (Switzerland), Arnoldo Jose Gabaldon (Venezuela), Luis Gomez-Echeverri (Colombia), Pat Gruber (United States), Michael Gucovsky (Israel), Peter Haas (United States), Scott Hajost (United States), Parvez Hassan (Pakistan), Gudrun Henne (Germany), Jim Hickman (United States), T. Christine Hogan (Canada), Joy Hyvarinen (Finland), Jesse Johnson (United States), Ilona Kickbusch (Germany), Maritta Koch-Weser (Germany), Koh Kheng Lian (Singapore), Milwako Kurosaka (Japan), Alexander Likhotal (Russian Federation), Karin Lissakers (United States), Frank

Loy (United States), Wangari Maathai (Kenya), Andrew Mack (Australia), Dan Martin (United States), Claudia Martinez (Colombia), Julia Marton-Lefèvre (France), Bill McCalpin (United States), Kristin Morico (United States), Sascha Müller-Kraenner (Germany), Daudi Mwakawago (Tanzania), Dhesigan Naidoo (South Africa), Sunita Narain (India), Derek Osborn (United Kingdom), Boyce Papu (South Africa), Franz Xaver Perrez (Switzerland), Kenneth Prewitt (United States), Karl Rábago (United States), Tom Rautenberg (United States), Julie Richardson (United Kingdom), Mark Ritchie (United States), Michael Roux (Australia), Kim Samuel-Johnson (Canada), Mark Schapiro (United States), P.J. Simmons (United States), Udo Simonis (Germany), Sandra Smithey (United States), Tom Spencer (United Kingdom), Matthew Stilwell (Australia), Charlotte Streck (Germany), Simon Tay (Singapore), Beth Tener (United States), Alvaro Umaña (Costa Rica), Simon Upton (New Zealand), Annabell Waititu (Kenya), Joke Waller-Hunter (the Netherlands), Wang Canfa (China), Patricia Waruhiu-Wangai (Kenya), John Waugh (United States), Makarim Wibisono (Indonesia), Xiangmin Liu (China), and Kees Zoeteman (the Netherlands).

An outstanding team of Yale students provided invaluable support in research, editing, and organizing the book. We wish to acknowledge the assistance of Elizabeth Allison, Andres Luque, Shafqat Hussain, and Tyler Welti. Pierre-Luc Arsenault stepped in as an editorial assistant and has worked wonders. We wish to pay special tribute to Emily Noah whose extraordinary skills in research, writing, editing, and graphic design advanced not only the book effort but also the Global Environmental Governance Project more generally.

Jane Coppock, the series editor, and Melissa Goodall, editorial assistant, at the Yale School of Forestry & Environmental Studies deserve special recognition and thanks. Simply said, without them this book would not have been possible. Their contribution to every stage of the process and every page of the volume is invaluable. We are also grateful to Barbara Ruth, Carolyn Deere, and Irina Faion for their assistance at critical moments.

A book is not just about writing. Its ultimate purpose is to convey an idea. In this regard, we are grateful for the use of David Walker's quilt art on the book cover, which communicates the myriad ways in which humanity is interwoven and interrelated. Dottie Scott's resourceful assistance with the page layout was indispensable to the production of the book on a tight schedule. We are also appreciative of the efforts of the team at Yale's Reprographics and Imaging Services (RIS) where the book was produced. The Yale F&ES book series has used these digital publishing services for many years, and the existence of a facility where books can be designed, printed, bound, and mailed, utilizing the latest in digital technology, has enabled many an author to get ideas into print at a speed that was once considered inconceivable. On this particular project, our thanks go to Maura Gianakos and Peter Johnson for the overall graphic design of the book, and to Joseph Cinquino who, as always, managed the printing and production process with efficiency and grace.

This project could not have gone forward without substantial support from several funders. The John D. and Catherine T. MacArthur Foundation helped launch the Global Environmental Governance Project in 1998 and has continued to support its activities. Contributions from the Heinrich Böll Foundation, the Rockefeller Foundation, the Rockefeller Brothers Fund, and the Global Environment and Trade Study (and its funders including the Ford Foundation and the Japan Foundation Center for Global Partnership) have allowed the project to continue and expand.

Publishing a book is not the end of this sweeping project. While this volume marks a major landmark in the Global Environmental Governance Project, it also denotes the beginning of an expanded policy and outreach effort. Building on its four-year initiative, the Yale Center for Environmental Law and Policy, in cooperation with the Globus Institute for Globalization and Sustainability in the Netherlands, and the Commission on Globalization, has established a Global Environmental Mechanism (GEM) Policy Action Group. The goals of this Policy Action Group are to: (1) define a thoughtful, yet rigorous agenda for global environmental governance reform; (2) open a "back channel" dialogue among government officials, NGO leaders, academics, and business community representatives on ways to strengthen global environmental institutions; (3) create a constituency for sustained involvement in a reform initiative; and (4) work toward the implementation of the reform agenda.

We hope that, with the publication of this collection of reform visions and options, the group of authors and collaborators can assist decisionmakers around the world in beginning to define ambitious yet feasible ways of converting global environmental governance challenges into opportunities.

New Haven, Connecticut
July 2002

Foreword

Strobe Talbott

Governance is the greatest challenge facing the international community. In fact, only if the nations of the world cooperate in establishing institutions and rules in support of the global common good will the phrase "international community" have practical meaning. Otherwise, sovereign nations will live, and very likely die, not in a community at all but in a Hobbesian jungle.

The overarching common goal can best be defined in the negative: avoiding catastrophe for the planet. Because of humankind's mastery of technology, we now have the capacity to destroy ourselves. We can do so today and quickly, in a thermonuclear war; or we can do so tomorrow, more slowly but no less completely, through the ruination of our environment. This book addresses that danger and what it will take to avert it.

In their thoughtful, rigorous, comprehensive, and readable chapters, the scholars and practitioners assembled here discuss options and opportunities for better management of our ecological interdependence. The authors, all in the forefront of their fields, draw on several areas of scientific expertise, including international law, economics, biological sciences, and environmental policy; they also represent a variety of national perspectives spanning five continents. Yet they share a conviction that traditional national policy and international diplomacy are no longer sufficient, either in pace, scope or substance. Retarding and reversing the damage that we are already inflicting on our environment requires an unprecedented, coordinated, long-term effort involving ambitious, innovative, and flexible coalitions of state and non-state actors, especially non-governmental organizations that tap into the resources, knowledge, and activism of citizens.

Making the case for environmental governance is an intellectual challenge as well as a political one. Hence the opportunity — and the obligation — of leading institutions like the Yale School of Forestry & Environmental Studies to contribute to the debate.

The Yale Center for the Study of Globalization is proud to have supported this venture. Those of us involved in the founding of the Center in 2001 have stressed that globalization is not a policy or an option. It's not good or bad. It's not something to be for or against. It's a fact of life — something to be understood and managed. Yet globalization is, for better or worse, subject to human behavior. We can maximize the positive aspects of globalization, diminish the risks, and counter the threats. In that sense, we've often said, globalization is like the weather, which not only manifests the forces of nature but shows the effects of human profligacy and short-sightedness.

This book tackles head on that aspect of globalization — including what it has to say about the weather, how it's changing, and how we, the international community, can change the way it's changing.

Readers will have a chance to join the authors in better understanding the problem of global environmental degradation and thereby being part of the solution, which is global governance.

The Global Environmental Agenda: Origins and Prospects

James Gustave Speth

SUMMARY

We have been moving rapidly to a swift and pervasive deterioration of our environmental assets. In response, there has been an upsurge of international environmental law and diplomacy, a vast outpouring of impressive scientific research, and thoughtful policy analysis. What has emerged over the past two decades is the international community's first attempt at global environmental governance.

Two developments were needed before the international environmental movement could be born: (1) environmental policy had to be legitimized at the national level, and (2) the life-sustaining processes of the biosphere had to be perceived as a common concern of all peoples. The first phase of global environmental governance has been instrumental in raising domestic and international awareness for environmental issues, but overall it has been marked more by failure than success. The threatening trends that spurred international attention twenty years ago persist essentially unabated, ozone depletion being the principal exception. It is clearly time to launch a second phase, moving us from talk to action.

Three broad paths to environmental governance can be discerned. First, new institutions and norm-setting procedures are needed at the international level. Second, bottom-up initiatives from non-government organizations (NGOs), businesses, local governments, and other actors should be encouraged. Third, we need to address more directly the underlying causes of environmental degradation, such as population growth, poverty and underdevelopment, inadequate technologies, and market failure brought on by failure to insist on environmentally honest prices.

THE NEW ETHICAL IMPERATIVE

We have entered a new period in our relationship with the natural world. Human influence is pervasive and deep. We impact hugely on the great life support systems of the planet. We are now at the planetary controls, whether we like it or not. Scientist Peter Vitousek and his co-authors stated the matter forcefully in a 1997 article in *Science*:

> All of these seemingly disparate phenomena trace to a single cause – the growing scale of the human enterprise. The rates, scales, kinds, and combinations of changes occurring now are fundamentally different from those at any other time in history; we are changing earth more rapidly than we are understanding it. We live on a human-dominated planet – and the momentum of human population growth, together with the imperative for further economic development in most of the world, ensures that our dominance will increase…. Humanity's dominance of Earth means that we cannot escape responsibility for managing the planet. (Vitousek et al., 1997)

Scientists are generally a cautious lot, so when our most respected scientists issue a plea for "active management of the planet," we must take notice. Aldo Leopold, perhaps the most famous graduate of the school that I now serve as dean, noted that "one of the penalties of an ecological education is that one lives alone in a world of wounds." There is a lot of bad news in the world of environmental affairs, but there is good news as well. One piece of good news is that the plea of Vitousek is but the latest in a long line of appeals from the scientific community, urging governments and others to take the task of protecting the global environment more seriously.

Starting in the 1980s, governments and others did indeed take notice and began the process of assuming responsibility for planetary management. What has emerged over the past two decades is the international community's first attempt at global environmental governance. All is not well yet in this new arena, but it is important to acknowledge what has been accomplished.

Before examining these accomplishments in global governance of the environment, however, a quick observation about vocabulary is in order. "Global governance" does not imply a global government, nor does it include only the actions of governments. Many non-governmental organizations (NGOs), businesses, and communities are already playing large roles in the emergence of global environmental governance as we know it today.

It is also interesting to contrast the use of language in the environmental field and the field of economics.

The phrase "managing the global economy" comes rather easily. It is frequently heard because it is a priority enterprise of governments, multilateral financial institutions, and many others. But "managing the global environment"? It still sounds futuristic, but it shouldn't. The global environment is more of an integrated system than the global economy. It is even more fundamental to human wellbeing. It is impacted powerfully by human activities, and it requires collective management.

ORIGINS OF THE GLOBAL ENVIRONMENTAL AGENDA

An agenda of the principal large-scale environmental concerns of the international community has been defined. In response to this agenda, there has been an upsurge of international conferences, negotiations, action plans, treaties, and other initiatives. New fields of international environmental law and diplomacy have been born. There has been a vast outpouring of impressive and relevant scientific research and policy analysis. Increasingly sophisticated actions by an ever-stronger international community of environmental and other NGOs have flourished, ranging from the global to the local, from civil disobedience to analytical think-tank publications.

Both national governments and multilateral institutions, from the United Nations to the international development banks, have recognized these concerns, creating major units to address global-scale issues. While many multinational corporations are still in denial, others have become highly innovative and have moved ahead with impressive steps, often before their governments. In academia, international environmental affairs has become a major subject of intellectual inquiry and teaching. A large body of scholarly analysis now exists. And we are fast-approaching another of those milestone events: the 2002 World Summit for Sustainable Development in Johannesburg, which follows the 1972 Stockholm Conference on the Human Environment and the 1992 Rio Earth Summit.

Large-scale environmental concerns have attracted increasing attention from governments, NGOs, multilateral agencies, and even the business community. How did this agenda emerge? How were the issues identified and framed? What has been accomplished to date in the area of global environmental governance? By whom? How did these actors gain recognition and political traction?

The Rise of Domestic Concern: The U.S. Environmental Movement

To put these issues in perspective, it is useful to start in the 1960s with the emergence of the modern era of environmental concern. It was driven by domestic, mostly local, issues: local air and water pollution, strip-mining, highway construction, noise pollution, dams and stream channelization, clear-cutting of forests, hazardous waste dumps, nuclear power plants, exposures to toxic chemicals, oil spills, suburban sprawl. Concern about these issues gathered strength throughout the 1960s.

In the United States, this concern led to the National Environmental Policy Act in December 1969, and to the first Earth Day a few months later. Within the short span of a few years in the early 1970s, the Environmental Protection Agency and the Presidential Council on Environmental Quality were established, the Clean Air and Water Acts and other major federal legislation were passed, and the federal courts were deluged with lawsuits brought by a new generation of environmental advocacy organizations, often funded by major U.S. foundations. It was during this period that groups like the Natural Resources Defense Council and the Environmental Defense Fund were launched.

The new environmental movement handed the business community a long string of defeats, and it often left scientists anxious in their efforts to keep up. Economists were aghast, and ecologists, even lawyers, were lionized. Large majorities of the public were strongly pro-environment. The news media were full of stories, and the government responded with far-reaching, expensive requirements and tough deadlines for industry. A tipping point — a phase change — was reached. What was once impossible became inevitable. The fire was lit.

How did this happen? A number of factors came together (Speth, 1985, 1988). First, there was the rising demand for environmental quality in an increasingly affluent post-war population. Between 1950 and 1970, U.S. per capita income rose by fifty-two percent. People sought the amenities of the suburbs, and by 1970 there were more Americans in the suburbs than in cities or rural areas. National Park visitation doubled between 1954 and 1962 and doubled again by 1971 (U.S. Council on Environmental Quality, 1979).

Second, pollution and blight were blatant and inescapable. Smog, soot, and the resultant smarting eyes and coughs from air pollution, streams and beaches closed to fishing and swimming because of water contaminants, plastic trash and toxic chemicals that would not go away, birds threatened by DDT, pesticide poisoning, fish kills, power plants and highways in the neighborhood, marshes filled for new track houses and streams channelized for navigation and drainage – all these threats were highly visible and impossible to ignore.

Third, the social upheavals of the 1960s had given rise to a new generation of questioning, politically active, and socially concerned young people. The civil rights and anti-war movements showed that political activism could work. Some of the active figures were also not so young. Based on the teach-ins used to protest the Vietnam War, Wisconsin Senator Gaylord Nelson came up with the concept of a national teach-in for the environment, and thus launched what became the first Earth Day.

Fourth, there was a widespread view that major corporations were getting away with murder. Eloquent writers emerged to make the case: Ralph Nader wrote *Unsafe at Any Speed* in 1965. Rachel Carson published *Silent Spring* in 1962. The play had to have a villain, and corporate America was it.

Fifth, the likely opposition – the business community – was caught off guard, without time to marshal its troops or gather its ammunition. Even environmental NGOs were surprised. The Sierra Club's executive director later noted that they "were taken aback by the speed or suddenness with which the new forces exploded....We were severely disoriented" (Shabecoff, 1993).[1]

Finally, there were the major precipitating events: the Cuyahoga River in Cleveland bursting into flames, the Interior Department's proposal to flood the Grand Canyon, and, most significantly, the Santa Barbara oil spill in 1969. The rest, as they say, is history.

PRINCIPAL CHARACTERISTICS OF

THE EARLY ENVIRONMENTAL AGENDA

The global-scale challenges that concern us today were almost totally absent from the discussion in the 1960s and 1970s. Only global population growth and protection of the ozone layer were included in the concerns of the time.

There was no major body of science – or group of scientists – pushing these issues forward. Some individual scientists played major roles – Paul Ehrlich, John Holden, Barry Commoner, and George Woodwell among them. But the issues were advanced mainly by events and by the realities of people's everyday experiences.

Similarly, there was little need to try to define and promote an agenda. The agenda was defined by everyday incidents and the accumulation of actions in response. It was Lois Gibbs and her efforts at Love Canal, for example, that put the issue of abandoned hazardous waste sites on the agenda, not scientists or the government, and it happened after much of the early environmental legislation had been passed.

---

1   Shabecoff's *A Fierce Green Fire: The American Environmental Movement* contains an excellent survey of today's environmental movement. See also the U.S. Council on Environmental Quality, *Environmental Quality: Tenth Annual Report*, 1979.

The Emergence of Global Issues

If this was the domestic scene, where were the global-scale issues of primary concern to us? Much as the domestic agenda of the 1970s was forming in the 1960s, the global change agenda was quietly taking shape in the 1970s. Throughout the 1970s, a steady stream of publications with a planetary perspective emerged, calling attention to global-scale concerns. Most were authored by scientists with the goal of taking their findings and those of other colleagues to a larger audience. A number of these reports were path-breaking, defining the global environmental agenda, but not all of them met with universal acclaim.

SEMINAL GLOBAL ENVIRONMENTAL REPORTS — 1970-1978[2]

1970   *Man's Impact on the Global Environment*, Report of the Study of Critical Environmental Problems (a scientific group assembled at MIT)

1971   *This Endangered Planet*, Richard Falk

1972   *Exploring New Ethics for Survival*, Garrett Hardin

1972   *Only One Earth*, Barbara Ward and Rene Dubos

1974   *The Limits to Growth*, Donella Meadows et al.

1978   *The Human Future Revisited*, Harrison Brown

1978   *The Twenty-Ninth Day*, Lester Brown

There were also numerous reports from scientific groups, especially panels and committees organized by the International Council of Scientific Unions, the U.S. National Academy of Sciences, the International Union for the Conservation of Nature (IUCN), and the United Nations Environment Programme (UNEP). These reports included the now famous 1974 study by Rowland and Molina, explaining the potential of CFCs to deplete the ozone layer. Their work remains the only environmental research to date to win the Nobel Prize. Also among these documents was the *Charney Report*, which was published by the U.S. National Academy of Sciences in 1979, and

[2]   For complete citations, see reference section at the end of this chapter.

told us most of what we needed to know about climate change to take action. These reports and the steady stream of publications from Lester Brown and his team at the Worldwatch Institute collectively laid out the key issues.

Then, starting around 1980, a series of reports appeared seeking to pull together all of these issues into a coherent agenda for international action.

SEMINAL GLOBAL ENVIRONMENTAL REPORTS – 1980-1990[3]

1980   *World Conservation Strategy,* IUCN and UNEP

1980   The Global 2000 Report to the President, U.S. Council on Environmental Quality

1981   *Global Future: Time to Act,* U.S. Council on Environmental Quality

1982   *The World Environment: 1972-1982,* UNEP scientific team (Holdgate et al.)

1983   *Environmental Research and Management Priorities for the 1980s,* an international group of scientists organized by the Royal Swedish Academy of Sciences

1987   *Our Common Future,* World Commission on Environment and Development (the Brundtland Commission Report)

Predominantly scientific efforts were designed to bring global-scale challenges forcefully to the attention of governments. These syntheses collectively stressed ten principal environmental concerns:

- Loss of crop and grazing land due to desertification, erosion, conversion of land to non-farm uses, and other factors;

- Depletion of the world's tropical forests, leading to loss of forest resources, serious watershed damage (erosion, flooding, and siltation), and other adverse consequences;

- Mass extinction of species, principally from the global loss of wildlife habitat, and the associated loss of genetic resources;

---

3   For complete citations, see reference section at the end of this chapter.

- Rapid population growth, burgeoning Third World cities, and ecological refugees;

- Mismanagement and shortages of freshwater resources;

- Overfishing, habitat destruction, and pollution in the marine environment;

- Threats to human health from mismanagement of pesticides and persistent organic pollutants;

- Climate change due to the increase in greenhouse gases in the atmosphere;

- Acid rain and, more generally, the effects of a complex mix of air pollutants on fisheries, forests, and crops;

- Depletion of the stratospheric ozone layer by CFCs and other gases.

Clearly this was a new agenda, very different from the one that sparked the first Earth Day in 1970.

STAGE-SETTING DEVELOPMENTS

Political scientist Keith Caldwell has noted that two developments were needed before the international environmental movement could be born: environmental policy had to be legitimized at the national level, and the life-sustaining processes of the biosphere had to be perceived as a common concern of all peoples.

Caldwell sees the 1972 UN Conference on the Human Environment, the Stockholm Conference, as crucially important in both respects (Caldwell, 1996). Ably led by Maurice Strong, the Stockholm Conference forced many national governments to develop domestic environmental programs – including those in Europe, which were lagging behind the United States at that point, though not today – and it legitimized the biosphere as an object of national and international policy and collective management.

The Stockholm Conference also had a further major consequence – the creation of UNEP – which, as noted above, had a major role in the 1970s in framing the global agenda. The United Nations Environment Programme made estimates of deforestation and promoted strategies of action, convened the 1977 international conference on desertification, and promoted international agreements on the protection of migratory species and the World Climate Program of the World Meteorological Organization, all in the 1970s.

By the mid-1980s, the intellectual and policy leadership of the scientific community, the NGO community (groups such as IUCN, Worldwatch, and the World Resources Institute), and UNEP had paid off: a new and international environmental agenda had been established, one that governments would have to address collectively in some way to be credible. The press for action on these ten issues was too strong to ignore. Intellectuals in the scientific and NGO communities had excellent media access to keep the pressure on and keep the issues in the public eye. It would take another decade for this to happen fully, but by the mid-1990s each of the ten challenges had become the subject of a major international treaty, plan of action, or other initiative (although the freshwater and marine initiatives are arguably too weak to count).

What we see, then, is that the global agenda emerged and moved forward due primarily to a relatively small, international leadership community in science, government, the UN, and NGOs. They took available opportunities to put these issues forward – indeed they created such opportunities – so that governments had little choice but to respond. The game that many governments played was to react, but not forcefully.

DOMESTIC ACTION AND GLOBAL INDIFFERENCE

Against this background, it is instructive to compare the emergence of the global agenda with the emergence of the original, predominantly domestic agenda a decade earlier. The differences have proven consequential in eliciting corrective action from governments. Several contrasts deserve close attention.

- The issues on the domestic agenda were acute, immediate, and understandable to the public. Issues on the global agenda tend to be more chronic, more remote (at least from the North), technically complicated, and thus more difficult to understand and relate to. These differences have translated into major disparities in the degree of public awareness and support.

- The global agenda did not spring bottom-up from actual impacts on people; rather, it was forged top-down at the international level by science (often disputed science), by NGOs (often with circumscribed credibility), and by a peanut-sized UN agency tucked away in Nairobi.

- Unlike the domestic agenda, respect for national sovereignty requires agreement from many governments, often with different rankings of priorities. No government can be compelled to agree nor obligated without its consent. Thus treaties are hard to attain, and forceful treaties are a rare commodity.

- The domestic agenda was largely translated into legislation before corporate and other opposition was aroused. Action on the global agenda has been pursued in the context of an alerted, prepared, and powerful opposition where corporate interests are viewed as threatened.

- The world's most powerful country led in the fight for national-level action in the 1970s, but has largely failed to provide international leadership on the global agenda. Indeed, the United States has frequently been the principal hold-out on international environmental agreements.

- The villainy of the global agenda is more ambiguous. The blame for global-scale environmental problems cannot rest solely on the shoulder of big corporations when lifestyles in the developed world, mismanagement by governments of both the North and the South, and other factors are so clearly implicated. Increasingly, pollution comes not from something going wrong, but from normal life.

- Domestic agendas can be addressed primarily through regulatory means, but the global agenda requires major expenditures by governments, including development assistance to the poorer countries.

In light of these barriers to progress, it is a wonder that any has been made at all. How should one assess the progress of the last two decades – the decades during which we have been "on notice" that we faced extraordinary global environmental challenges? As noted earlier, there is a significant list of accomplishments that have followed in the wake of the emergence of the new global agenda. But as also noted, there have been severe constraints on seeking concerted international action. How has the play of these forces worked out in the real world?

ASSESSMENT AND PROSPECTS

Looking back, it cannot be said that the generations of the 1960s and 1970s did nothing in response to the global call for action. Progress has been made on some fronts, but not nearly enough. There are outstanding success stories, but rarely are they commensurate with the problem.

For the most part, we have analyzed, debated, discussed, and negotiated these issues endlessly. My generation is a generation, I fear, of great talkers, overly fond of conferences. But on action, we have fallen far short. As a result, the threatening global trends highlighted twenty years ago are still very much with us, ozone depletion being the notable exception.

But if we have not succeeded in reversing these trends, perhaps we have laid a good foundation for rapid action today. In fact, the results of twenty years of international environmental negotiations are disappointing. It is not that what has been agreed, for example, in the conventions on climate change, desertification, and biodiversity, is useless. But these treaties are mostly frameworks for action; they do not drive the changes that are needed. The same can be said for the extensive international discussions on world forests, which have never reached the point of a treaty.

In general, international environmental law and its hundreds of treaties are plagued by vague agreements, minimal requirements, lax enforcement, and under-funded support. The weakness of most environmental treaties should not be a surprise, however; they were forged in negotiating processes that give maximum leverage to any country with an interest in protecting the status quo. Similarly, the international institutions created to address these issues – the UNEP and ECOSOC's Commission on Sustainable Development – are among the weakest multilateral organizations.

If the first phase of global environmental governance has been marked more by failure than success, it is clearly time to launch a second phase that corrects past mistakes and moves from talk to action.

GLOBAL ENVIRONMENTAL GOVERNANCE SCENARIOS

The World Business Council for Sustainable Development (WBCSD) has sketched several broad paths in environmental governance:

- The "FROG" – First Raise Our Growth – scenario calls for the resolution of economic challenges first. FROG is a business-as-usual scenario, leading to huge environmental costs, even in the eyes of business leaders.

- "GEOPolity" is a success scenario in which sustainability is vigorously pursued. In this case, people turn to government to focus the market on environmental and social ends and rely heavily on intergovernmental institutions and treaties.

- The final scenario is "Jazz." Jazz is not an acronym. It is a spirit, a world of unscripted initiatives, decentralized and improvisational. In this world, there is abundant information about business behavior; good conduct is enforced by public opinion and consumer behavior. Governments facilitate; NGOs are very active; business sees strategic advantage in doing the right thing (WBCSD, 1997).

The initial international response to the global change agenda has been to try to move the world from FROG to GEOPolity. It isn't working. Getting serious requires new action on three mutually supportive fronts.

Revising GEOPolity

The current world of GEOPolity is designed to fail. It can be redesigned for success by insisting on new norm-setting procedures and new institutions, including a Global Environmental Organization (GEO). The case for an effective GEO is as strong as that for an effective World Trade Organization (WTO). The international community knows how to create plausible multilateral arrangements and has often done so in other, mostly economic, areas (Speth, 2002).

Taking Jazz to Scale

A second path to the future is to implement measures that can take Jazz to scale. Jazz is the most exciting arena for action today, with an outpouring of bottom-up, unscripted initiatives from business, NGOs, governments, and others:

- Seven large companies, including DuPont, Shell, BP, and Alcan, have agreed to reduce their CO_2 emissions fifteen percent below their 1990 levels by 2010. Indeed, Alcan is reported to be on track to reduce its emissions twenty-five percent below 1990 levels by 2010, and DuPont is on schedule to reduce emissions by sixty-five percent.

- Eleven major companies, including DuPont, GM, and IBM, have formed the Green Power Market Development Group and committed to develop markets for 1,000 megawatts of renewable energy over the next decade.

- Home Depot, Lowes, Andersen, and others have agreed to sell wood (to the degree that it is available) only from sustainably managed forests certified by an independent group using rigorous criteria. Unilever, the largest processor of fish in the world, has agreed to do the same regarding fish products.

NGOs have played important roles in forging these corporate initiatives. They are the real maestros of Jazz. Local governments, universities, and other entities have also contributed. Over 500 local governments have now joined a campaign to reduce greenhouse gas emissions (Speth, 2002).

Attacking the Drivers of Deterioration

The third and most important path to sustainability is to address more directly the underlying drivers of environmental degradation (Speth, 1995).

- *Population.* Analyses suggest that an escalation of proven non-coercive approaches could lead to a leveling off of global population at eight and a half billion people in this century. This will not happen without adequate support for the United Nations' Cairo Plan of Action.

- *Poverty and underdevelopment.* Poverty is an important contributor to environmental deterioration: the poor often have little choice other than to lean too heavily on a declining resource base. But improved development prospects are also needed because the only world that works is one in which the aspirations of poor people and poor nations for fairness and justice are being realized. The views of developing countries in international negotiations on the environment are powerfully shaped by preoccupation with their own compelling economic and social challenges and distrust of the intentions and policies of industrialized countries. Sustained and sustainable development provides the only context in which there is enough confidence, trust, and hope to ground the difficult measures needed to realize environmental objectives.

Eliminating large-scale poverty is no longer an impossible dream. It could be accomplished in the lifetimes of today's young people. But, as with population, achieving these goals is limited by inadequate development assistance, in this case compounded by protectionist trade regimes and heavy debt burdens.

- *Technology.* The only way to reduce pollution and resource consumption while achieving expected economic growth is to bring about a wholesale transformation in the technologies that today dominate manufacturing, energy, transportation, and agriculture. Across a wide front, environmentally sophisticated technologies are either available or soon can be. From 1990 to 1998, when oil and natural gas use grew globally at a rate of two percent annually, and coal consumption did not grow at all, wind energy generation grew at an annual rate of twenty-two percent and photovoltaics at sixteen percent. Denmark now gets fifteen percent of its energy from wind; Japan last year installed 100 megawatts of photovoltaic power. Transformation of the energy sector must rank as the highest priority.

- *Market signals.* Needed changes in technology and consumption patterns will not happen unless there is a parallel revolution in pricing. The corrective most needed now is environmentally honest prices. Full cost pricing is thwarted today by the failure of governments to eliminate environmentally perverse subsidies (estimated globally at $1.5 trillion per year) to ensure that external environmental costs are captured in market prices (Myers and Kent, 2001). We have no reason to expect major environmental improvement while these distortions persist.

CONCLUSION

There is no great mystery about *what* must be done. What does remain a great mystery is *how* we get on that path. Political systems alternate between incremental drift and rapid change – a pattern of punctuated equilibria. The global environment has been addressed incrementally, whereas we need major reform, a phase change, a tipping point, a rapid shift to a new equilibrium akin to the outpouring of U.S. domestic environmental concern in the 1960s and 1970s.

It is possible that we are seeing the birth of something like this shift in the anti-globalization protests, in the far-reaching and unprecedented initiatives being taken by some private corporations, in the growth of NGOs and their innovations, in scientists speaking up and speaking out, and in the outpouring of climate and other environmental initiatives by the religious community. We certainly must hope that something new and vital is afoot.

There are many hopeful signs that things are beginning to change for the better, but we are still at the early stages of the journey to sustainability. Meanwhile, the forward momentum of the drivers of environmental deterioration is great. As former Presidential Science Advisor Jack Gibbons is fond of saying, "If we don't change direction, we'll end up where we're headed!" And today we are moving rapidly to a swift, pervasive, and appalling deterioration of our environmental assets. There is still world enough and time, but the next few decades are crucial. The next doublings of the world economy cannot resemble those of the past.

REFERENCES

Brown, Harrison. 1978. *The Human Future Revisited: The World Predicament and Possible Solutions.* New York: W. W. Norton.

Brown, Lester. 1978. *The Twenty-Ninth Day: Accommodating Human Needs and Numbers to the Earth's Resources.* New York: W. W. Norton.

Caldwell, Lynton K. 1996. *International Environmental Policy: From the Twentieth to the Twenty-First Century.* 3rd ed. Durham, NC: Duke University Press.

Charney, J.G. 1979. *Carbon Dioxide and Climate: A Scientific Assessment.* Washington, D.C.: National Academy of Sciences.

Falk, Richard. 1971. *This Endangered Planet.* New York: Random House.

Hardin, Garrett. 1972. *Exploring New Ethics for Survival: The Voyage of the Spaceship Beagle.* New York: Viking Press.

Holdgate, Martin W., Mohammed Kassas, and Gilbert F. White. 1982. *The World Environment 1972-1982.* Nairobi, Kenya: United Nations Environment Programme.

IUCN. 1980. *World Conservation Strategy: Living Resource Conservation for Sustainable Development.* Gland, Switzerland: International Union for Conservation of Nature and Natural Resources.

McNeill, J. R. 2000. *Something New Under the Sun: An Environmental History of the Twentieth Century World.* New York: W. W. Norton.

Meadows, Donella H. et al. 1974. *The Limits to Growth.* New York: Universe Books.

Myers, Norman, and Jennifer Kent. 2001. *Perverse Subsidies.* Washington, D.C.: Island Press.

Rowland, Sherwood, and Mario Molina. 1974. "Stratospheric Sink for Chlorofluoromethanes: Chlorine Catalysed Destruction of Ozone." *Nature* 249: 810-814.

Salomon, Jean-Jacques. 1995. "The 'Uncertain Quest': Mobilising Science and Technology for Development." *Science and Public Policy* 22 (1): 9-18.

Shabecoff, Philip. 1993. *A Fierce Green Fire: The American Environmental Movement.* New York: Hill & Wang.

Speth, James Gustave. 1985. *Protecting our Environment: Toward a New Agenda.* Washington, D.C.: Center for National Policy.

_____. 1988. "Environmental Pollution: A Long-Term Perspective." In *Earth '88: Changing Geographic Perspectives: Proceedings of the Centennial Symposium,* edited by Earth '88. Washington, D.C.: National Geographic Society.

_____. 1995. "The Transition to a Sustainable Society." *Proceedings of the National Academy of Sciences* 89 (3): 870-872.

_____. 2002. "Recycling Environmentalism." *Foreign Policy,* July/August 2002.

Study of Critical Environmental Problems. 1970. *Man's Impact on the Global Environment: Assessment and Recommendations for Action.* Cambridge, MA: MIT Press.

U.S. Council on Environmental Quality. 1979. *Environmental Quality: Tenth Annual Report.* Washington, D.C.: Government Printing Office.

U.S. Council on Environmental Quality. 1980. *The Global 2000 Report to the President – Entering the Twenty-First Century.* Washington, D.C.: Council on Environmental Quality and United States Department of State.

U.S. Council on Environmental Quality. 1981. *Global Future: Time to Act: Report to the President on Global Resources, Environment, and Population.* Washington, D.C.: Council on Environmental Quality and United States Department of State.

UNEP. 2002. *Global Environment Outlook 3.* Nairobi, Kenya: United Nations Environment Programme. Available from http://www.grid.unep.ch/geo/geo3/index.htm

Union of Concerned Scientists. 2001. "Warning to Humanity." *Renewable Resources Journal* 19 (2): 16-17.

Vitousek, Peter M., Harold A. Mooney, Jane Lubchenco, and Jerry M. Melillo. 1997. "Human Domination of Earth's Ecosystems." *Science* 277 (5325): 494-499.

Ward, Barbara, and Rene Dubos. 1972. *Only One Earth: The Care and Maintenance of a Small Planet.* New York: W. W. Norton.

WBCSD. 1997. *Exploring Sustainable Development: Global Scenarios 2000-2005.* Geneva, Switzerland: World Business Council for Sustainable Development.

World Commission on Environment and Development. 1987. *Our Common Future.* New York: United Nations.

World Resources Institute. 2000. *World Resources 2000-2001: People and Ecosystems.* New York: Oxford University Press. Available from http://www.wri.org/wri/wr2000/toc.html

Worldwatch Institute, ed. 2001. *Vital Signs 2001: The Environmental Trends That Are Shaping Our Future, 2001 Edition.* New York: W. W. Norton.

Flying Blind: Assessing Progress Toward Sustainability

David Hales and Robert Prescott-Allen

SUMMARY

For development to be sustainable, it must combine a robust economy, rich and resilient natural systems, and flourishing human communities. Rational pursuit of these goals demands that we have clear policy targets, operationalize them in terms of actions and results, devise analytical tools for deciding priority actions, and monitor and evaluate our progress. Goals that are not measurable are unlikely to be achieved. We invest in what we measure, and over time we become what we reward. Without valid and reliable assessment methodology and tools, we run the risk of achieving unintended and unanticipated results, and of wasting much of our investment.

When the nations of the world convene in Johannesburg, South Africa for the World Summit on Sustainable Development, it will again be apparent that our worthwhile dreams have exceeded our capacity to manage effectively, in large measure because we have no systematic, valid, and reliable way to evaluate our progress, and no fixed point of responsibility for this task.

This chapter offers a challenge to governments whose rhetoric calls for democratic participation, transparent actions, and real results, but whose practical actions fall short of these aspirations. There are no other commitments remotely achievable for the Johannesburg Summit that could be more valuable than a legally binding agreement to create the means to authoritatively, candidly, and openly assess progress toward sustainable development.

THE SUSTAINABILITY CHALLENGE

As the gavel fell on the adoption of *Agenda 21: Programme of Action for Sustainable Development* in June 1992 in Rio de Janeiro, there was a strong sense that the nations of the world were on the road to sustainability. The catalytic force of the Earth Summit led to the Convention on Biodiversity, the Framework Convention on Climate Change, and the Convention on Desertification, all of which entered into force during the 1990s. While the specifics of financial resources and technology transfer were intentionally left vague, the basis for a global partnership, seemed to be in place.

Institutions were devised for the implementation of the Rio outcomes. In 1993, the General Assembly of the United Nations established the UN Commission on Sustainable Development to "review progress" on each chapter of Agenda 21 and assess overall headway. In 1997, the Kyoto Protocol was negotiated to operationalize the Framework Convention on Climate Change, including legally binding targets for reduction of greenhouse gas emissions. An Intergovernmental Panel on Forests and an Intergovernmental Forum on Forests have been established to apply the Forest Principles in programs for action at the national level.

At every level, although not in every place, the roles of civil society, transnational corporations, and non-governmental organizations (NGOs) have evolved. More than sixty countries have formed national commissions for sustainable development, and more than four hundred cities and municipalities have adopted local versions of Agenda 21. Many corporations seem anxious to be seen as responsive to societal calls to play their part in raising environmental and labor standards worldwide. In 2000, the Organisation for Economic Co-operation and Development (OECD), together with representatives of business, labor, and civil society, produced *Guidelines for Multinational Enterprises*, one of several examples of texts encouraging corporate social responsibility. The World Economic Forum also routinely discusses corporate accountability and the role of corporations in promoting sustainable development.

Yet in 2002, as the gavel is raised to convene nations and their development partners in Johannesburg for the World Summit on Sustainable Development, a working definition of sustainable development remains elusive (Esty, 2001a) and the institutional support structures for sustainable development at national and international levels dysfunctional to the point of irrelevance (Upton, 2000).

A fundamental reason for high levels of dissatisfaction, discord, and unease is the lack of capacity to show real progress against the goals set by the Rio Conference.

THE RIO DECADE: ASSESSING PROGRESS

Principle 1 of the Rio Declaration states that a "healthy and productive life in harmony with nature" is at the core of sustainable development and is an entitlement of people around the globe. Much has changed since 1992, but in terms of achieving the goal of sustainability, what have these developments meant? The answer, simply put, is that we don't know. A summary tour of "facts" serves to illustrate this uncertainty.

Are people richer or poorer?

The World Bank argues that poor people the world over have increased their incomes, are better educated, and are living healthier and more productive lives. However, when these figures are disaggregated by country, it is difficult to determine how much of the progress alluded to by the Bank has occurred in the past ten years. In many of the least developed countries, annual per capita income has decreased (UN, 1999). The gap between rich and poor has grown wider in many places. By 2000, the income of the richest fifth of the world's people was seventy-four times that of the poorest fifth, and the assets of the richest two hundred individuals exceeded the combined wealth of the less wealthy forty percent of the world's population (UNDP, 1999).

The economies of some countries – Singapore, South Korea, Hong Kong, and Taiwan, for example – have done well. Indonesia, Thailand, and Argentina made apparent economic progress for the first part of the Rio Decade, and have faced economic disasters since. In other nations, little has changed. Average incomes in sub-Saharan Africa continue to be stagnant, as they have been since the 1960s, and many of the transition economies of Eastern Europe and Central Asia have suffered through sharp rises in poverty in the 1990s.

Is there enough food for everyone?

Overall food production is sufficient to feed the current global population of more than six billion people. Yet, the inability to transport and distribute that food, interruptions in food supply due to political instability, and chronic poverty have led to unremitting malnutrition in many urban areas and across sub-Saharan Africa. There are no major stocks of food fish that are not experiencing stress and decline, and many are collapsing.

Has quality of life improved?

Life expectancy has risen slightly, with gains in developing countries marginally outpacing those in the developed world (World Resources Institute, 1998). There have been substantial medical breakthroughs, but new threats to human health have also emerged. Major strides have been made in the reduction of diseases that have plagued so many for so long.[1] At the same time, AIDS, the leading cause of death in sub-Saharan Africa, has reduced life expectancy in twenty-nine African countries by seven years (UNFPA, 1999). Children the world over continue to die of treatable illnesses and maladies such as diarrhea, and preventive health care and affordable medicines are unavailable to most of the world's people.

Are societies more fair and just?

The importance of good governance and democratic participation in the authoritative allocation of resources has been emphasized in the negotiated outcomes of every development-related international conference of the decade. Elected governments at the national level have increased from 66 (out of 167) in 1987, to 121 (out of 192) at the end of 2001. In many places, however, democratic reforms are fragile at best, and many of the world's poor associate the growth of poverty with the spread of democracy.

Are women and men treated equally?

The role of women in many societies has changed substantially, and the international community clearly recognizes that gender equality is

---

[1] For example, iodine deficiency has been reduced in many parts of the world, and river blindness has been eliminated in eleven countries in West Africa, opening new lands to cultivation and adding years of productive labor. *Dracunculiasis* (guinea worm) cases have dropped from over three million per year, spread over Africa and Asia, to less than 10,000, mostly in the Sudan. Polio is now confined to ten nations, compared to more than 150 in 1992.

a fundamental part of social justice. Women now hold more than ten percent of all national parliamentary seats, and the percentage of female cabinet ministers worldwide has risen from 3.4 in 1987 to 6.8 in 1996. However, two-thirds of the illiterate adults in the world are women and two-thirds of the children who are not in school around the world are girls (UN, 1997).

Is the environment better off?

The world continues to lose habitats and animal and plant species at an astounding rate. The capacity of natural systems to respond to stress has thus decreased, resulting in floods, droughts, and other severe natural disasters. During the 1990s, there was a net loss of forest cover, although the rate of annual loss seems to have declined compared to the rate of annual loss over the decade from 1980 to 1990. Developed countries have increased their forest cover since Rio, while developing countries show substantial deforestation. The health of the world's coral reefs has declined significantly since 1992, with more than half of coral ecosystems currently considered endangered or threatened (Wilkinson, 2000). Efforts to abate land-based marine pollution seem to have had only limited local effect. As Speth argues in this volume, many of the key environmental trend lines are deeply worrisome.

Are human demands on the environment sustainable?

Increasing human populations and inefficient patterns of consumption continue to put additional pressure on already strained resources and natural systems. Every second since the adjournment of Rio has seen the birth of three new souls, each one of whom needs 1,400 calories and four gallons of water a day to survive. Half of all humanity now lives in cities, most of which are situated in coastal areas and river valleys literally on top of some of the world's most productive agricultural lands and marine ecosystems.

Humans have long affected regional weather, yet this generation is the first to demonstrably affect the Earth's climate. Synthetic endocrine disruptors – copycat hormones – are capable of changing basic life processes in ways that are difficult to anticipate. The development of genetically modified species holds great potential for food security but has generated serious concerns for unanticipated and irreversible consequences to human and ecosystem health.

WHERE ARE WE ON THE SUSTAINABILITY CURVE?

Combining these facts and figures does not provide a comprehensive picture of progress toward global sustainability. At best, we can say that some human lives have improved and some are under greater duress. Some natural systems seem to be doing better, others have been irrevocably changed, and none remain unaffected. And the problem is no less serious at lower governance levels. Assessing progress is equally difficult at regional, national, and local scales. National averages mask substantial differences among groups and places within countries, just as global figures obfuscate disparities among nations.

Even when the economy and the environment are considered separately, it is difficult to summarize whether we are better or worse off than a decade ago. From consideration of unconnected facts, even if they gave a valid picture of the "economy" or the "environment," it is impossible to conclude just where we are in the transition to sustainability.

Achieving sustainability requires defining its components in measurable terms and clearly fixing the responsibility to assess progress comprehensively.

THE VALUE OF MEASUREMENT

We approach the tenth anniversary of Agenda 21 with few nations having adopted definitions of success in achieving sustainability and little practical clarity at the international level. Although the Millennium Goals[2] and the Monterrey Consensus[3] are substantial steps in the right direction at the international level, we still have no reliable roadmap to follow. Making progress toward sustainability is like going to a des-

---

2   The eight Millennium Goals are set forth in the United Nations Millennium Declaration of September 2000: (1) Eradicate extreme poverty and hunger; (2) Improve maternal health; (3) Achieve universal primary education; (4) Combat HIV/AIDS, malaria, and other diseases; (5) Promote gender equality and empower women, (6) Ensure environmental sustainability, (7) Reduce child mortality; and (8) Develop a global partnership for development.

3   The Monterrey Consensus is the final document adopted at the conclusion of the UN Financing for Development conference on March 22, 2002, in Monterrey, Mexico, wherein heads of state and government pledged to take a major step toward eradicating poverty and achieving sustainable economic growth around the world. For more information about the conference and the full text of the Consensus, see http://www.un.org/esa/ffd/

tination we have never visited before, equipped with a sense of geography and the principles of navigation, but without a map or compass.

Rational pursuit of sustainable development demands that we have clear goals, that we operationalize those goals in terms of measurable results, that we devise analytical tools for deciding priority actions, and that we monitor and evaluate our progress (Prescott-Allen, 2001). A more quantified approach to sustainable development is necessary.

Goals that are not measurable are unlikely to be achieved. We invest in what we measure, and over time, we become what we reward. Without a valid and reliable assessment methodology, we run the risk of achieving unintended and unanticipated results, and of wasting much of our investment in the future.

A core set of indicators, marking goals and achievements, could help restructure our understanding of complex environmental and socioeconomic problems and redefine our thinking about appropriate response strategies. Measurement provides an empirical foundation for setting goals, for evaluating performance, for calculating the impact of our activities on the environment and society, and for benchmarking (IISDnet, 2000a).

Good data and information provide the tools for detecting aggregate effects and "tragedies of the commons" in the making. Given the spatial and temporal dispersion of environmental problems, quantification of trends and impacts is critical to the understanding of possible cause and effect relationships and the initiation of a policy response. Moreover, numerical analyses facilitate the evaluation of policy success or failure and allow for faster redefinition of alternatives. Facts, figures, and time series data on key indicators can narrow the range of disputes and reduce the polarization that often marks policy debates – whether about global climate change or pollution of a local lake (Esty, 2001b).

Information systems can transform policy options as well. Comparative analysis helps to target investment, spur competition, and trigger innovation. Better and cheaper data also tend to increase transparency and permit greater accountability. A quantified approach to environmental policymaking, therefore, could lead to better decisionmaking, improved performance, and greater efficiency by reducing uncertainty, enhancing comparative analysis, defining points of leverage, benchmarking, and revealing best practices (Esty, 2002).

MEASUREMENT TOOLS

Information is critical to sound decisionmaking. Its collection and presentation, however, are vital to its relevance and impacts. The tracking and aggregation of data are carried out at several levels and with multiple purposes. Some of the most widely employed tools include accounts, indicators, indices, and assessments.

Accounts

Accounts are selective collections of numerical data, converted to a common unit (money, weight, area, or energy). They can reveal how many people are working, and whether there are more or fewer jobs. They can reveal the number of acres of wetlands in a particular jurisdiction, and whether that number is increasing or decreasing. Monetary and environmental accounting, the predominant approaches to measuring progress, are indispensable, but insufficient tools for measuring sustainable development. Collections of facts rarely allow for communication and consensus building among those who have different values and perceptions.

The most influential accounting system is the System of National Accounts, codified and adopted by the United Nations in 1953 and most recently revised in 1993. The system records asset changes, income, and costs that can be measured and compared in monetary terms. It measures almost everything upon which humans can put a price, but excludes everything that humans usually consider priceless – from parenting and education to forests and air. The most common indicators derived from the System of National Accounts are the Gross Domestic Product (GDP) and the Gross National Product (GNP).[4]

---

4   The Gross Domestic Product (GDP) measures the total added value of enterprises operating in a particular country and the Gross National Product (GNP) measures the total added value of enterprises owned by citizens of a particular country. For example, goods produced by an American-owned firm operating in Japan would be included in the United State's GNP and in Japan's GDP.

Both GDP and GNP are inappropriate measures for human and ecosystem wellbeing. They show income, but not income distribution. They do not distinguish between productive and destructive activities, or between sustainable and unsustainable ones. Forest fires, hurricanes, cancer, crime, and disease all add to the GDP because dealing with them requires money to change hands.

It is as if a business kept a balance sheet by merely adding up all transactions without distinguishing between income and expenses, or between assets and liabilities. This leads to an overestimate of income and encouragement of economic policies that cannot be sustained. We need a different measure of progress, a clear guide through the jumble of contradictory statistics.[5]

Indicators, Indices, and Assessments

The primary alternatives to using accounts rely on assessments. Assessments assemble, summarize, organize, interpret, and possibly reconcile pieces of existing knowledge, and communicate them in a simplified manner. They are context-specific and do not attempt to be complete, but rely instead on measuring specific representative aspects, or indicators. Because they can be selective, assessments are better equipped than accounts to cover the wide range of issues necessary for an adequate portrayal of human and environmental conditions.

Indicators represent a particular attribute, characteristic, or property of a system (Gallopin, 1997). They require numerical data and time series to express trends. When a collection of indicators is aggregated mathematically, an index is produced. Indices simplify complex phenomena and make it possible to gauge the general status of a system (IISDnet, 2000a; WEF, 2002).

5 While other approaches have been proposed, including the Index of Sustainable Economic Welfare (ISEW) (Daly and Cobb, 1994) and the Genuine Progress Indicator (GPI), the Achilles heel of these and similar approaches is the difficulty of converting data to monetary units. For things that are traded, the market price is used. For things that have marketplace equivalents, oil in underdeveloped reserves for example, the market price is an adequate surrogate. For everything else, contingent values or estimated cost of social and environmental damage must be substituted. This reliance on monetary units as a single measurement obscures the great diversity of methods, data sources, and assumptions that are actually used. Moreover, monetary indicators cannot be forced to measure or explain non-monetary values.

A number of assessment initiatives have been launched in the past few years as alternatives to traditional measurement practices focusing on one or several systems. Among the most effective efforts are the Human Development Report, the Living Planet Index, the Ecological Footprint, the Environmental Sustainability Index, the Compass of Sustainability, the Dashboard of Sustainability, and the Wellbeing Assessment. These indices differ in scope, in the weight given to the environment, and in the basis used for converting indicator measurements to performance scores. Table 1 (pp 42-43) provides a brief overview of several key assessment initiatives.

THE VALUE AND PROMISE OF INTEGRATED ASSESSMENTS

Rio defined sustainability in economic, social, and environmental terms, and postulated the interdependence and indivisibility of these factors. We have learned, often to our chagrin, and usually to our frustration, that gains in economic welfare can often be offset by environmental costs, and that environmental protection can lead to social costs. We need integrated assessment methodologies that will serve as navigational tools, allowing us to define starting points and benchmarks along the way so that we can learn as we go.

Integrated assessments seek to provide relevant information to decisionmakers rather than merely to advance understanding for its own sake. They also bring together a broader set of areas, methods, or degrees of certainty than would typically characterize a study of the same issue within the bounds of a single research discipline (CIESIN, 1995). Integrated assessments separate signal from noise and help make sense of the signals. They meet the need for substantive information and, when developed in a participatory fashion, provide the additional benefits of consensus on broad goals and support for difficult political actions. Integrated assessments enable improved coordination and targeting of resources. They can help decisionmakers understand the linkages between short- and long-term needs and between apparently diverse goals by illuminating both connections and thresholds of impact. In addition, integrated assessments provide mechanisms by which individuals can evaluate the sustainability of their own behavior and hold governmental officials and private corporations accountable.

THE BELLAGIO PRINCIPLES FOR ASSESSING
SUSTAINABLE DEVELOPMENT

In 1996 the International Institute for Sustainable Development convened assessment specialists at the Rockefeller Foundation's Conference Center in Bellagio, Italy to develop principles to guide the assessment of progress toward sustainable development. The Bellagio Principles state that assessments should meet the following ten criteria:

1) Guiding vision and goals: Assessments should be guided by a clear vision of sustainable development and goals that define that vision.

2) Holistic perspective: Assessments should include review of the whole system as well as its parts and consider the wellbeing of sub-systems and both positive and negative consequences of human activity in monetary and non-monetary terms.

3) Essential elements: Assessments should consider equity and disparity within the current population and between present and future generations.

4) Adequate scope: Assessments should adopt a time horizon long enough to capture both human and ecosystem time scales.

5) Practical focus: Assessments should be based on an explicit set of categories that link visions and goals to indicators.

6) Openness: Assessments should have transparent methods and accessible data; they should make explicit all judgments, assumptions, and uncertainties in data and interpretation.

7) Effective communication: Assessments should be designed to meet the needs of the users and aim for simplicity in structure and language.

8) Broad participation: Assessments should obtain broad representation of key professional, technical, and social groups, while also ensuring the participation of decisionmakers.

9) Ongoing assessment: Assessments should develop a capacity to repeat measurement to determine trends and be responsive to change and uncertainty and adjust goals and frameworks as new insights are gained.

10) Institutional capacity: Continuity of assessing progress should be assured by clearly assigning responsibility and support in the decisionmaking process, providing institutional capacity for data collection, and supporting development of local assessment capacity.

Source: IISDnet (2000b), http://iisd1.iisd.ca/measure/bellagio1.htm

Table 1   Leading Assessment Initiatives

Method	Institution	Categories of measurements	Description
Human Development Report	United Nations Development Programme http://www.undp.org/hdr2000/english/HDR2000.html	*People* · Life expectancy at birth · Education (school enrollment and adult literacy rate) · GDP per capita	Includes four separate indices: · Human Development Index (categories of measurements refer to this index only) · Gender-related Development Index · Gender Empowerment Measure · Human Poverty Index (separate indices for developed and developing countries)
Environmental Sustainability Index	World Economic Forum (Yale Center for Environmental Law and Policy, Yale University and Center for International Earth Science Information Network, Columbia University) http://www.ciesin.org/indicators/ESI/downloads html#report	*Environment* · Environmental systems · Reducing environmental stresses · Reducing human vulnerability · Social and institutional capacity · Global stewardship	Includes twenty indicators of environmental sustainability classified in five categories. Each indicator includes several variables, for a total of sixty-eight variables.
Living Planet Index	World Wide Fund for Nature http://www.panda.org/livingplanet/LPR00/lpindex.cfm	*Environment* · Animal species in forests · Animal species in freshwater ecosystems · Animal species in marine ecosystems	Averages three indices, which monitor the changes over time in animal species in three different types of ecosystems.
Ecological Footprint	Redefining Progress http://www.panda.org/livingplanet/LPR00/ecofoot.cfm	*Environment* · Area of cropland required to produce crops consumed · Area of grazing land required to produce animal products · Area of forest required to produce wood and paper · Area of sea required · Area of land required · Area of forest required to absorb CO_2 emissions	Estimates a population's consumption of food, materials, or energy, by adding up six estimates of different types of areas required to produce the resources consumed by that population. The Ecological Footprint is measured in "area units."

Method	Institution	Categories of measurements	Description
Compass of Sustainability	AtKisson + Associates http://www.iisd.org/cgsdi/compass.htm	*Nature* *Economy* *Society* *Wellbeing of individuals*	An instrument panel for each of the four broad categories provides both quantitative and qualitative information about progress toward sustainability. In each of the four categories, there is a minimum of three indices (stocks, flows and responses) and ten indicators. The four categories are summed into a Sustainable Development Index
Dashboard of Sustainability	Consultative Group on Sustainable Development Indicators http://iisd.ca/cgsdi/dashboard.htm	*Environment* *Economy* *Society* *Institutions*	Graphic combination of indicators of three or four categories (the first three plus or minus Institutions) into a Policy Performance Index
Wellbeing Assessment/ Barometer of Sustainability	PADATA (Robert Prescott-Allen), World Conservation Union (IUCN), International Development Research Centre (IDRC) www.iucn.org/info_and_news/press/wonback.doc	*Ecosystem* *People* Combines the indicators into: · Human Wellbeing Index · Ecosystem Wellbeing Index · Wellbeing Index · Wellbeing/Stress Index	The Barometer of Sustainability is the only performance scale designed to measure human and ecosystem wellbeing together without submerging one in the other. Its two axes enable socio-economic and environmental indicators to be combined independently, keeping them separate to allow analysis of people-ecosystem interactions.

CASE STUDY: WELLBEING ASSESSMENT

Wellbeing Assessment (Prescott-Allen, 2001) is an integrated assessment methodology that can be used in both public and private sectors and from local to global levels. The basic hypothesis of Wellbeing Assessment is that sustainable development results from effective pursuit of human wellbeing *and* ecosystem wellbeing, and that the interaction between the subsystems can be measured and indexed.

Wellbeing Assessment defines human wellbeing as "a condition in which all members of society are able to determine and meet their needs and have a large range of choices to fulfill their potential" and ecosystem wellbeing as "a condition in which the ecosystem maintains its diversity and quality (and thus its capacity to support people and the rest of life) and its potential to adapt to change and provide a wide range of choices and opportunities for the future" (Prescott-Allen, 2001).

Measurements

Wellbeing Assessment measures the wellbeing of people and ecosystems separately, yet considers them jointly by organizing the information into two subsystems with five components each:

People	Ecosystem
• Health and Population	• Land
• Wealth	• Water
• Knowledge and Culture	• Air
• Community	• Species and Genes
• Equity	• Resource Use

Wellbeing Assessment identifies features of each dimension and organizes them into a hierarchy of progressively more specific and measurable parts. Indicators are chosen on the basis of representativeness, reliability, and feasibility. This procedure establishes a logical link between the subsystems and indicators, draws attention to elements that cannot be measured or on which there are no data, and leads to comprehensive consideration of human and ecosystem wellbeing.

Methodology

Indicators are combined using the Barometer of Sustainability, a performance scale with two axes, one for human wellbeing, the other for ecosystem wellbeing. Performance criteria – good, fair, medium, poor, and bad levels of performance – are defined for each indicator, enabling indicator measurements to be converted to scores and displayed on the axes.

Scores can be combined into higher level indices and ultimately into a Human Wellbeing Index, an Ecosystem Wellbeing Index, a Wellbeing Index, and a Wellbeing/Stress Index.[6] Because of the ability to include a large number of indicators, scores in Wellbeing Assessment are robust, and present a comprehensive picture less affected by a lack of data or by inaccurate data on individual indicators. Although underlying weights given to various variables and other assumptions can be debated, the indices provide clear, rapidly communicated pictures of a society's human and ecosystem wellbeing, how close a society is to its goal of sustainability and how it compares with other societies, the rate and direction of change, and major strengths and weaknesses of the human and natural systems of the entity being assessed.

THE ASSESSMENT CHALLENGE

More information and data do not necessarily mean greater knowledge or efficiency. A flood of unconnected and often apparently contradictory facts can swamp the flow of useful information for decisionmaking. Assessing progress thus presents both a governance and a methodological challenge.

From a governance perspective, authority and responsibility for data collection, analysis, and assessment are scattered, the process is dominated by special interests, and long-range planning and strategic decisionmaking are undermined. At every level, the capacity to collect and report data is fragmented and narrowly focused. When data are collected, they are assembled for specific and immediate purposes and then forgotten or poorly stored, usually separated from the assumptions, values, and purposes used in their collection. Differences in collection methodologies are often obscured over time, and incompatible data are combined in ways that, at best, dilute meaning.

---

6 Figure 1 shows a graphic representation of the Human Wellbeing Index and the Ecosystem Wellbeing Index.

Figure 1   Human and Ecosystem Wellbeing Indices

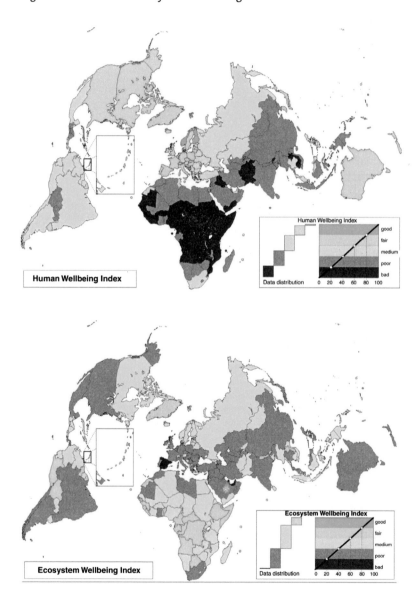

Source: Prescott-Allen, Robert. 2001. *The Wellbeing of Nations: A Country-by-Country Index of Quality of Life and the Environment.* Washington, D.C.: Island Press.

From a methodological perspective, we must learn how to define sustainability in terms of indicators that can be tracked and monitored, understood and applied by decisionmakers, and that allow us to efficiently manage our investments of time, money, labor, and thought. And yet, even if we have such effective indicators, we still run the risk of having an unintelligible hodgepodge of information on our hands.

Numbers, moreover, are not value neutral (Esty, 2002). "Northern" bias must be recognized and addressed.

There is a tendency to think of "developed countries" as countries that have achieved sustainability. In fact, nations with a high standard of living irreversibly change their own natural systems, while potentially imposing excessive pressure on the global environment. Successful assessment methodologies will have to make evident and understandable the linkages between consumption, deployment of advanced technology, and resource impact, both local and global.

Assessments must also function adequately at various scales, from local to global, and must lend themselves to aggregation and disaggregation without loss of validity and reliability. They must allow for regional and global comparisons while retaining national and local relevance. That means, at a minimum, that the actions of all countries must be assessed on the same basic factors and measures, but that any system adopted at an international level must lend itself to expansion via local participation to reflect additional values, conditions, and aspirations.

Examples of misleading global indicators abound, and pictures painted with broad brushes, as at the beginning of this chapter, can be both too rosy and too dire, often simultaneously. But to successfully address these challenges, we will need to assess progress on multiple fronts and at several levels simultaneously, and make decisions, the consequences of which are anticipated and intended.

NEXT STEPS: JOHANNESBURG AND BEYOND

After a decade of investment and action, results are difficult to document and almost impossible to interpret. When the nations of the world convene in South Africa in August 2002 for the World Summit on Sustainable Development, it will again be apparent that our worthwhile dreams have exceeded our capacity to manage effectively, in large measure because we have no systematic, valid, and reliable way to evaluate our progress, and no fixed point of responsibility for this task.

The Monterrey Consensus emphasized the international commitment to the goals of the Millennium Declaration, namely, "to eliminate poverty, improve social conditions and raise living standards, and protect our environment." The achievement of these goals will require an effective and transparent system for mobilizing public resources as well as strong, accountable institutions and measurement of results. The response from Johannesburg must be unequivocal and should include the following elements:

- A set of common *indicators* on which nations can collect and periodically report, allowing national and local governments to tailor or add indicators of particular significance to a local context;

- A common, scientifically sound *methodology* for integrating data sets into assessments of sustainability;

- The establishment of *national obligations to collect and report* social, economic, and environmental data, with sanctions for non-reporting;[7]

- Clear *standards* for periodic assessment of progress toward sustainability;

- The creation of an independent *International Scientific Panel on Sustainability*, similar to the Intergovernmental Panel on Climate Change under the UN Framework Convention on Climate Change, with the authority and responsibility to collect and assemble data, and report fully, objectively, and publicly on progress toward achieving sustainability;

---

7 Nations that do not report in a timely or adequate way could be ineligible for membership in successor bodies to the Commission on Sustainable Development, and have their voting privileges in multilateral environmental agreements suspended, for example.

- *Commitment to fund* these assessments and the activities of the Scientific Panel on Sustainability, such as commitment from donor countries to meet all costs of national reporting from the least developed countries, including capacity building.

CONCLUSION

The essential link between responsibility and accountability is a valid and reliable measurement of change over time. This link was not forged at Rio and has not been addressed since. Despite the flood of data over the past decade, information regarding the performance of governments and society in the pursuit of sustainability has been neither systematically collected nor transparently and objectively reported. We know little more today than we did ten years ago regarding our progress and the overall effectiveness of our actions.

Governments are inherently uneasy about committing to goals and managing for results, although none can deny that both steps are necessary for good governance. If they avoid the issue in Johannesburg as they did in Rio, we need only look at the experience of the last ten years to see the prospects for the next decade: more futile and inconclusive discussions, more sterile political debates over who is not meeting their obligations, and more wasteful investments nationally and internationally. We will continue to "fly blind."

There are no other binding commitments ("Type I Outcomes") remotely achievable for the World Summit on Sustainable Development that could be more valuable than a commitment to creating the means to authoritatively assess progress toward sustainable development.

REFERENCES

CIESIN. 1995. *Thematic Guide to Integrated Assessment Modeling of Climate Change.* Center for International Earth Science Information Network [cited June 9 2002]. Available from http://sedac.ciesin.org/mva/iamcc.tg/TGHP.html

Daly, Herman E., and John B. Cobb. 1994. *For the Common Good: Redirecting the Economy Toward Community, the Environment, and a Sustainable Future.* 2nd ed. Boston, MA: Beacon Press.

Esty, Daniel C. 2001a. "A Term's Limits." *Foreign Policy* (126): 74-75.

_____. 2001b. "Toward Data-Driven Environmentalism: The Environmental Sustainability Index." *The Environmental Law Reporter* 31: 10603-10612.

_____. 2002. "Why Measurement Matters." In *Environmental Performance Measurement: The Global Report 2001-2002,* edited by Peter R. Cornelius. New York: Oxford University Press.

Gallopin, G. 1997. "Indicators and their Use: Information for Decision Making." In *Sustainability Indicators: A Report on the Project on Indicators of Sustainable Development,* edited by Bedrich Moldan, Suzanne Billharz, and Robyn Matravers. Chichester: John Wiley & Sons.

IISDnet. 2000a. *Measurement and Indicators for Sustainable Development.* International Institute for Sustainable Development [cited June 8 2002]. Available from http://iisd.ca/measure/default.htm

_____. 2002b. *Bellagio Principles.* International Institute for Sustainable Development [cited June 9 2002]. Available from http://iisd1.iisd.ca/measure/bellagio1.htm

Prescott-Allen, Robert. 2001. *The Wellbeing of Nations: A Country-by-country Index of Quality of Life and the Environment.* Washington, D.C.: Island Press.

UN. 1997. *Women at a Glance.* United Nations Department of Public Information [cited June 9 2002]. Available from http://www.un.org/ecosocdev/geninfo/women/women96.htm

_____. 1999. *World Economic and Social Survey 1999*. New York: United Nations. Available from http://www.un.org/esa/analysis/wess/wess99.htm

UNDP. 1999. *Human Development Report 1999: Globalization with a Human Face*. New York: United Nations Development Program. Available from http://hdr.undp.org/reports/global/1999/en/default.cfm

UNFPA. 1999. *State of the World Population 1999*. New York: United Nations Population Fund. Available from http://www.unfpa.org/swp/1999/contents.htm

Upton, Simon. 2000. "Roadblocks to Agenda 21." In *Earth Summit 2002*, edited by Felix Dodds. London: Earthscan.

WEF. 2002. *Environmental Sustainability Index 2002*. Geneva, Switzerland: World Economic Forum. Available from http://www.yale.edu/envirocenter/esi/esi.html

Wilkinson, Clive. 2000. *Status of Coral Reefs of the World: 2000*. Queensland, Australia: Australia Institute of Marine Science. Available from http://www.aims.gov.au/pages/research/coral-bleaching/scr2000/gcrmn2000.pdf

World Resources Institute. 1998. *World Resources 1998-99: Environmental Change and Human Health*. New York: Oxford University Press. Available from http://www.wri.org/wri/wr-98-99/wr98-toc.htm

The North-South Knowledge Divide: Consequences for Global Environmental Governance

Sylvia Karlsson

SUMMARY

This chapter argues that there is a knowledge divide between the North and the South resulting from the substantial difference in accumulated scientific knowledge about the two regions and their current unequal capacities for generating new knowledge. It outlines the consequences of the divide for global environmental governance, including the risk that (1) issues of the South will be less visible on the global governance agenda, (2) that "globalized" knowledge generated in other ecological zones and socioeconomic settings is less representative for conditions in the South, and (3) that as a result, the South is unable to participate on equal terms in global governance.

This chapter further discusses two main strategies for addressing these consequences. The first strategy involves improving the generation of new knowledge about the South. This could be accomplished by strengthening the scientific community in the South, encouraging the scientific community in the North to carry out more research on the South, and expanding the groups that participate in the generation of new knowledge. The second strategy entails changing how decisionmakers in global institutions deal with scientific knowledge. This could be done by facing uncertainty with greater resolve, making better use of existing knowledge about the South, and incorporating alternative sources of knowledge.

THE NORTH-SOUTH KNOWLEDGE DIVIDE

> I see not just a gulf, but a yawning gulf, between the industri-
> alized countries and the developing countries in terms of sheer
> numbers of scientists and engineers. (Serageldin, 1998: 43)

The world's scientific community is heavily dominated by developed
countries, whether one looks at resources, the number of researchers,
or scientific "production." OECD countries contribute ninety-four
percent of the indexed scientific literature. Moreover, measures of
inequality between countries are more pronounced in scientific
expenditures than in income: although the average per capita income
of the thirty OECD countries is about sixty times greater than that of
the roughly fifty countries classified by the World Bank as "low-
income economies," average expenditures on science and technology
per capita in the former are 250 times greater than those in the latter
(Sagasti and Alcalde, 1999). More than ninety-six percent of world
patents are registered by Japan, the countries of Western Europe, and
the United States (Shrum and Shenhav, 1995).

The number of scientists/engineers per million inhabitants in
developing countries is 200 on average, while in developed countries,
it is 2,800 on average (Serageldin, 1998). Of course, the picture varies
greatly across developing countries, and a number of them have significant research capacity. India, for example, has the third most pop-
ulous scientific community in the world (Kandlikar and Sagar, 1999:
121). Africa, on the other hand, with fifty-three countries, has only nine
merit-based science academies (Hassan, 2001).

Developed and developing countries tend to group into two very
rough physical and climatic categories. Developing countries, which I
refer to here as the "South," are primarily located in sub-tropical or
tropical ecosystems. Developed countries, or the "North," occupy
mainly temperate and arctic climates and ecosystems.[1] Many
commentators point out that the amount of research in environment-

---

[1]   Obviously this categorization of the world into South and North is a gross simplification.
Exceptions, for example, include Australia and the southernmost parts of the United States in
the North, and the extensive arid regions of the South. Both categories encompass countries
with vastly different levels of economic development, among other differences. The World
Bank, for instance, uses four categories in its classification of economies by income (World
Bank, 1999). Nevertheless, because I wish to focus on the distinctions between *both* ecosystems and socioeconomic systems (see discussions in later sections), I confine the discussion
in this chapter to the two categories of North and South.

related disciplines such as biology, ecology, and ecotoxicology carried out in sub-tropical and tropical regions is very small compared to research in non-tropical latitudes (Bourdeau et al. 1989; Lacher and Goldstein, 1997). In addition, the North and its temperate and arctic ecosystems are sometimes cited as the "normal" or "standard" type in ecological sciences (Pomeroy and Service, 1986).

The knowledge divide comprises multiple gaps – in basic environmental and social data, monitoring of change, assessments, and more comprehensive research on human and social systems.

The Data Gap

The data gap is fundamental, since data availability is critical for monitoring, assessment, and further research. As stressed by Hales and Prescott-Allen in this volume, even in industrialized countries, data are often too limited or too disparate to be usable.[2] In developing countries, however, "even the most basic statistics are often lacking" (UN Economic and Social Council, 2001) and "[m]onitoring and data collection infrastructure of most developing countries is severely handicapped or non-existent" (UN System-Wide Earthwatch, 2000).

The data gap is manifest for both local and global issues. Information on mercury poisoning among populations in the Amazon, for example, is largely absent, and yet pollution levels of mercury from gold mining operations are significant (Lacher and Goldstein, 1997). Knowledge in the South about the effects of the use of agricultural pesticides on human health and ecosystems is also eextremely limited (Karlsson, 2000).

In the area of global environmental change, the North carries out almost all basic research and analysis, and the relevance of the results for developing countries is not usually assessed (Gutman, 1994). Yet, it is those countries that are most likely to be negatively affected by global

---

2   The scope of this gap is spelled out in the Environmental Sustainability Index (WEF, 2002). As Esty (2002) argues, the importance of sound data as the foundation for environmental decision-making – at the global, regional, national, local, and corporate scales – cannot be overstated.

warming (Redclift and Sage, 1998).[3] One of the exceptions to this pattern is India, which has a community of climate researchers. Their research focus, however, has been almost exclusively on the impact of climate change on coastal zones and agriculture, and hardly any of the results have been published (Kandlikar and Sagar, 1999).

The limited contribution to the body of scientific knowledge on global environmental issues from developing country scientists is not only a reflection of the unequal research capacity, but is also a result of different research priorities. Environmental issues of more acute local importance, rather than on a global scale, are engaging scientists in developing countries (Biermann, 2001; Gupta, 2000; Commission on Developing Countries and Global Change, 1992).

The knowledge divide between North and South regarding environmental issues could, from a historical perspective, be seen as just a phase of the scientific development process. It could be regarded as simply a knowledge gap that remains to be filled through more research. However, when science, both natural and social, is entering the policy process as the basis for environmental governance at the global, regional, and national levels, the knowledge divide becomes more than a purely scientific issue. It may have political consequences.

CONSEQUENCES OF THE DIVIDE FOR GLOBAL ENVIRONMENTAL GOVERNANCE

The international policy debate is in no small part shaped by the arguments emerging from scientific research and analysis (Kandlikar and Sagar, 1999: 133). Policymakers put strong faith in science, particularly in natural science, to discover environmental threats, interpret the

---

3   The IPCC finds that most of the less-developed regions are particularly vulnerable to climate change, both because a larger share of their economies is in climate-sensitive sectors and because they lack the resources to adapt. For example, small island states and low-lying coastal areas are especially vulnerable to a rise in sea level and to storms and have a limited capacity to respond to such events (IPCC, 2001: 16).

consequences, and even suggest policy options. At the global governance level, this is illustrated by the fact that "scientists represent the
only members of civil society to be consistently asked to advise government representatives" (UNEP, 2000: 13).

There are a number of scientific advisory processes at the global
level through which scientists are invited to give advice on environmental issues. Scientific expertise is sought in intergovernmental
bodies like the Intergovernmental Panel on Climate Change (IPCC), in
ad hoc expert groups to various conventions, in bodies that develop
technical standards and global assessments on the state of environmental knowledge, or in capacity building and multilateral aid
projects.

These scientific advisory processes contribute in three principal
ways to intergovernmental deliberations (UNEP, 2000):

- Catalyzing action by using science to set the terms of the debate;

- Ensuring a significant scientific component in negotiations;

- Establishing authoritative scientific standards for policy deliberations, decisions, and implementation.

Science is of significant importance to global deliberations.
Relevant questions in relation to the North-South knowledge divide
then become:

- What knowledge do decisionmakers in global institutions consider?

- If the desired knowledge is available, how it is used?

- What type of influence does it have on the content and character
  of global environmental governance?

Issues of the South Remain Off the Global Agenda

Many argue that environmental issues addressed by governance at the
global level tend to be those on the priority agenda of Northern countries (Agarwal, Narain, and Sharma, 1999; Gutman, 1994). These are
usually issues of a "global character," often including climate change,
ozone depletion, and biodiversity. While the effects of climate change
are likely to be most adverse and severe primarily for developing countries, these countries are the ones faced with more pressing immediate

concerns. Redcliff and Sage (1998), for example, claim that for many in the South, the global environmental agenda is "essentially a Northern agenda, of little relevance to them." The issues on which attention is focused are often far from the experience of environmental degradation of poor people in hamlets, villages, towns, and mega-cities in large parts of the world, where "the 'environment' consists of problems associated with health, shelter, and food availability" (Redcliff and Sage, 1998: 501). These environmental issues, which the South prioritizes, are less visible on the global agenda.

The comparative invisibility of environmental issues prioritized by the South can be linked to the North-South power gradient within the current international system, where the more powerful countries set the agenda. Nevertheless, it can also be argued that Northern dominance in setting the agenda is often supported by the invocation of science.

It is difficult for the South to put up science-based arguments for alternative issues to prioritize. As Gutman (1994: 390) argues, the South "is unable to express its environmental priorities or assess the costs and benefits of the international environmental agenda put forward by the North." Agarwal et al. comment on the power of scientific discourse in setting the agenda, and how that handicaps the South:

> The focus on science can easily divert attention from problems that have a focus in other issues like poverty. A science-based environmental agenda is more likely to be an agenda determined by the science-rich North, which can neglect the environmental concerns of the poor nations. (Agarwal, Narain, and Sharma, 1999: 5)[4]

Issues of the South – Invisible Even When on the Agenda

While the discussion above is concerned with the issues that make it to the global governance agenda, there are issues that are already on

---

4   Agarwal et al. here make use of the common definition of scientists as natural scientists, in this case environmental scientists. I would argue that scientists in other disciplines, such as sociology, economics, and development studies, do focus on other issues like poverty as subjects of study.

the agenda but whose relevance for countries in the South remains invisible due to lack of scientific data.

The Sanitary and Phytosanitary Agreement
The WTO agreement on Sanitary and Phytosanitary measures (SPS Agreement) illustrates this point.[5] With increasing trade and stricter standards established in importing countries, the issue of pesticide residues in agricultural products has gained in importance. The Agreement mandates that standards for the levels of pesticide residues in traded agricultural products — the Maximum Residue Limits set by the Codex Alimentarius — should be accepted by all parties to the Uruguay Agreements. These standards have thus become, indirectly, legally binding for the member countries of the WTO.

Developing countries, however, have problems in generating residue trial data because the industry, which provides these data, only does so for crops of major economic importance (Codex Alimentarius Commission, 1997). The absence of Maximum Residue Limits for pesticides on crops that developing countries export can be a serious hindrance to trade.

Industrialized countries have well-developed and enforced national legislation, as well as the capacity to produce residue trial data. Developing countries, on the other hand, often lack this capacity. Therefore, the globally agreed upon rules are least useful for those countries which in theory would benefit most from such coordinated regulations.

Toxic Substances
Another case in point can be found in the provisions of the multilateral environmental agreements that address toxic substances posing health or environmental risks. The process of adding substances to the agreements requires a large amount of data showing the level and type of risk. Notably, the Convention on the Prior Informed Consent Procedure for Certain Hazardous Chemicals and Pesticides in International Trade (the Rotterdam Convention) of 1998 includes as one of

5   For a detailed description of the Sanitary and Phytosanitary Agreement and its implications for developing countries, see Karlsson (2000).

the essential criteria for adding further hazardous pesticide formulations to the Convention the "reliability of the evidence that the use of the formulation" causes health problems (United Nations, 1998).

In this and other cases, developing countries face the risk of having their priority substances of concern not addressed due to lack of hard evidence of the health effects. There is little research in these countries on risks from chemicals. The types of specific chemical risks they face — which often come from the particular socioeconomic, institutional, and cultural circumstances in which the substances are used in developing countries — may therefore not appear on the priority lists of Northern countries. For instance, pesticides that may be used under strict safety conditions and without significant risks in developed countries, may pose significant health risks in developing countries when used by uneducated farmers without protective gear.

Inappropriately "Globalized" Knowledge

Another consequence of the knowledge divide occurs when "globalized" knowledge is not appropriate for situations and problems in the South. At the global level, scientific knowledge is often collected, analyzed, and summarized into assessments of particular environmental problems. These efforts create a scientific foundation for decisionmaking at the global level.

When most of the information assembled at the global level, or incorporated into global models, is generated in non-tropical latitudes and in developed countries, the assessments may be less valid for environmental problems in the South for the following reasons:

- There are unique ecosystems and species of both ecological and economic importance in the South that are only marginally present in some developed countries (e.g., rain forests, mangroves, and coral reefs), and may not be sufficiently accounted for in global assessments.

- There is a range of managed systems (agricultural, silvicultural, and aquacultural) equally unique to the tropics and sub-tropics.

- Northern analysts may have unfounded assumptions, among other things, about patterns of human behavior – for example, that agricultural workers will wear protective clothing at all times while spraying pesticides.

• The type of diet, body weight, and general health conditions assumed in the determination of tolerable levels of toxic substances in the human body may be different. A level of contamination by a substance in a food crop that is a marginal part of the diet can be relatively higher than in a food crop that serves as the staple food. People already weakened from other diseases or malnutrition may also be more sensitive to toxic substances than the average healthy person in a developed country.

The lack of good data, as well as the knowledge and science divide, contribute to the relative invisibility of Southern issues on the global governance agenda. In the area of climate change, for example, assessments have sometimes been inaccurate. The Indian Methane Campaign was launched in 1991 in response to climate change studies done abroad, including a study by the U.S. Environmental Protection Agency (EPA, 1990), which attributed large emissions of methane to Indian sources. The campaign made its own assessment of Indian methane emissions and denounced the EPA's findings (Kandlikar and Sagar, 1999: 123).

Biermann (2001) cites the Indian scientists' criticism of the IPCC regarding the lack of a separate chapter in their report on the monsoon, which is a central concern for research on climate change from their perspective. Furthermore, the modeling of the cost of carbon emission mitigation carried out for developing countries by scientists in the North is not satisfactory because "it is generally characterized by a lack of sensitivity to the differences between developed and developing countries" (Kandlikar and Sagar, 1999: 130).

Although it might be expected that data from the North would be misleading if merely extrapolated to the South, the extrapolation is done time and again. Of course, tendencies to disregard local variability on both global and local environmental issues can be interpreted as a pragmatic approach when there is a lack of local data. Whatever the reason, however, biases and inappropriateness for the conditions in developing countries are strongly noted in the South, particularly by scientists who are often excluded from the global scene. The knowledge divide can thus impair global deliberations, when they are based on an unsatisfactory understanding of the geographically distinct causes and effects of the global problems.

Inadequate Participation of Developing Countries in Global Governance

Another major consequence of the North-South knowledge divide pertains to the inadequate participation of developing countries in the provision of knowledge for global policy and action. The lack of national scientific capacity weakens the position of developing countries in multilateral negotiations and their participation in the conventions. Even in institutions designed to be "global," such as the IPCC, there is an enormous disparity in North-South participation.[6] Not only do developing country officials lack scientific input from their own researchers, but they also experience significant difficulty in coping with the masses of scientific and economic documents coming from the West.

The lack of developing country science raises the question of a Northern bias in global assessments. It appears that the Northern bias may be more pronounced as one moves further from basic science (Kandlikar and Sagar, 1999). Moreover, global environmental assessments often fail to explicitly address value considerations, such as equity (Biermann, 2001), which is of particular relevance to developing countries.

In the environmental domain, both the strong dependence on science (natural science in particular), and the tendency to disguise value judgments by "scientizing"[7] the debate, increase the need to focus on the lack of participation of developing countries in scientific advisory processes. It is easy to fall into complacency by assuming that one need not pay so much attention to geographical representativeness because science is "objective" and, therefore, whoever is not involved in the decisionmaking would have arrived at the same conclusions (Yearley, 1996: 118). Many researchers have pointed to the limits to complete objectivity in research and to the cultural dependence and implicit value judgments in natural science (Jasanoff, 1996).

---

6   In the 1996 IPCC Working Group I there were 158 authors from the United States, 61 from the United Kingdom, 3 from India, and 7 from China. The relative participation looked similar in Working Group II. Working Group III had 30 participants from the United States, 5 from the United Kingdom, 7 from India, and 2 from China (Kandlikar and Sagar, 1999).

7   Jasanoff (1996: 173) defines the act of "scientizing" an issue as "at once to assert that there are systematic, discoverable methods for coping with it and to suggest that these approaches can be worked out independently of national or sectarian interests."

With the value connotations associated with science, and particularly its application in policy, it is clear that the present participation of the South in deliberations on global environmental governance, both scientific and political, is inadequate. It is a question of equity and fairness to present more balanced knowledge-based voices from developing countries in these arenas.

BRIDGING THE KNOWLEDGE DIVIDE: CHANGING THE GENERATION OF KNOWLEDGE

Acknowledging the existence of a knowledge divide between the North and the South and its consequences prompts the question of what can be done to address the situation. Over the long term, bridging the North-South knowledge divide will require measures aimed at reducing the divide itself. Increasing the generation of scientific knowledge in the South and of the South will be critical in this respect. Four strategies could be pursued: (1) strengthening the data and science foundations of the South; (2) strengthening the scientific community in the South; (3) encouraging more research on the South among Northern scientists; and (4) expanding the groups capable of generating scientific knowledge.

Strengthening Southern Data and Science

The most straightforward way to bridge the knowledge divide is to commit resources to strengthening the data and science foundations on which global environmental governance efforts depend. The value of baseline data comparable across countries is clear (Esty, 2002). Such metrics allow for trends to be tracked, problems spotted, policies evaluated, and "best practices" identified. Enormous potential gains could be achieved across many environmental problem areas simply by moving laggards toward the performance of those at the leading edge. Because of the belief that poverty and environmental degradation are causally linked (World Commission on Environment and Development, 1987), it would be essential to improve data on sustainable development and socioeconomic indicators as well as data on environmental factors.

POSSIBLE GLOBAL ENVIRONMENTAL GOVERNANCE MEASURES

- A global environmental data initiative to track a set of key socio-economic and ecological and environmental public health indicators in all countries of the world on a methodologically consistent and comparable basis;

- Beyond building a global environmental database, a true commitment to closing the North-South knowledge gap, which would entail capacity building in the South. The developing world needs more scientists, economists, and researchers of all sorts;

- Building up this capacity, requires (as discussed below) sustained commitments to education for several decades.

Strengthening the Scientific Community in the South

Part of the responsibility for strengthening the scientific community *in* the South lies in the hands of developing countries themselves who need to prioritize investment in science. But their efforts alone will not suffice. The role for bi- and multilateral aid agencies and Northern and international research programs in building this capacity is critical.

A number of actors are already involved in such capacity building, from national space agencies to UN organizations, from the international academic community to individual researchers (Fuchs, Virji, and Fleming, 1998; EUMETSTAT, 1997; UN Economic and Social Council, 1997). It is even increasingly the case that international scientific advisory processes have as a goal the facilitation of national level capacity building (UNEP, 2000).

However, much capacity building is currently aimed at financing more Ph.D. degrees for developing country citizens, providing funds for large scale cooperation projects on global environmental change research, and granting travel money to bring scientists from the South to scientific conferences and expert meetings. These efforts do not suffice to provide developing country scientists with a basic research infrastructure.

Research funding is predominantly nationally based. Up until now, there has been no explicit mandate in global environmental governance (such as in the UN Environment Programme and the Global Environment Facility) to fund basic research based on the competitive merits of research proposals. Most of the resources go to assessments of previous research rather than the generation of new knowledge.

> **POSSIBLE GLOBAL ENVIRONMENTAL GOVERNANCE MEASURES**
>
> Establishment of small "micro research grants" for individual research projects in countries with limited research capacity.[8] Existing expert bodies under multilateral environmental agreements or other UN bodies could administer these grants. These agencies would have the best overview of the specific research gaps hampering their work.

Similar to the success in the field of micro credit, where very little money goes a long way for development in poor communities, rather humble research grants for salaries and equipment might lead to substantial research results in many developing countries. When combined with assistance to make the results internationally available, such measures could make significant contributions to reducing the knowledge divide.

Increasing the Number of Northern Scientists Working on the South

The second approach to increasing knowledge of environmental and human systems in the South is to strengthen the scientific community of the North *for* the South, by increasing the number of Northern scientists who conduct field studies in the South. When they carry out their work in close partnership with local scientists, they benefit in their own research from local knowledge and experience while also contributing to the capacity of their Southern partners. This approach may necessitate capacity building for the Northern research community on local ecological and socioeconomic contexts in the South.[9]

---

8 I am grateful to Dr. Arthur L. Dahl for this suggestion and for contributing valuable input to discussions on global governance measures in general.

9 Dasgupta (1998: 22) argues for such an approach among economists who study environmental issues.

Northern scientists could learn to better incorporate the priorities and realities of the South, both within research and policy processes.

POSSIBLE GLOBAL ENVIRONMENTAL GOVERNANCE MEASURES

- Establishing of clear communication channels between UN bodies, such as convention secretariats, and Northern funding agencies, such as research councils and private foundations. Priority research areas could thus be suggested;

- Convening UN expert meetings in the South, even if the majority of experts are from the North, combined with field trips with local experts.

Expanding the Number of Groups that Generate New Scientific Knowledge

The third approach to reducing the knowledge gap is to expand the groups that participate in the generation of scientific knowledge. The limited numbers of scientists in the South, and the extremely limited resources available for monitoring and research activities, warrant more innovative approaches. For example, if high school students across these countries, as part of their education, gathered basic data on environmental and social parameters under the guidance of researchers and with the support of the educational infrastructure, the cadre of observers and the amount of data collected would increase dramatically. There are already a number of successful examples where this has been tried.

School children, non-governmental organizations, major groups, and amateur volunteers have helped to collect data and fill data gaps, and the UN Secretary-General has encouraged the Commission on Sustainable Development to develop this further (UN Economic and Social Council, 2001).

Including these new groups in science production is not only a pragmatic approach to collecting data; it would also contribute to an aspect of human development that all should be entitled to:

> The intellectual tools and approaches of science should be made accessible in all countries, and to all levels of the population, in order to allow all persons to be active participants in finding solutions to environmental problems and defining appropriate forms of sustainable development. (UN Economic and Social Council, 1997)

A complementary approach would be to make the newest global data (satellite images, for example) available for natural resource management decisions at the local level.

POSSIBLE GLOBAL ENVIRONMENTAL GOVERNANCE MEASURES

- Strengthening support for projects that incorporate training for various civil society groups and the private sector, enabling them to participate in data collection;
- Promoting the development of simple monitoring and research methods that could be used by local groups;
- Establishing various central cores of stable funding for long-term monitoring projects on specific environmental degradation problems;
- Encouraging the international scientific community to make its results public and available in usable forms for local populations and decisionmakers.

Making the tools of the scientific enterprise available to larger sections of the population of the world would not only bridge the knowledge divide, but is likely to increase the level of trust between various stakeholders in decisionmaking processes, from the global to the local level.

BRIDGING THE KNOWLEDGE DIVIDE: CHANGING DECISIONMAKING

Another approach to bridging the knowledge divide would be to take the divide at face value and to focus on how it is addressed in governance, trying to change the way decisionmakers deal with knowledge and uncertainty. Getting global institutions to change their decision-making processes to reduce the negative consequences of the existing knowledge divide could entail three strategies: (1) facing uncertainty with more care and rigor; (2) making better use of available knowledge; and (3) considering alternative knowledge in the policymaking process.

Dealing with Uncertainty

Facing uncertainty with more care will entail greater acknowledgement of the limits of knowledge, clearer focus on underlying assumptions, and, at times, a precautionary approach.

Those engaged in global environmental policymaking must take more care to construct their analyses on solid foundations. Special attention must be given to getting data from the South. Modeling must be done in ways that reflect the experiences and realities of the developing world. Where extrapolations or assumptions are used, the basis for these starting points should be made explicit. Ranges of values and the use of multiple scenarios can also help to ensure that uncertainties are addressed in ways that generate a more neutral analytic foundation for global environmental action.

Utilizing Existing Scientific Knowledge in the South

A second approach that global institutions could adopt is to make better use of the scientific knowledge about the South that is available. It will take effort to find these data. Travel may be necessary to physically collect them, as this knowledge is unlikely to be catalogued and found through the databases of libraries accessible over the internet. It may require spending more time to locate scientists from the South – or scientists from the North whose specialty is environmental impacts in the South – and more resources to bring them to meetings in scientific advisory processes at the global level. It will certainly require some investment in verifying and quality-controlling the data found. Simultaneous translation at meetings may also be necessary, as language frequently is an obstacle to contributions from Southern scientists.

A lot of science from the South never reaches the international science arena. Many, especially younger, researchers in the South publish in local journals, particularly in the fields of agriculture, silviculture, and aquaculture (IDRC, 1991). In many cases, the language barrier prevents scientists from publishing in international journals and they are confined to the domestic or regional science community. Funds for the translation of some of this body of knowledge would help to close the knowledge gap.

Considerable information and analyses are also generated by agencies, domestic and foreign, governmental and non-governmental, which work directly on environmental management and sustainable development in the South. Much of the research and writing in the development community, such as internal project reports, usually remains in the gray literature and never reaches the scientific journals (Kammen and Dove, 1997). This literature could be made more accessible and incorporated into global-level discussions.

POSSIBLE GLOBAL ENVIRONMENTAL GOVERNANCE MEASURES

- Systematic efforts to bring forth "hidden" scientific knowledge to scientific advisory processes at the global level;

- Broadening the disciplines represented in global decision processes, i.e., including the social sciences, to expand the base of data and information (UNEP, 2000);

- New commitments of resources for assisting scientists from the South in making their research results internationally available – both through publications and through participation in international meetings.

Incorporating Other Sources and Types of Knowledge

The third approach to changing decisionmaking requires a somewhat different mindset within global institutions, in order to broaden the categories of knowledge that are considered. It would ask decision-

makers to acknowledge that highly validated science cannot do everything and that there may be value in examining the wealth of experience captured in local and traditional knowledge, especially of indigenous people.

The knowledge divide looks different if one includes local knowledge. For example, local people may have considerable knowledge of
species interconnections, natural variations in biogeophysical factors
in the local context, and an integrated understanding of how their
own actions influence the natural resources they depend on, even if
they cannot express this knowledge in the language of modern science.[10] There is a considerable amount of local knowledge in these categories that could be of value to decisionmaking. One scientific advisory body that has started to discuss how to approach traditional
knowledge is the Committee on Science and Technology of the
Convention to Combat Desertification (UNEP, 1998). Non-governmental organizations (NGOs) are also a potential channel through
which such local experiences could reach the global level.

POSSIBLE GLOBAL ENVIRONMENTAL GOVERNANCE MEASURES

- Systematic dialogue between government-appointed experts in
  scientific advisory bodies and NGOs to explore ways of sifting out
  the valuable local experiences of communities that do not nor-
  mally participate in policymaking processes. Such an exchange
  could in turn encourage the participation of scientists from multiple disciplines and the formulation of further research priorities;[11]

- Scientific validation of alternative types of knowledge. To this
  end, scientists should be encouraged to collect and "test" local
  knowledge. Traditional knowledge should be "systematized" and
  put to the tests of normal scientific validation and peer-review;

- Dissemination of alternative types of knowledge and information
  to policymakers through the normal scientific channels.

---

[10] In many cases, this knowledge is in the process of being lost because people migrate to urban
areas, are forced off their land, etc.

[11] I am grateful to Professor Anders Hjort of Ornäs for contributing this suggestion.

CONCLUSION

> The world is divided into two civilisations that interact strong-
> ly, albeit in a one-sided way. One civilisation is based on the
> growth of scientific knowledge, the other demonstrates a more
> or less passive acceptance of results generated by the first.
> (Salomon, 1995: 9)

While Salomon makes this statement in the context of a general discussion of the role of science and technology for development, this
chapter argues that the gist of his conclusion is also applicable to environmental governance at the global level, despite a significant and
growing scientific enterprise in many developing countries. The natu-
ral-science-dominated discourse on global environmental issues, the
reluctance to take action under uncertainty, and the limited scientific
capacity of the South put developing countries at a disadvantage in the
global environmental governance arena.

The "globalization" of knowledge based largely on findings in
Northern societies and ecosystems presents additional obstacles for
developing countries in global deliberations. Possible approaches to
addressing the knowledge divide and its negative consequences on
global environmental governance, discussed in this chapter, can be
summarized as follows:

MEASURES TO BRIDGE THE KNOWLEDGE DIVIDE	
Changing the Generation of of Knowledge	**Changing Decisionmaking**
• Launch an initiative to collect baseline environmental data across all countries of the world;	• Face uncertainty more carefully and rigorously;
• Strengthen the scientific com-munity in the South;	• Use available knowledge about the South better;
• Strengthen the scientific com-munity in the North researching in the South;	• Identify, test, and, where appropriate, incorporate alternative sources of knowledge.
• Expand the groups participating participating in the generation of new knowledge.	

The knowledge divide and its consequences cannot be considered a problem of the South alone, but rather a collective problem for the international community, since the North and the South are ultimately part of the same physical and social whole. Any serious approach to addressing the knowledge divide should consider not only the goal of making global environmental governance more equitable and more broadly knowledge-based, but also the deeper underlying issue of what it means for people to be involved in the generation of knowledge about their own realities.

REFERENCES

Agarwal, Anil, Sunita Narain, and Anju Sharma, eds. 1999. *Green Politics.* New Delhi: Centre for Science and Environment.

Biermann, Frank. 2001. "Big Science, Small Impacts – In the South? The Influence of Global Environmental Assessments on Expert Communities in India." *Global Environmental Change* 11 (4): 297-309.

Bourdeau, Philippe, J. A. Haines, W. Klein, and C. R. K. Murti, eds. 1989. *Ecotoxicology and Climate, With Special Reference to Hot and Cold Climates.* Vol. 38. Chicester, United Kingdom: John Wiley and Sons, Ltd.

Codex Alimentarius Commission. 1997. *Problems Relative to Pesticide Residues in Food in Developing Countries.* Rome: Food and Agriculture Organization and World Health Organization.

Commission on Developing Countries and Global Change. 1992. *For Earth's Sake: A Report from the Commission on Developing Countries and Global Change.* Ottawa, Canada: International Development Research Center.

Dasgupta, P. 1998. "Shifting Responsibilities for Knowledge to Advance a Sustainable South." In *Organizing Knowledge for Environmentally and Socially Sustainable Development,* edited by T. H. Ismail Serageldin, Joan Martin-Brown, Gustavo Lopez Ospina, Jeann Damlamian and Tariq Husain. Washington, D.C.: World Bank.

EPA. 1990. *Methane Emissions and Opportunities for Control.* Washington, D.C.: United States Environmental Protection Agency.

Esty, Daniel C. 2002. "Why Measurement Matters." In *Environmental Performance Measurement: The Global Report 2001-2002,* edited by Daniel C. Esty and Peter R. Cornelius. New York: Oxford University Press.

EUMETSTAT. 1997. *Annual Report on Developing Country Activities.* Toulouse, France: Committee on Earth Observation Satellites.

Fuchs, Roland, Hassan Virji, and Cory Fleming. 1998. *START Implementation Plan 1997-2002.* Stockholm: International Geosphere-Biosphere Programme. Available from http://www.start.org/Publications/Documents/START_Implementation_Plan.pdf

Gupta, Joyeeta. 2000. "North-South Aspects of the Climate Change Issue: Towards a Negotiating Theory and Strategy for Developing Countries." *International Journal of Sustainable Development* 3 (2): 115-135.

Gutman, Pablo. 1994. "Developing Countries and International Environmental Negotiations: The Risks of Poorly Informed Choices." *Society and Natural Resources* 7: 389-397.

Hassan, Mohamed H. A. 2001. "Can Science Save Africa?" *Science* 292 (5522).

IDRC. 1991. "The Global Research Agenda: A South-North Perspective." *Interdisciplinary Science Reviews* 16 (4): 337-344.

IPCC. 2001. *Climate Change 2001: Impacts, Adaptation and Vulnerability.* Geneva, Switzerland: Intergovernmental Panel on Climate Change. Available from http://www.ipcc.ch/pub/tar/wg2/

Jasanoff, Sheila. 1996. "Science and Norms in Global Environmental Regimes." In *Earthly Goods, Environmental Change and Social Justice,* edited by Fen Osler Hampson, and Judith Reppy. Ithaca, NY: Cornell University Press.

Kammen, Daniel M., and Michael R. Dove. 1997. "The Virtues of Mundane Science." *Environment* 39 (6): 10-41.

Kandlikar, Milind, and Ambuj Sagar. 1999. "Climate Change Research and Analysis in India: An Integrated Assessment of a South-North Divide." *Global Environmental Change* 9 (2): 119-138.

Karlsson, Sylvia. 2000. *Multilayered Governance: Pesticides in the South – Environmental Concerns in a Globalised World.* Linköping, Sweden: Department of Water and Environmental Studies, Linköping University.

Lacher, Thomas E., and Michael I. Goldstein. 1997. "Tropical Ecotoxicology: Status and Needs." *Environmental Toxicology and Chemistry* 16 (1): 100-111.

Pomeroy, D. E., and M. W. Service. 1986. *Tropical Ecology.* New York: Longman Scientific & Technical.

Redclift, Michael, and Colin Sage. 1998. "Global Environmental Change and Global Inequality." *International Sociology* 13 (4): 499-516.

Sagasti, Francisco, and Gonzalo Alcalde. 1999. *Development Cooperation in a Fractured Global Order: An Arduous Transition.* Ottawa, Canada: International Development Research Center.

Salomon, Jean-Jacques. 1995. "The 'Uncertain Quest': Mobilising Science and Technology for Development." *Science and Public Policy* 22 (1): 9-18.

Serageldin, T. H. Ismail. 1998. "The Social-Natural Science Gap in Educating for Sustainable Development." In *Organizing Knowledge for Environmentally Sustainable Development,* edited by T. H. Ismail Serageldin, Joan Martin-Brown, Gustavo Lopez Ospina, Jeann Damlamian and Tariq Husain. Washington, D.C.: World Bank.

Shrum, Wesley, and Yehouda Shenhav. 1995. "Science and Technology in Less Developed Countries." In *Handbook of Science and Technology Studies,* edited by Sheila Jasanoff et al. Newbury Park, United Kingdom: Sage Publishers.

UNEP. 1998. *Report on International Scientific Advisory Processes on the Environment and Sustainable Development.* Nairobi, Kenya: United Nations Environment Programme. Available from http://earthwatch.unep.net/about/docs/sciadv.htm

_____. 2000. *The Second Report on International Scientific Advisory Processes on the Environment and Sustainable Development.* Nairobi, Kenya: United Nations Environment Programme. Available from http://earthwatch.unep.net/about/docs/sciadv2.htm

UN. 1998. *Convention on the Prior Informed Consent (PIC) Procedure for Certain Hazardous Chemicals and Pesticides in International Trade.* New York: United Nations. Available from http://www.fao.org/ag/agp/agpp/pesticid/pic/Download/fin_e.pdf

UN Economic and Social Council. 1997. *Commission on Sustainable Development, Fifth Session, 7-25 April 1997. Overall Progress Achieved Since the United Nations Conference on Environment and Development. Report of the Secretary-General, Addendum, Science for Sustainable Development.* New York: United Nations. Available from http://www.un.org/documents/ecosoc/ cn17/1997/ecn171997-2add25.htm

_____. 2001. *Commission on Sustainable Development, Ninth Session. Information for Decision-Making and Participation (Chapter 40, Agenda 21), Report of the Secretary-General.* New York: United Nations.

UN System-Wide Earthwatch. 2000. *International Expert Meeting on Information for Decision-Making and Participation.* Geneva, Switzerland: United Nations Environment Programme. Available from www.unep.ch/earthw/ottawabk.htm

WEF. 2002. *Environmental Performance Measurement: The Global Report 2001-2002.* Geneva, Switzerland: World Economic Forum.

World Bank. 1999. *World Development Report 1998/99, Knowledge for Development.* New York: Oxford University Press. Available from http://www.worldbank.org/wdr/wdr98/contents.htm

World Commission on Environment and Development. 1987. *Our Common Future.* New York: United Nations.

Yearley, Steven. 1996. *Sociology, Environmentalism, Globalization.* London: Sage Publications.

The Role of NGOs and Civil Society in Global Environmental Governance

Barbara Gemmill and Abimbola Bamidele-Izu

SUMMARY

This chapter identifies five major roles that civil society might play in global environmental governance: (1) collecting, disseminating, and analyzing information; (2) providing input to agenda-setting and policy development processes; (3) performing operational functions; (4) assessing environmental conditions and monitoring compliance with environmental agreements; and (5) advocating environmental justice. Three case studies – the Crucible Group, TRAFFIC, and global ecosystem assessment processes – illustrate the success NGOs have had in stepping up to these roles.

International decisionmaking processes seek legitimacy through the involvement of civil society, yet formal mechanisms for NGO participation within the UN system remain limited. Ad-hoc civil society participation should be replaced by a strengthened, more formalized institutional structure for engagement. The chapter offers concrete suggestions for such measures, including:

- Wider use of the "commission" model for long-term, substantive involvement of civil society in global policymaking processes;
- Assistance for the development of NGO networks;
- Development of standards for civil society participation and engagement in international decisionmaking processes;
- Creation of a comprehensive database of information and analysis at different geographic and political levels;
- Involvement of a larger part of the public in issue spotting, assessment, and monitoring functions;
- Support for knowledge-generating institutions in developing countries.

INTRODUCTION

Globalization has considerably weakened traditional governance processes. Increasing global economic integration has reduced the power of national governments while granting other economic and political actors access to the world stage. The 1990s witnessed a dramatic increase in the involvement of non-governmental organizations (NGOs) in global governance (Charnovitz, 1997).

NGOs and other civil society groups are not only stakeholders in governance, but also a driving force behind greater international cooperation through the active mobilization of public support for international agreements.

Enabling the constructive participation of civil society in global environmental governance is thus one of the most important tasks for policymakers concerned with the effectiveness of global governance (Gemmill, Ivanova, and Chee, 2002).

This chapter explores the potential for strengthened roles for civil society, and especially non-governmental organizations, within a new or a restructured global environmental governance system. We argue that civil society should play a major role in five key areas:

- Information collection and dissemination;

- Policy development consultation;

- Policy implementation;

- Assessment and monitoring;

- Advocacy for environmental justice.

We further contend that existing structures do not enable civil society to fulfill these roles effectively and offer suggestions for reform measures to facilitate the participation of civil society in global environmental governance.

WHO AND WHAT IS CIVIL SOCIETY?

The first step in examining civil society participation is describing exactly who is included within the delineation of civil society. In the broadest sense, civil society has been characterized as a sphere of social life that is public but excludes government activities (Meidinger, 2001). Michael Bratton describes civil society as social interaction between the household and the state characterized by community cooperation, structures of voluntary association, and networks of public communication (Bratton, 1994). The term civil society is generally used to classify persons, institutions, and organizations that have the goal of advancing or expressing a common purpose through ideas, actions, and demands on governments (Cohen and Arato, 1992).

The membership of civil society is quite diverse, ranging from individuals to religious and academic institutions to issue-focused groups such as not-for-profit or non-governmental organizations. In the realm of environmental governance, NGOs are the most prominent actors and therefore comprise the main focus of this chapter. NGOs are:

> Groups of individuals organized for the myriad of reasons that engage human imagination and aspiration. They can be set up to advocate a particular cause, such as human rights, or to carry out programs on the ground, such as disaster relief. They can have memberships ranging from local to global. (Charnovitz, 1997: 186)[1]

NGOs involved in environmental governance are highly diverse, including local, national, regional, and international groups with various missions dedicated to environmental protection, sustainable development, poverty alleviation, animal welfare, and other issues.

The diversity of civil society and its value to official intergovernmental processes on the environment are acknowledged in Agenda 21, the comprehensive sustainable development blueprint adopted at the 1992 Rio Earth Summit. The document does not make use of the term civil society, although it expressly recognizes the members of civil society as a major constituency.

---

[1] Charnovitz further points out that, "Indeed, some NGO's are more 'global' than intergovernmental organizations. For example, the International Amateur Athletic Federation includes twenty-one more members than the United Nations" (Charnovitz, 1997).

The Commission on Sustainable Development (CSD), responsible for implementing Agenda 21, classifies civil society into the following Major Groups:[2]

- Women

- Children and Youth

- Indigenous Peoples and Communities

- Non-governmental Organizations

- Workers and Trade Unions

- The Scientific and Technological Community

- Business and Industry

- Farmers

All of the Major Groups are officially recognized by the United Nations through an accreditation mechanism developed specifically for NGOs (Pace, 2002).

A noteworthy question connected to the definition of civil society is whether business and industry should be included in this social grouping. While Agenda 21 considers business and industry part of civil society, some observers contend that, because they already have considerable influence over international governance processes through informal lobbying opportunities and formal influence channels, business and industry should not be included in civil society (Meidinger, 2001). Because this chapter focuses on the participation of NGOs, it is not essential to resolve the business and civil society delineation question within these pages, although determining how business should participate within governance is clearly of great importance.

OVERVIEW OF CIVIL SOCIETY PARTICIPATION: EXPANDING NGO INVOLVEMENT

The participation of civil society in global governance is increasing in significance, but is not unprecedented. NGO involvement is usually considered a late-twentieth-century phenomenon, but in fact it has

---

2   The CSD also recognizes the role of local authorities, which are removed enough from the international intergovernmental process to be considered civil society in the context of the institution.

occurred for over two centuries (Charnovitz, 1997). The recent rate of proliferation of non-governmental organizations, however, is notable. In 1948, for example, the United Nations listed forty-one consultative groups that were formally accredited to participate in consultative processes; in 1998, there were more than 1,500 organizations with varying degrees of participation and access (Simmons, 1998). Numerous factors, from the development of information technology to the greater awareness of global interdependence to the spread of democracy, explain the rise of NGOs.[3]

The United Nations is the intergovernmental organization that has most openly recognized and endorsed the need to collaborate with the non-governmental sector (Weiss, 1999).[4] Historically, the UN cooperated with NGOs primarily as partners in the implementation of certain programs, particularly in the areas of emergency response, human rights, and election monitoring.

Due to their critical role in service delivery and implementation, civil society organizations have long been recognized as "partners" of the UN system, especially in environmental negotiations.

Over the past decade, environmental NGO activity within UN processes has intensified. Prior to the 1990s, while various social movements may have utilized the UN as a global forum to call attention to particular agendas, the focus was not on influencing the official UN deliberations. Through the process leading up to the 1992 United Nations Conference on Environment and Development (UNCED), environmental organizations began intense internal capacity building efforts to gain more sophisticated understanding of the international policymaking process (Conca, 1996). Some of the innovations at the time – most notably, parallel NGO fora held alongside UN conferences – are now a routine element of intergovernmental deliberations (Fomerand, 1996).

---

3 Interestingly, the first intergovernmental environmental summit, the 1972 UN Conference on the Human Environment, is cited as one factor behind the rise in NGOs (Conca, 1996).

4 Other intergovernmental bodies, such as the World Trade Organization, the International Monetary Fund, and the G-7 have no provisions for formal involvement of non-governmental organizations, see Esty (1998) and Charnovitz (1996).

The UN Conference on Environment and Development was of particular significance to NGOs. Agenda 21 declared the need for new forms of participation:

> The United Nations system, including international finance and development agencies, and all intergovernmental organizations and forums should, in consultation with non-governmental organizations, take measures to . . . enhance existing or, where they do not exist, establish mechanisms and procedures within each agency to draw on the expertise and views of non-governmental organizations in policy and program design, implementation and evaluation. (UN, 1994: Chapter 27)

The 1992 Earth Summit thus affirmed that the commitment and genuine involvement of non-state actors are critical to reaching sustainable development goals.

Throughout the 1990s, NGOs continued to focus on official UN deliberations and the international policy arena. A variety of channels have served NGOs in their purpose of participating and influencing international deliberations. NGOs sought accreditation at international intergovernmental conferences where they could lobby government delegates, organize briefings, and even officially address plenary sessions. A number of government delegations to international conferences are now formally including NGO representatives. In the preparatory process for the 1996 UN Conference on Human Settlements (Habitat II), for example, NGOs and local authorities participated in the informal drafting groups that drew up the *Declaration and Programme of Action*. Within the policymaking circle of the United Nations Economic Commission for Europe (UNECE), NGOs had a say in establishing the agenda and other aspects of the negotiations process for the 1998 Aarhus Convention on Public Access to Information, Participation in Decisionmaking and Access to Environmental Justice. In both of these cases, a special, semi-official status was accorded to civil society representatives.

Successes and Challenges in Civil Society Participation: Differing Roles and Rules for Engagement

New forms of NGO participation have changed the nature of international environmental policymaking. The international community has begun to recognize that effective global action requires meaningful stakeholder involvement in international policymaking and implementation (Wapner, 2000). NGO involvement in global environmental governance can take a variety of forms (Esty, 1998, 2002; Charnovitz, 1997):

- *Expert advice and analysis.* NGOs can facilitate negotiations by giving politicians access to competing ideas from outside the normal bureaucratic channels;

- *Intellectual competition to governments.* NGOs often have much better analytical and technical skills and capacity to respond more quickly than government officials;[5]

- *Mobilization of public opinion.* NGOs can influence the public through campaigns and broad outreach;

- *Representation of the voiceless.* NGOs can help vocalize the interests of persons not well-represented in policymaking;

- *Service provision.* NGOs can deliver technical expertise on particular topics as needed by government officials as well as participate directly in operational activities;

- *Monitoring and assessment.* NGOs can help strengthen international agreements by monitoring negotiation efforts and governmental compliance;

- *Legitimization of global-scale decisionmaking mechanisms.* NGOs could broaden the base of information for decisionmaking, improving the quality, authoritativeness, and legitimacy of the policy choices of international organizations.

Civil society's involvement in global environmental governance has enriched the process and strengthened outcomes in a number of places and in a number of ways.[6] In fact, it is the participation of nongovernmental groups that makes the process "global" and not simply

---

5 For a further discussion of the need for both "competition" and "cooperation" from NGOs in global-scale policymaking, see Esty and Geradin's argument in *Regulatory Competition and Economic Integration: Comparative Perspectives* (2001).

6 For a detailed assessment of the value of multi-stakeholder participation in environment and sustainable development policymaking processes, see Hemmati (2001).

**CHANNELS FOR NGO PARTICIPATION
IN INTERNATIONAL ORGANIZATIONS**

1. NGO representatives can be included on a national delegation to an international conference to advise delegates from their government (Cairo Population Conference in 1994);

2. Representatives from a NGO can be included on a national delegation to an international conference to represent the NGO and conduct negotiations (International Labor Organization);

3. NGOs can send delegates to semi-public international conferences (IUCN has a membership that includes 699 NGOs as well as states and government agencies);

4. An international organization can set up an advisory group that includes experts from NGOs, who do not represent the NGO (UN Advisory Board on Disarmament Matters);

5. An international organization can give NGOs an opportunity to participate in ongoing policy development (Convention on International Trade in Endangered Species);

6. An international organization can enlist NGOs to help in implementing programs (UN High Commissioner for Refugees);

7. An international organization can give NGOs an opportunity to participate (not necessarily in a negotiating role) in an official conference to draft a treaty (ECOSOC);

8. An international organization can give NGOs an opportunity to participate in preparatory committees for an international conference (Rio Earth Summit in 1992, Johannesburg Summit on Sustainable Development in 2002);

9. An international organization can hold a special session to give NGOs an opportunity to make presentations (General Assembly on sub-Saharan Africa in 1986);

10. An international organization can include NGOs as members (International Commission for Scientific Exploration of the Mediterranean Sea).

Source: Charnovitz, Steve. 1997. "Two Centuries of Participation: NGOs and International Governance." *Michigan Journal of International Law* 18(2): 281-282.

"international." While many governments agree that NGO participation is indispensable,[7] many also feel that the drawbacks of civil society participation may outweigh the benefits. Arguments and concerns abound on both sides. Some are fretful that NGOs might constitute special interest groups, and that their participation would invariably result in policy distortions. Others fear that intergovernmental decisionmaking processes would become bogged down by NGOs, which are not necessarily representative of or accountable to their particular constituencies (Nichols, 1996). Decisionmakers are also anxious that NGOs may seek to usurp the sovereign powers of governments.

However, some of these concerns may be overstated, considering the advantages of civil society involvement. Civil society can help build the political will for a new approach to development that integrates environmental and social goals. Non-governmental organizations can serve as alternatives to weak or inadequate democratic institutions, as avenues for more inclusive dialogues, and as conduits for disseminating information on activities and issues within the international system.

These and other significant characteristics of civil society participation in governance are explored in the following three case studies.

The Crucible Group: Harnessing the Power of Diverse Voices

The Crucible Group is a multinational, multidisciplinary gathering of experts that first met officially in 1993 to discuss the control and management of agricultural genetic resources. The initial goal was to identify issues, trends, and use options. While agricultural genetic resources are of crucial importance to biotechnology and genetic engineering, there are serious debates surrounding their ownership and control as well as the equitable sharing of benefits. The group — twenty-eight individuals from nineteen countries — included grassroots organizers, farmers, trade diplomats, agricultural research scientists, intellectual property specialists, and agricultural policy analysts from both the North and South.[8]

Recognizing the diversity of perspectives and priorities, the group did not seek consensus, but was able to agree on twenty-eight recom-

---

[7] Many European governments, for example, provide a very significant part of the budget of non-governmental organizations.

[8] For more information on the Crucible Group and its activities, see http://www.idrc.ca/books/725/preface.html

mendations for policymakers. The first summary of the deliberations and the recommendations, *People, Plants, and Patents: The Impact of Intellectual Property on Trade, Plant Biodiversity, and Rural Society*, was published in 1994 (IDRC, 1994). Having now evolved into the Crucible Group II, with more than forty-five participants from twenty-five countries, the group has continued to meet to revisit many unresolved issues and consider a number of new ones. As a neutral forum, the Crucible Group II has promoted open discussion among participants who might otherwise never have been at the same table. The Group launched a second volume, *Seeding Solutions: Policy Options for Genetic Resources*, at the April 2002 Conference of Parties to the Convention on Biological Diversity. The report provides valuable input into the debate and development of guidelines on intellectual property issues, rights of farmers, mechanisms for benefit sharing, and appropriate governance structures for conservation of plant genetic resources.

Several conclusions can be drawn from the Crucible Group experience:

- A dialogue does not have to produce consensus to be useful for governance purposes;

- A process designed to include non-state actors will reflect a broader spectrum of views and may generate more creative approaches to solving problems;

- A process where government and non-government participants are equal partners in a project is more likely to generate "buy in" and thus useful results.

Not all governance projects involving civil society, however, have achieved a balance of influence among participants. In fact, multi-stakeholder dialogues – especially those that are of very short duration – are losing favor with many in civil society. Some feel that the term stakeholder undermines communities and individuals struggling for their rights and that it implies equality among participants, which is not always the case. Clearly, for multi-stakeholder processes to serve as a vehicle for meaningful civil society participation, they must provide mechanisms for open, long-term discussions and deliberations.

The Global Environment Outlook and the UN Millennium Ecosystem Assessment: Helping to Fill Research and Analytical Gaps

One of the most important roles that NGOs can play in global environmental governance is to provide up-to-date information on critical issues. Governments often turn to NGOs to fill research gaps that stand in the way of effective decisionmaking. Certain NGOs, such as the World Resources Institute (WRI) and IUCN — The World Conservation Union,[9] have crafted their mandates around the role of information provider. These groups are dedicated to the production of accurate, up-to-date research and data on the most pressing environmental issues.

Whereas governmental bodies and intergovernmental organizations often lack analytical capacity or are hampered by bureaucratic constraints and other obligations, NGOs can focus on a dynamic research agenda, and move quickly to address new issues.

The Global Environment Outlook (GEO) of UNEP and the recently launched UN Millennium Ecosystem Assessment are good examples of formalized non-governmental assessment processes and inter-organizational networking.[10] At the core of these processes lies a global network of collaborating groups responsible for regional inputs. Global system assessment is integrated with local environmental reporting. NGOs and other non-state actors such as academic and research institutions are the main contributors, providing reports and data analysis. In the case of the GEO assessment, the final reports are reviewed by government representatives before publication. NGOs have not yet been allowed participation in the verification process.

These large-scale assessments require considerable amounts of funding. The contributions of charitable organizations, such as the

---

9 IUCN – The World Conservation Union is an important example of collaboration between state and non-state actors. While formally an NGO, this organization includes a number of state agencies among its members.

10 Different reports of the UNEP's Global Environment Outlook Report Series can be viewed at http://www.unep.org/GEO/index.htm For more information about the Millennium Ecosystem Assessment, its activities, and publications, see http://www.millenniumassessment.org/en/index.htm.

United Nations Foundation, for international environmental research are indispensable. Funding matters do raise some concerns in terms of the autonomy of NGO research and analysis. The complicated dependence that NGOs and many academic and research institutions have on governmental and other donor funding concerns some observers in terms of the freedom civil society members have in conducting the research and analysis they contribute to governance processes. The funding situation, however, is not likely to change. Financial relationships and dependencies should therefore be transparent and open to scrutiny.

TRAFFIC: Ensuring Effective Implementation

A third example of civil society fulfilling an essential environmental governance role is provided by TRAFFIC, the wildlife monitoring network for the 1975 Convention on International Trade in Endangered Species of Wild Fauna and Flora (CITES).[11]

TRAFFIC is a partnership between WWF — World Wide Fund For Nature and IUCN — The World Conservation Union. It was established in 1976 to assist the CITES Secretariat in implementing the provisions of the Convention. The Convention covers more than 30,000 species of animals and plants and has been endorsed by over 150 countries (Rosser, Haywood, and Harris, 2001). The diversity of the traded goods covered under CITES, which range from medicinal herbs to exotic pets, requires a level of international, on-the-ground coordination that would be difficult for a single intergovernmental institution (Wijnstekers, 2001).

TRAFFIC is a key component in the implementation of CITES. The NGOs behind the partnership are able to utilize their resources worldwide to operate twenty-two offices in eight regional programs, making TRAFFIC the world's largest wildlife trade monitoring organization (TRAFFIC, 2001). Its program priorities are threatened species and ecoregions, resource security, and international cooperation. Members lobby decisionmakers to ensure that trade in plant and animal species does not pose a threat to species conservation, and collaborate with governments and the private sector in developing economic incentive programs to encourage sustainable trade. TRAFFIC has been particularly successful in data collection, on-the-ground inves-

---

[11] For more information about TRAFFIC, see http://www.traffic.org/

tigative tasks, and in-depth research. Through its research and out-reach initiatives, TRAFFIC has become a key resource for governments and other NGOs, providing decisionmakers with critical information and analysis and prompting initiatives to ensure sustainable trade.

STRENGTHENING CIVIL SOCIETY PARTICIPATION IN GLOBAL ENVIRONMENTAL GOVERNANCE

As indicated by the three cases discussed above, civil society – name-ly, the NGO community – has particular strengths to bring to global environmental governance. The creativity, flexibility, entrepreneurial nature, and capacity for vision and long-term thinking often set NGOs apart from governmental bodies. A revitalized global environmental governance regime would thus benefit from greater participation of NGOs in global policy processes. What follows is a discussion of five key potential roles for civil society organizations in a strengthened global environmental governance system.

Information-Based Duties

As shown by the Global Environment Outlook and Millennium Ecosystem Assessment processes, NGOs have much to offer in the way of information collection, dissemination, and analysis. Numerous other examples exist in which NGOs serve a key information-based role. One of the most significant relates to the Conferences of Parties and other meetings held in conjunction with multilateral environ-mental agreements such as the UN Convention on Biological Diversity and the UN Framework Convention on Climate Change. Often, the meetings are distinguished less by what is said in plenary session than by the wealth of research and policy documents produced by NGOs and other civil society constituents and released specifically to coin-cide with the official events. Many conference delegates read these opinion papers and other documents, which often shed new light on the costs of inaction and the options for change. Another common opportunity for civil society members to provide input into intergov-ernmental negotiations comes in the form of a single statement devel-oped by NGOs present and released at the close of the official event.

Measures to improve the utility of information exchange could include:

- *Wider acceptance and use of the "commission" model.* Short-term consultations often yield less valuable information than do multi-stakeholder commissions (similar to the World Commission on Dams) provided with sufficient investment of time and resources.[12]

- *Assistance in the formation of networks.* UN convention secretariats, for example, could facilitate ongoing, high-level multi-stakeholder knowledge networks that make a directed effort to bring expertise to bear on science and policy challenges, including perspectives from marginalized groups.

- *Mechanisms to support "give and take."* While officials may read the opinion pieces and research documents NGOs release, there is often little feedback and very limited opportunities for back and forth dialogue. The institution of "notice and comment" processes, formal advisory panels, and other informal mechanisms for information exchange between government officials and NGOs could pay real dividends.

- *Efforts to agree to disagree.* Seeking "consensus" is often a mistake. Consensus can be difficult to reach, resulting in prolonged discussions of watered-down conclusions, "forced" agreements, and a failure to communicate valid perspectives. An acceptance on the part of intergovernmental decisionmakers of a civil society statement reflecting *multiple* opinions would often be more useful.

Inputs into Policy Development

Over the past decades, NGOs have assumed a more active role in the process of agenda-setting and policy development (Porter, 2000). NGOs have been instrumental in notifying the public, governments, and international organizations of critical new issues for many years. In 1945, NGOs pushed for inserting human rights language into the UN Charter and have been active in that policy domain since. Global environmental issues gained prominence in the 1970s also as a result of NGO activities. In the 1980s, forestry concerns were included on the agenda of intergovernmental deliberations under the pressure of NGOs (Humphreys, 1996). In 1997, six NGOs played a key role,

---

12 For a discussion of the World Commission on Dams, see Streck, this volume.

through the International Committee to Ban Landmines, in convincing governments to embrace the successful intergovernmental landmine treaty (Weiss, 1999).

The ability of NGOs to place issues on the global agenda does much to enhance their ability to participate in the later stages of decisionmaking. As pointed out by former Canadian Foreign Minister Lloyd Axworthy, "Clearly, one can no longer relegate NGOs to simple advisory or advocacy roles ... They are now part of the way decisions have to be made" (cited in Simmons, 1998). The question of what constitutes meaningful civil society participation in decisionmaking, however, is still being explored as NGOs and intergovernmental bodies continue to develop working relationships.

To this end, the development of a structure for civil society participation and engagement in international decisionmaking processes is necessary. Currently, modalities of involvement vary from being a full partner as in the case of the International Labor Organization[13] to denial of access (even as observers) as in the case of the World Trade Organization. While each international agency would need to tailor participation standards to its particular objectives, a minimum set of criteria should be elaborated. The following elements need to be addressed:

- Clear *articulation of rules*, rights, and commitments to consultation with civil society beyond time-limited NGO fora;

- Clearly delineated *selection criteria* for NGO participation in consultations and advisory groups, placing an emphasis on diversity;

- Establishment of *guidelines* for the process of NGO contributions;

- Commitment to *respectful treatment* of NGO documents;

- *Support for publication* and dissemination of NGO submissions to delegates at relevant international meetings;

- *Formalized submission process* for NGO recommendations and comments to intergovernmental bodies;

---

[13] The International Labor Organization was established in 1919 with a tripartite governance structure – governments, business, and labor are equal partners in the decisionmaking process of the organization.

- Provision for *feedback and response* to NGO submissions by inter-governmental bodies or national governments;

- *Mechanism for monitoring* the implementation of these components.

A more formalized structure for NGO participation would be useful in addressing some of the current obstacles to civil society involvement in global environmental governance. The wariness that governments and others have of NGO involvement might be reduced if baseline standards defined the rights and responsibilities of governmental and non-governmental entities in a clear and consistent manner.

Operational Functions

As demonstrated by the example of TRAFFIC, the UN system usefully engages civil society entities as operational partners in many circumstances. The role of NGOs in implementation of worldwide policy efforts has greatly increased since the mid-1980s, when NGOs began to fill gaps left in the provision of services by reduced roles for many development agencies (Simon and Dodds, 1998). Non-governmental organizations are particularly useful in an operational context, as they can provide implementation tailored to specific conditions and can "make the impossible possible by doing what governments cannot or will not do" (Simmons, 1998). This is especially true with regard to the management of natural resources, which is often best handled by community-based organizations who have a stake in local environmental conditions and are free from many of the conflicting demands experienced by governments. And, in fact, the preamble to Section III of Agenda 21 underscores the need for individuals and groups, especially at the local level, to participate in decisions that may affect the communities in which they live and work.

A significant portion of the world's ecological "hot spots" are located in rural – often very poor – areas of developing countries. As a result, the burdens of ecological damage, as well as the burdens associated with ecological regeneration, are borne primarily by people in these areas (Agarwal, 1998). NGOs and other groups in the developing world typically are poorly funded, have little access to information, and often lack a visible presence or audible voice in international governance processes (Breitmeier and Rittberger, 2000). The activities of Shack/Slum Dwellers International, a network of grassroots development groups in fourteen countries, are illustrative of one way in which Southern groups can build greater presence on the international stage. Through the use of micro-financing and other programs, Shack/Slum Dwellers International leverages the resources of its member groups to provide them with financial support, information, and advice on development strategies and related issues. Using their collective power, the federation has developed a voice on the global policymaking stage (Edwards, 2001).

The operational functions of NGOs within a reformed global environmental governance system could be strengthened by:

- Expanded efforts at *inclusion of local, community-based groups* with knowledge of the issues at hand;

- *Capacity building* targeted at enhancing communication between local groups and other governance partners;

- Support for *initiatives to measure and monitor service delivery* by NGOs — and the use of benchmarking and the identification of "best practices" as a way to improve performance.

Assessment and Monitoring

Performance assessments and monitoring of environmental conditions undertaken by NGOs may hold decisionmakers in international arenas publicly accountable for decisions in ways that the intergovernmental system itself could never accomplish (Gaer, 1996). As Thomas Weiss notes, "NGOs are . . . capable of making sensitive or politically important information public – something that intergovernmental organizations often are reluctant or loathe to do because of their dependence on member states for resources" (Weiss, 1999). A number of NGO-led or assisted assessment initiatives are currently under way.

As shown by TRAFFIC, for example, environmental NGOs are critical actors in compliance monitoring of international agreements and in finding more accurate compliance data than governments are willing to provide. Much room exists, however, for greater civil society involvement in this important area of governance.

There is an urgent need to account for the needs of developing countries, to acknowledge the limitations they face in conducting monitoring and assessment activities, and to provide support for the enhancement of these functions within governments and civil society alike. Key measures that could facilitate the assessment and monitoring role of NGOs include:

- *Creation of a comprehensive database for information and analysis at different geographic and political levels.* NGOs are key providers of local environmental data and information. A coherent mechanism for data collection and analysis will encourage this function and facilitate a two-way information flow;

- *Involvement of a larger part of the population in assessment and monitoring functions.* The inclusion of civil society groups in data collection would greatly contribute to filling knowledge gaps as well as enhance knowledge development, increase interest, and promote engagement. This will be especially beneficial to developing countries;[14]

- *Support for knowledge-generating institutions in developing countries.* Universities are key generators of knowledge, yet they are among the most under-funded institutions in developing countries. Funding and communication technology transfer will be critical to their ability to perform these functions.

---

[14] For a detailed analysis of the gap between scientific capacities in developed and developing countries, its consequences for global environmental governance, and recommendations for bridging this knowledge divide, see Karlsson, this volume.

Advocacy for Environmental Justice

Over the past few decades, NGOs in many countries have been extremely effective in highlighting disparities in who bears environmental burdens and who gets the benefits of environmental investments. Some groups have issued reports. Others have brought public interest litigation to defend environmental rights as well as to clarify and enforce laws. If a reformed global environmental governance system were to include a dispute settlement mechanism, it is easy to see the potential contributions NGOs and other civil society members could make to such a structure. The submission of "friends of the court" opinions would be well-suited to the skills and interests of NGOs. In fact, the Aarhus Convention envisions a process by which NGOs could seek judicial remedy against other parties, such as national governments or private sector entities, for environmental harms or crimes.

CONCLUSION

Designing governance structures that draw NGOs into global-scale environmental problem solving, policymaking, and implementation remains an important global challenge. Civil society has much more to offer to intergovernmental processes. Indeed, the very legitimacy of international decisionmaking may depend on NGOs as a way to ensure connectedness to the publics around the world and substitute for true popular sovereignty, which international bodies, devoid of elected officials, lack. A number of UN projects and programs are already benefiting from the contributions of NGOs in areas as varied as information collection and dissemination, policy implementation, monitoring and assessment, norm-setting, and policy development. A revitalized global environmental governance system must facilitate both an expansion of these roles for NGOs and the development of better-defined processes of participation.

A number of difficulties remain. Civil society participation requires a significant commitment of time as well as substantial financial resources from governments and intergovernmental bodies. Diversity within the global civil society community precludes the reaching of a consensus position that could be easily channeled into intergovernmental negotiations. It is imperative that NGOs explore innovative forms of networking through regional coalitions, for example, to help ensure the inclusion of a multitude of voices from developing countries and to make civil society involvement in governance more effective.

The contributions from civil society participation need to be enhanced through a strengthened, more formalized structure for engagement. UN programs seek legitimacy for their policies through the involvement of civil society, yet formal mechanisms for NGO participation within many parts of the UN system remain limited.

An improved governance structure would acknowledge the role of NGOs and other members of civil society and devise formal channels for participation. Ad-hoc acceptance of civil society participation should be replaced by institutional arrangements among UN member states, UN agencies, and NGOs.

REFERENCES

Agarwal, Anil. 1998. "Globalization, Civil Society and Governance: The Challenges for the 21st Century." Paper read at NORAD's Environment Day, in Oslo, Norway.

Bratton, Michael. 1994. *Civil Society and Political Transition in Africa.* Boston, MA: Institute for Development Research.

Breitmeier, Helmut, and Volker Rittberger. 2000. "Environmental NGOs in an Emerging Global Civil Society." In *The Global Environment in the Twenty-First Century: Prospects for International Cooperation,* edited by Pamela Chasek. Tokyo, Japan: United Nations University. Available from http://www.ciaonet.org/book/chasek/

Charnovitz, Steve. 1996. "Participation of Non-Governmental Organizations in the World Trade Organization." *University of Pennsylvania Journal of International Economic Law* 17: 331-357.

_____. 1997. "Two Centuries of Participation: NGOs and International Governance." *Michigan Journal of International Law* 18 (2): 183-286.

Cohen, Jean L., and Andrew Arato. 1992. *Civil Society and Political Theory.* Cambridge, MA: MIT Press.

Conca, Ken. 1996. "Greening the UN: Environmental Organisations and the UN System." In *NGOs, the UN, and Global Governance,* edited by Thomas G. Weiss and Leon Gordenker. Boulder, CO: Lynne Rienner.

Edwards, Michael. 2001. "A New Model for Civil Society?" *Alliance* 6 (4): 10-19.

Esty, Daniel C. 1998. "Non-Governmental Organizations at the World Trade Organization: Cooperation, Competition, or Exclusion." *Journal of International Economic Law* 1 (1): 123-148.

_____. 2002. "The World Trade Organization's Legitimacy Crisis." *World Trade Review* 1 (1): 7-22.

Esty, Daniel C., and Damien Geradin. 2001. "Regulatory Co-opetition." In *Regulatory Competition and Economic Integration*, edited by Daniel C. Esty and Damien Geradin. New York: Oxford University Press.

Fomerand, Jacques. 1996. "UN Conferences: Media Events or Genuine Diplomacy?" *Global Governance* 2 (3): 361-376.

Gaer, Felice D. 1996. "Reality Check: Human Rights NGOs Confront Governments at the UN." In *NGOs, the UN, and Global Governance*, edited by Thomas G. Weiss and Leon Gordenker. Boulder, CO.: Lynne Rienner.

Gemmill, Barbara, Maria Ivanova, and Yoke Ling Chee. 2002. "Designing a New Architecture for Global Environmental Governance." *World Summit for Sustainable Development Briefing Papers*, International Institute for Environment and Development (IIED), London. Available from http://www.poptel.org.uk/iied/test/searching/ring_pdf/wssd_21_international_environmental_governance.pdf

Hemmati, Minu. 2001. *Multi-Stakeholder Processes for Governance and Sustainability: Beyond Deadlock and Conflict*. London: Earthscan Publications.

Humphreys, David. 1996. *Forest Politics: The Evolution of International Cooperation*. London: Earthscan Publications.

IDRC. 1994. *People, Plants, and Patents: The Impact of Intellectual Property on Trade, Plant Biodiversity, and Rural Society*. Ottawa, Canada: International Development Research Centre.

Meidinger, Errol. 2001. "Law Making by Global Civil Society: The Forest Certification Prototype." Baldy Center for Law and Social Policy, State University of New York at Buffalo, Buffalo, NY. Available from http://www.iue.it/LAW/joerges/transnationalism/documents/Meidinger.pdf

Nichols, Philip. 1996. "Extension of Standing in World Trade Organization Disputes to Nongovernment Parties." *University of Pennsylvania Journal of International Economic Law* 17(1): 295-329.

Pace, William. 2002. "Governance and Civil Society." Paper read at UNEP Civil Society Consultation on International Environmental Governance. February 12, 2002.

Porter, Gareth. 2000. *Global Environmental Politics*. Boulder, CO: Westview Press.

Rosser, Alison, Mandy Haywood, and Donna Harris. 2001. *CITES: A Conservation Tool*. Cambridge, United Kingdom: IUCN Species Survival Commission. Available from http://www.iucn.org/themes/ssc/pubs/CITES/CITESToolEng.pdf

Simmons, P. J. 1998. "Learning to Live with NGOs." Foreign Policy, Fall 1998: 82-96. Available from http://www.globalpolicy.org/ngos/issues/simmons.htm

Simon, David, and Klaus Dodds. 1998. "Introduction: Rethinking Geographies of North-South Development." *Third World Quarterly* 19 (4): 595-606.

TRAFFIC. 2002. *About TRAFFIC*. [cited June 28 2002]. Available from http://www.traffic.org/about/

UN. 1994. *Agenda 21: The United Nations Programme of Action for Sustainable Development*. New York: United Nations. Available from http://www.un.org/esa/sustdev/agenda21text.htm

Wapner, Paul. 2000. "The Transnational Politics of Environmental NGOs: Governmental, Economic, and Social Activism." In *The Global Environment in the Twenty-First Century: Prospects for Internaitonal Cooperation*, edited by Pamela Chasek. Tokyo, Japan: United Nations University. Available from http://www.ciaonet.org/book/chasek

Weiss, Thomas G. 1999. "International NGOs, Global Governance and Social Policy in the UN System." Globalism and Social Policy Programme, STAKES, Helsinki, Finland. Available from http://www.stakes.fi/gaspp/occasional%20papers/gaspp3-1999.pdf

Wijnstekers, Willem. 2001. *The Evolution of CITES*. Geneva, Switzerland: CITES Secretariat. Available from http://www.cites.org/common/docs/Evol_2001.pdf

Regional Environmental Governance: Examining the Association of Southeast Asian Nations (ASEAN) Model

Koh Kheng Lian and Nicholas A. Robinson

SUMMARY

Regional systems of environmental management are an essential component of global environmental governance, complementing governance efforts at the national and global levels. This chapter analyzes the role and functions of the Association of Southeast Asian Nations (ASEAN) in the environmental domain as one model for regional governance.

ASEAN's tradition emphasizes non-interference in its members' domestic affairs, seeks consensus and cooperation, and aims to facilitate national implementation of regional agreements. Two main areas have served as a focal point for regional environmental cooperation within ASEAN: management of shared natural resources (biodiversity) and pollution control (air pollution from forest fires).

The ASEAN experience in environmental management illustrates the strengths and limitations of environmental governance at the regional level, with important lessons for the global level. The organization's emphasis on cooperation favors regional policy and soft law formulations. However, the general lack of concrete instruments for translating ASEAN commitments into national level action has hindered implementation of effective programs. ASEAN's limitations could be reduced if the organization were understood as an essential, but not exclusive, part of an environmental governance system, working and cooperating with international organizations to solve problems and implement solutions.

REGIONAL ENVIRONMENTAL GOVERNANCE

Global sustainable development requires actions to be taken in each country in accordance with national capacities. The key to success in addressing transboundary harms is a structure that connects international policymaking with national implementation. National action can be encouraged through strengthened global networks, improved data and information systems, and new financing arrangements, but work at the national level remains critical.

The regional level represents a critical middle ground between the global and national scales (Dua and Esty, 1997). Contiguous states may collaborate to sustain shared ecosystems and solve common problems. Indeed, many transboundary issues appear first at the regional level, affecting several neighboring countries. Pollution of a shared river basin or loss of habitat across the migration range of a species, for example, are as relevant at the regional as at the national level. No country can cope effectively with shared environmental problems on its own. Regional systems of environmental management are thus essential to securing agreements for, and implementation of, specific action programs (Kimball, 1999).

Regional integration of national activities for sustainable development can be advanced through measures such as harmonization of standards, joint development of environmental management systems, and collaborative capacity building projects. None of this will happen, however, without an effective institutional framework to facilitate it.

THE ASSOCIATION OF SOUTHEAST ASIAN NATIONS

The Association of Southeast Asian Nations (ASEAN) was founded in 1967 to encourage stable relations among Indonesia, Malaysia, Singapore, the Philippines, and Thailand, and to resist the destabilizing influences of the war in Vietnam. To promote stability, ASEAN fostered economic, social, and cultural cooperation in the spirit of equality and partnership. The Association subsequently expanded its membership to include Brunei Darussalam, Cambodia, Laos, Myanmar (Burma), and Vietnam.[1]

During the first phase of cooperation, the national ASEAN Secretariats carried out projects without a formal treaty system. Subsequently, ASEAN has developed increasingly sophisticated measures for policy coordination. The Association seeks to meet its goal of closer cohesion and economic integration by building a recognized ASEAN community. In 1997, the ASEAN heads of state and government gathered in Kuala Lumpur to mark the Association's 30th anniversary. The outcome document of that meeting, *ASEAN Vision 2020*, attests to the achievements of the past thirty years and elaborates a vision for the future of the region:

> That vision is of ASEAN as a concert of Southeast Asian Nations, outward looking, living in peace, stability, and prosperity, bonded together in partnership in dynamic development and in a community of caring societies. (ASEAN, 1997)

The Hanoi Plan of Action, 1999 – 2004, was formulated pursuant to ASEAN Vision 2020 and covered some fifteen areas relating to the environment.

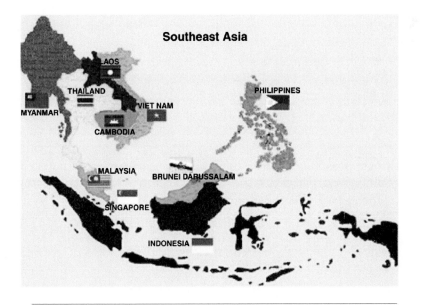

---

[1] Brunei Darussalam joined in 1984, Vietnam in 1995, Laos and Myanmar in 1997, and Cambodia in 1999.

The "ASEAN Way"

Regional cooperation to build stable relations in Southeast Asia has become known as the "ASEAN Way," a collaborative approach emphasizing three fundamental standards:

- Non-interference or non-intervention in other member states' domestic affairs, as underscored in the United Nations Charter, Article 2(7);

- Consensus building and cooperative programs rather than legally binding treaties (but in an exceptional situation, a binding agreement may be possible);

- Preference for national implementation of programs rather than reliance on a strong region-wide bureaucracy.

The emphasis on consensus is also reflected in ASEAN methods for dispute resolution. In the Pacific region, due to the influence of the British Commonwealth, most disagreements are settled with formal judicial methods (Cameron and Ramsay, 1996). Disagreements between the nations of ASEAN, on the other hand, are generally settled through conciliation and consultation, which is seen as a way to minimize tensions and avoid unnecessary conflicts (Narine, 1999).

ASEAN Organizational Framework for Managing Environmental Matters

There is no core ASEAN bureaucracy. The small Secretariat, based in Jakarta, has a limited facilitation role. Activities are undertaken by each ASEAN member state at the national level. ASEAN embraces the tenet of common but differentiated responsibilities. Members agree on common measures, decide how to implement them, and contribute according to their capabilities, acknowledging that ASEAN member states have achieved different levels of development and therefore have different capacities for action.

When ASEAN was established in 1967, environmental management was not expressly recognized as a concern (Koh, 1996). ASEAN integrated the environment into its complex system of regional consultations on economic, social, technical, and scientific development following the Stockholm Conference on the Human Environment in 1972.

ASEAN's Senior Officials on the Environment carry out a series of activities in the environmental domain:

- Preparing for ASEAN's regional participation in international environmental governance deliberations;

- Establishing guidelines pertaining to pollution, biodiversity, climate change, forests, and related environmental matters;

- Working toward harmonization of environmental standards for ambient air and river quality.

In each country, National Focal Points are responsible for carrying out ASEAN initiatives. Member states are increasingly willing to assume greater responsibilities to increase ASEAN's environmental effectiveness, as demonstrated by the Philippines' decision to host ASEAN's Regional Centre for Biodiversity Conservation and Malaysia's agreement to manage the Marine Turtle Conservation Program. The current framework for ASEAN environmental management and cooperation is reflected in its institutional architecture (see Figure 1). This structure facilitates cooperation among ASEAN member states and enhances the Association's ability to cooperate with other countries.

A Summit of the ASEAN heads of state and government, ASEAN's highest decisionmaking body, is held every three years. These high-level panels pave the way for intermediate, ministerial-level meetings, and provide proposals for decisions to be adopted by consensus at the ministerial level. Ministerial meetings by sector – including agriculture and forestry, economics, energy, environment, finance, labor, regional haze, rural development and poverty alleviation, science and technology, and social welfare – are convened in tandem with the Summit. Every three years, well before the meeting of the heads of state and government, ASEAN holds a Ministerial Meeting on the Environment.

Figure 1   ASEAN's Organizational Framework

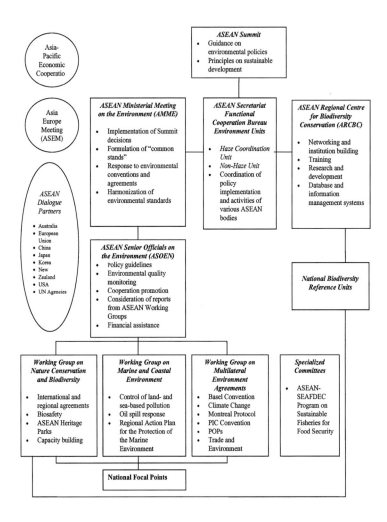

APPROACHES TO SOLVING ENVIRONMENTAL PROBLEMS

The "ASEAN Way" faces new challenges as it knits together programs across the ten Southeast Asian states, yet the very fact that the ASEAN Way is regarded as a defined approach, distinct from the more formalistic parliamentary decisionmaking systems of Europe and North America, is evidence for the proposition that ASEAN bears close study by those interested in strengthening regional and global environmental governance.

ASEAN's approach to environmental governance and its institutional responsibilities and achievements can be illustrated by its efforts to manage biodiversity conservation and to address transboundary air pollution from forest fires.

Biodiversity Conservation: Addressing Global Priorities Using Regional Management

Southeast Asia is a "mega-rich" region in terms of biological diversity. These resources require careful conservation management. Unsustainable logging and conversion of forests into agricultural land have had adverse impacts on biodiversity across the region. Biodiversity conservation has thus become an issue of significant interest to ASEAN member states (Koh, 2002). Recognizing the need to share information and to shape a common approach to biodiversity, member states initiated a Working Group of ASEAN Senior Officials on the Environment and an ASEAN Regional Centre for Biodiversity Conservation. The four core functions of the Centre illustrate the problem solving approach that ASEAN has adopted regarding environmental concerns:

* *Networking and Institution Building*
  Strong national institutions are critical for the implementation of regional policies. To this end, a network of national biodiversity reference units has been established, connecting scientific knowledge and promoting information exchange. The network is also charged with the task of developing and implementing an exchange program for academics and researchers from ASEAN institutions, as well as designing policies for biodiversity conservation.

* *Data and Information Management*
  Sound data on natural resources and environmental trends are critical for the effective design of policies and their implementa-

tion. The Biodiversity Centre creates, shares, and maintains electronic data repositories regarding biodiversity and has the capacity to link its records to other international databases.

- *Research and Development*
  The accumulation of scientific knowledge and understanding is seen as critical in the environmental domain where many uncertainties persist. The Biodiversity Centre has taken on the role of coordinating regional efforts in determining research priorities, organizing conferences to finalize the regional research agenda, and providing funds for applied biodiversity research activities.

- *Education and Training*
  The sustained build up of capacity for the execution of common policies and decisions is an important governance function. The Biodiversity Centre assists institutions in formulating their training needs, and designs and carries out training and education programs.

Across the region, in cooperation with the European Union, the ASEAN Regional Centre for Biodiversity Conservation is creating management systems for biological conservation as a foundation for sustaining the region's natural resources. The Centre serves as the main focal point for networking and institutional linkage among ASEAN member countries, and with other regional organizations, to enhance the region's capacity to promote biodiversity conservation.[2] The process also prepares the ASEAN members to participate in the Conference of Parties to the Convention on Biological Diversity.

Transboundary Air Pollution: Addressing National Issues with Regional Impacts
Air pollution from burning biomass in Southeast Asia has become a recurrent environmental challenge that causes serious adverse economic and health impacts (Tan, 1996). The use of fire to transform forest areas into agricultural land has uncontrollable consequences during the dry periods that the region experiences as a result of El Niño climate oscillations. This problem is particularly serious in Indonesia, where the practice of forestland burning is largely prohibited by statute, but where enforcement is hindered by lack of community education, inadequate administrative capacity, and corruption. Once fires spread out in dry weather, the capacity to extinguish them

---

2 For more information on these programs, see http://www.arcbc.org.ph

is limited and the smoke becomes a transnational pall, known as "haze." As a result, ambient air quality standards are breached and breathing the air in certain cities throughout the region becomes a health hazard (Tay, 1998).

In 1995, ASEAN adopted the Cooperation Plan on Transboundary Pollution, which included measures for addressing transboundary atmospheric pollution, transboundary ship-borne pollution, and transboundary movement of hazardous wastes. The Cooperation Plan demonstrated a region-wide level of commitment and spirit of cooperation on environmental issues that had not been seen before.

Unlike biodiversity, however, haze is a sub-regional issue, involving the original ASEAN member states. Thus, rather than employing the typical ASEAN-wide working group structure, a Haze Technical Task Force was developed. The Cooperation Plan has been largely ineffective, unfortunately, because it lacks an operational agenda. In the absence of targeted mitigation activities, the region suffered a major bout of transboundary air pollution in 1997. Progress has been too slow to effectively avert the recurrence of the haze (Robinson, 2001; Tan, 1999; Tay, 1998, 1999), reflecting the preference of the states of ASEAN for cooperative and consensual discussions, or soft law, over the adoption of international agreements, or hard law.[3]

The recent landmark ASEAN Agreement on Transboundary Haze Pollution, however, signed on 10 June 2002 in Kuala Lumpur, demonstrates that in a crisis situation, ASEAN members can rally together to reach consensus on a hard law instrument. The Agreement seeks to:

- Prevent land and forest fires through better management policies;

- Establish operational mechanisms to monitor land and forest fires;

- Strengthen regional land and forest fire-fighting capability and other mitigating measures.

Under the Agreement, parties oblige themselves to:

- Develop information systems, including monitoring, assessment, and early warning to prevent and monitor transboundary haze pollution;

---

3 This reluctance is also evident in the 1985 ASEAN Agreement on the Conservation of Nature and Natural Resources, negotiated with the cooperation of the International Union for the Conservation of Nature and Natural Resources (IUCN), which remains to be ratified by enough states to enter into force.

- Provide necessary information regarding haze pollution originating within their borders;

- Take legislative, administrative, and other relevant measures to implement the Agreement.

An ASEAN Coordinating Centre for Transboundary Haze Pollution Control was also established to facilitate cooperation among the parties. Similar to the ASEAN Regional Centre for Biodiversity Conservation, its functions comprise data and information collection and analysis, networking, and capacity building. The Centre for Transboundary Haze Pollution Control is mandated with information clearinghouse functions regarding environmental threats, scientific capacities, technological options, and financing possibilities. It does not possess enforcement power. Whether the policies promoted by the Centre will be fully implemented at the national level remains to be seen, however, since there are no enforcement mechanisms and agencies at the ASEAN level.

EVALUATION OF ASEAN'S CONTRIBUTION TO ENVIRONMENTAL GOVERNANCE

What can we learn from the ASEAN record of regional environmental governance? First, ASEAN draws on a strong sense of regional identity to bring together diverse cultures and political traditions to promote cooperation and to shape common policies. Second, it does so by respecting each country's internal procedures, and building capacity within each nation to meet agreed program objectives. Third, ASEAN's emphasis on consensus and capacity building is ill equipped to deal with urgent events, as demonstrated by the lack of adequate response to regional fires and haze. This inadequacy has led some ASEAN commentators to call for a stronger emphasis on the implementation of policy and the initiation of necessary reforms (Tay, Estanislao, and Soesastro, 2001).

When ASEAN's environmental policies are considered in light of the region's environmental needs, several key strengths become apparent:

- *Adaptation capacity.* In many instances, ASEAN has demonstrated an ability to adapt to new circumstances. ASEAN overcame the reunification of Vietnam in 1975, Vietnam's invasion of Cambodia in 1979, and the end of the Cold War in the early 1990s, when the organization was expected to disband (Funston, 1999);

- *Effective regional policy formulation.* ASEAN has been remarkably successful in shaping a common regional environmental policy framework (see box on ASEAN Sustainability Framework).[4] By respecting each country's internal procedures, ASEAN has facilitated cooperation;

- *Stable relationships among members.* The non-interventionist approach has contributed to building relatively stable relations among member states. The community building process has facilitated social and political interaction, rather than interference, and has reduced intra-ASEAN tensions (Snitwongse, 1995);

- *Sound foundation for implementation.* ASEAN's consensus building process has created a sound foundation for implementation. For instance, the Working Group on Nature Conservation and Biodiversity has drafted an ASEAN framework agreement on access to genetic resources, which may be effective in shaping a common approach among the administrations and parliaments of the ASEAN States, or may form the basis for a new regional hard law instrument. It also is likely to minimize – in advance – possible regional trade disputes on the subject.

Despite the proliferation of policies on sustainable development, declarations, resolutions, plans of action, and programs, the implementation of agreements within ASEAN is usually rather slow. Some of the key limitations and barriers to effectiveness include:

- *Non-intervention.* The "ASEAN Way" follows too blindly the principle of non-intervention, undermining the possibility of adopting practical measures to cope with regional problems. Diplomats, political leaders, and scholars have urged ASEAN to re-examine the meaning of its non-interventionist norm (Tay, Estanislao, Soesastra, 2001);

- *Inadequate support.* Lack of expertise, information and data, funding, and organizational support within ASEAN have often led to suboptimal results;

---

4 This common policy framework is the product of ASEAN Action Plans between 1978 and 1992, culminating in a Strategic Plan, 1994-98 (Koh, K.L. 1996), which was implemented to establish a region-wide process for implemention of *Agenda 21*.

ASEAN SUSTAINABILITY FRAMEWORK

ASEAN's policies, in soft law instruments, set forth a common regional policy framework for sustainable development with the following policy guidelines (Koh, 1996):

- **Environment Management.** Endorse and employ environmental impact assessments, optimal land use plans, and town and country planning or zoning plans;
- **Nature Conservation.** Develop new practicable approaches for preserving forest wildlife and ecosystems; monitor the quality of environment and natural resources to enable compilation of ASEAN state of the environment reports;
- **Marine Conservation.** Develop practicable methods for management of pollution discharges;
- **Industry.** Ensure reasonable control of waste discharges at the early stages of project formulation; recycle waste; develop suitable systems for control of toxic and hazardous waste;
- **Education and Training.** Enhance public awareness; introduce environmental subjects in schools and universities; provide technical training in environmental information systems; encourage wider involvement in environmental management; promote cooperation among governments, NGOs, universities, and business communities within ASEAN;
- **Environmental Legislation.** Develop appropriate legislation to support proper management in the development of the environment;
- **Information Systems.** Establish monitoring programs for surveillance of sensitive environmental resources; promote use of remote sensing to establish databases; develop comprehensive environmental information systems to facilitate decisionmaking;
- **Enhanced ASEAN Joint Action.** Facilitate closer cooperation of the ASEAN member states to act in unison in incorporating environmental concerns into economic policies to provide better foundation for natural resource management;
- **International Cooperation.** Establish cooperation with developed and developing countries and international agencies for transfer of technology; share experiences in the management of the environment.

- *Inadequate information.* The absence of a monitoring and surveillance mechanism limits the ability of ASEAN to gather information on environmental trends and risks and to respond effectively;

- *Lack of a dispute resolution mechanism.* Because the ASEAN Way emphasizes decisionmaking through consensus building, it lacks an effective dispute settlement process. Thus, ASEAN often opts for conflict avoidance rather than conflict resolution (Narine, 1999: 360).

Learning from Success and Failure

In the ten years since the UN Conference on Environment and Development, ASEAN has done much to both integrate all Southeast Asian nations into one region, and to regard the region as a shared ecosystem. The political cooperation and economic negotiations toward more liberalized trade relations will be facilitated by the establishment of a sound, common environmental policy framework.

The "ASEAN Way," with its non-interventionist approach, has promoted building stable relations, agreeing upon general policy, and fostering capacity building measures. However, arresting environmental degradation patterns also requires affirmative action – which by definition must be interventionist, albeit in agreed ways, based on scientific knowledge.

A number of measures would enable significant improvement in that direction:

- The Association could create a regional "cooperation team" to be deployed throughout the region to prevent or contain environmental catastrophes, using appropriate information and scientific knowledge. Such a system is already in place for marine oil spills and could be replicated for terrestrial environmental problems. ASEAN could draw on its rich history of cooperation to create such teams. This would enhance respect for sovereignty, not undermine it, as the inability to avert an environmental disaster is a greater loss of sovereign authority than cooperation to control the harm.

- ASEAN might agree to establish eco-labeling schemes for palm oil and timber products in order to address the capital investment that is a cause of the forest fires in Indonesia and deforestation throughout the region. This scheme would enable consumers to make informed market decisions and would help deter the illegal process of setting fires to clear land.

- ASEAN could mete out sanctions against palm oil companies that are responsible for the fires, rather than pursuing a conciliatory approach of negotiating behind closed doors, "saving face" for their neighbors.

ASEAN has adopted a reactive rather than a proactive approach to environmental protection. Since there has been intermittent warfare throughout the region for fifty years, reluctance to intervene in member states' affairs is understandable. Nonetheless, ASEAN member states should differentiate illegitimate or hostile meddling in each other's affairs from the promotion of effective policies and environmental justice across the region.

In the case of Indonesian forest fires, for instance, neither those states whose nationals invest in the Indonesian palm oil plantations or timber operations that instigate forest burning, nor Indonesia, whose resources are being damaged, should tolerate the injury to other ASEAN states from the haze. The prevalent regional attitude of deference towards the domestic affairs of one's neighbors can thus lead to violations of Principle 21 of the Stockholm Declaration, which stresses that states have "the sovereign right to exploit their own resources pursuant to their own environmental policies *and* the responsibility to ensure that activities within their jurisdiction or control do not cause damage to the environment of other states or of areas beyond the limits of national jurisdiction." As Singapore Ambassador Tommy Koh has observed, "ASEAN's corporate culture prevented Indonesia's neighbors from engaging her in a free and candid exchange of views."[5] Others in the region have arrived at similar conclusions.[6]

---

5 Quoted in *The Straits Times*, 10 July 1998, at page 48.

6 For instance, at the ASEAN Foreign Ministers Meeting of the member countries held in Manila in 1998, Thailand urged ASEAN to adopt the principle of "flexible engagement." The Thai foreign Minister Surin Pitsuwan stated: "Perhaps it is time that ASEAN's cherished principle of non-intervention is modified to allow ASEAN to play a constructive role in preventing or resolving domestic issues with regional implications." This proposal was only supported by the Philippines.

An analysis of the ASEAN Way in light of the organization's successes and failures reveals that ASEAN is better equipped to deal with issues where members' interests converge than problems where members have opposing interests. Indeed, ASEAN's consensus-based approach works well when all countries in the region share similar goals, but when states' interests diverge, this same approach leads countries to evade issues and avoid negotiations.

ASEAN has been shown to be effective in dealing with the management of common natural resources such as biodiversity. In the case of the Indonesian haze, however, pollution from one country is causing damages in neighboring areas, and the implementation of costly measures in Indonesia may be required to preserve the environment elsewhere in the region. Finding an effective solution to this issue may necessitate more serious measures and could accelerate the evolution of ASEAN from a regional body capable of arriving at an environmental policy consensus to one capable of implementing that consensus.

PROSPECTS FOR COOPERATION: THE REGIONAL-GLOBAL INTERFACE

Regional environmental governance structures are a part of an environmental governance architecture spanning the local and the global levels (Esty, 1999). Initiatives at the regional level complement, rather than substitute for, the policies and efforts of international institutions. To this end, global mechanisms need to facilitate regional environmental initiatives. Three major forms of cooperation between ASEAN, or other regional organizations, and international environmental governance institutions could be especially valuable: information systems, international best practices, and dispute settlement.

Information Systems

Global-level governance structures could serve as an important source of data and information, allowing for more effective regional policy formulation. A repository of data on environmental indicators from surveillance systems across regions would allow for the identification of risks, trends, causes, and possible responses. A Global Environmental Information Clearinghouse, as outlined by Esty and Ivanova in this volume, could serve in this capacity and fill in the data gap that hampers effective environmental policy at the regional and national levels. Moreover, a global mechanism for information gathering and dissemination would promote a two-way flow of information. National and regional agencies and non-governmental organizations could access a wide range of relevant data, allowing for better problem identification, prioritization, and resource deployment. At the same time, regional organizations could serve an intermediary repository function for local level information collection efforts and encourage broader engagement in the policy process by a larger segment of the general public (see Karlsson, this volume).

International Best Practices

Information sharing on implementation strategies, technologies, and policies may be another area of potentially essential cooperation between the global and regional levels. Best practices in problem solving on a range of issues could provide a useful tool for regions facing similar challenges. One area in which ASEAN could share its experience, for example, is in the efforts to resolve conflicts between trade and environmental interests, which "increasingly appear as flash points that divide nations, creating tensions that could cause some countries to renege on commitments to an open market" (Dua and Esty, 1997). ASEAN's shrimp exports were embargoed by the United States in 1996 on the grounds that shrimp trawlers in those countries did not use the turtle-excluding device, a tool that significantly reduces the number of deaths of sea turtles in shrimp harvesting.[7] The embargo prompted a concerted effort at protection, conservation, replenishment, and recovery of sea turtles and of their habitats, based on the best available scientific evidence, taking into account the environmental, socio-economic, and cultural characteristics of individual ASEAN members.[8] Information on best practices and policies con-

---

7 Malaysia and others challenged the U.S. trade restrictions under the dispute settlement procedures of the World Trade Organization. In October 2002, however, the WTO Appellate Body ruled in favor of the United States, confirming that the ban of shrimp represented a valid environmental concern compatible with WTO laws (USTR, 2001).

8 Under the agreement, each ASEAN country is to nominate specialists to form a Technical Experts Working Group, the purpose of which is to prepare a Marine Trade Conservation Programme and Work Plan for endorsement by the ASEAN Fisheries Working Group and approval by ASEAN agriculture and fisheries ministers.

cerning the effective management of trade and environment interests could form one of many areas of collaboration among regions, facilitated by a global information clearinghouse.

Dispute Settlement

International organizations could also assist regional bodies and member states in resolving disputes. As exemplified by ASEAN, when conciliation is not possible and interference with the national policies of a member state is not a viable option, resolving disputes becomes a significant challenge. However, countries may be willing to accept arbitration from an external court or organization that is trusted as impartial by all parties involved in the dispute. Resorting to such a venue would not conflict with the principle of non-intervention in domestic affairs, and might enable countries to reach agreement on a set of difficult issues. One example of a situation in which ASEAN members have referred to an international body is the dispute between Malaysia and Indonesia over the islands of Sipidan and Litigan, which was referred to the World Court (Narine, 1999: 377). Similar international arrangements could also be used for environmental matters.

CONCLUSION

Regional environmental governance through ASEAN offers valuable lessons for intra-regional cooperation. Notwithstanding the evident need within ASEAN countries to devote greater attention to implementation of shared policies, ASEAN has been successful in shaping a common regional environmental policy framework and establishing a basis for capacity building throughout the region. ASEAN's consensus building process may have created a sound foundation for future implementation of common policies. But the weaknesses of this process are evident too – especially where views, values, and interests diverge. Over the longer term, the flexibility of the "ASEAN Way" may, in fact, help ASEAN to build a stronger basis for regional action and effective policymaking. As emphasized by Ambassador Tommy T.B. Koh, chair of the UN Conference on Environment and Development in Rio:

The dream of a united Europe has been shared by Europeans for more than 300 years. That dream is still not completely realized. Viewed in this light, the progress that has been achieved by ASEAN in the last seven years has been quite remarkable. Although ASEAN was formed primarily for the purpose of promoting economic and cultural cooperation among the member nations, the two outstanding achievements of ASEAN to date have been the forging of a sense of community among the five member nations and what I will call confidence-building. (Koh, 1998)

Regional environmental governance represents an indispensable link between, and complement to, national and global initiatives. As illustrated by the ASEAN case, to be more effective, regional systems for environmental governance need to supplement cooperative policy formulation with effective mechanisms to facilitate implementation of policies at both the sub-regional and national levels.

REFERENCES

ASEAN. 1997. *ASEAN Vision 2020*. Kuala Lumpur, Malaysia: Association of Southeast Asian Nations.

Cameron, James, and Ross Ramsay. 1996. "Transnational Environmental Law Disputes." *Asia Pacific Journal of Environmental Law* 1 (1).

Dua, Andre, and Daniel C. Esty. 1997. *Sustaining the Asian Pacific Miracle: Economic Integration and Environmental Protection.* Washington, D.C.: Institute for International Economics.

Esty, Daniel C. 1999. "Toward Optimal Environmental Governance." *New York University Law Review* 74 (6): 1495-1574.

Funston, John. 1999. "Challenges Facing ASEAN in a More Complex Age." *Contemporary Southeast Asia* 21 (2): 205-219.

Kimball, Lee A. 1999. "International Environmental Governance: A Regional Emphasis on Structured Linkages Among Conventions and Intergovernmental Organizations." *Transnational Law Exchange* 2 (1): 6-10.

Koh, Kheng Lian. 1996. *Selected ASEAN Documents on the Environment* July 1996 (1).

_____. 2002. "Ecosystem Management Approach to Biodiversity Conservation: The Role of ASEAN." In *Capacity Building for Environmental Law in Asian and Pacific Regions*, edited by K. L. Koh. Manila: Asian Development Bank.

Koh, Tommy Thong Bee. 1998. *The Quest for World Order: Perspectives of a Pragmatic Idealist.* Singapore: Institute for Policy Studies, Times Academic Press.

Narine, Shaun. 1999. "ASEAN Into the Twenty-First Century: Problems and Prospects." *The Pacific Review* 12 (3): 357-380.

Robinson, Nicholas A. 2001. "Forest Fires as a Common International Concern: Precedents for the Progressive Development of International Environmental Law." *Pace Environmental Law Review* 18 (2): 459-504.

Snitwongse, Kusuma. 1995. "ASEAN's Security Cooperation: Searching for a Regional Order." *The Pacific Review* 8 (3): 518-530.

Tan, Allan K. J. 1999. "Forest Fires of Indonesia: State Responsibility and International Liability." *International and Comparative Law Quarterly* 48: 826-855.

Tan, Gerald. 1996. *ASEAN Economic Development and Co-operation.* Singapore: Times Academic Press.

Tay, Simon S. C. 1998. "The South-East Asian Forest Fires and Sustainable Development: What Should Be Done?" *Asia Pacific Journal of Environmental Law* 3: 205.

_____. 1999. "The Southeast Asian Fires and Sustainable Development: What Should Be Done About Haze?" *Indonesian Quarterly* xxvi (2): 99-117.

Tay, Simon S. C., Jesus P. Estanislao, and Hadi Soesastro. 2001. *Reinventing ASEAN.* Singapore: ISEAS, Seng Lee Press.

USTR. 2001. *U.S. Wins WTO Case on Sea Turtle Conservation: Ruling Reaffirms WTO Recognition of Environmental Concerns.* Washington, D.C.: USTR Press Releases, United States Trade Representative.

Global Public Policy Networks as Coalitions for Change

Charlotte Streck

SUMMARY

Numerous international agreements have been concluded over the past few decades, yet on a global scale environmental quality has deteriorated. Traditional legal and institutional arrangements for environmental protection have not lived up to the task. The time is ripe to complement the traditional governance system with innovative elements of "networked governance," bringing together governments, the private sector, and civil society organizations.

Over the last decade, global public policy networks have emerged as a possible element of such a governance structure. These open, flexible, and transparent structures have formed around issues of common interest. The World Commission on Dams, the Global Environment Facility, and the flexible mechanisms of the Kyoto Protocol are three examples of networks that have been instrumental in forging successful working arrangements. These models are worth examining more closely. Global public policy networks, coordinated by international organizations, might help to close the current gap between needs and results in global environmental governance.

THE LIMITS OF TRADITIONAL BUREAUCRACIES

Global problems demand global responses. Key issues that pose a direct threat to the common future of our planet include climate change, depletion of the ozone layer, loss of biodiversity, maritime pollution, and trade in hazardous waste, among others. Traditionally, global governance was viewed as intergovernmental cooperation to solve common environmental problems. Governments today are competing with private entities for power, influence, and representation (Reinicke, 1998; Strange, 1996, 1997). A world of growing international interdependence, increasing economic and political liberalization, and technological change cannot be regulated at the national level or by traditional intergovernmental cooperation alone (Rischard, 2001).

Several key characteristics distinguish today's reality from traditional governance contexts:

- National economies are increasingly integrated through trade and financial flows, the spread of knowledge, and the movement of people;

- Technological change and economic integration have created transnational economic and social networks of interdependence that are difficult to regulate through national legislation;

- Traditional bureaucracies often lack the knowledge and flexibility to react to today's complex and fast-moving governance challenges.

The instruments of international policymaking currently at our disposal – international treaties, institutions, and agencies – have proven insufficient to meet the challenges of an increasingly globalized and interdependent world in a timely and efficient manner. New institutional and operational responses are necessary to deliver measurable environmental results through an inclusive and transparent process. Flexible and integrative networks may show one way to address international problems more quickly and effectively than existing hierarchical and sluggish structures are able to.

Recent trends in international governance indicate that the focus has shifted from intergovernmental activities to multi-sectoral initiatives – from governance at the international level to governance across different levels, and from a largely formal, legalistic process to a less formal, more participatory and integrated approach.

EMERGING ALTERNATIVES: GLOBAL PUBLIC POLICY NETWORKS

Global public policy networks are a recent addition to the system of global governance. Such networks have appeared mainly at the international level, where a constant need for policy solutions and the lack of a central government leave room for innovative structures. They are multisectoral partnerships linking different sectors and levels of governance and bringing together governments, international organizations, corporations, and civil society.

Global public policy networks offer a promising model for how to handle new governance problems because complex political, economic, and social systems cannot be governed by a single sector – the public sector – or from a single level – the national level. Governance structures building on networks are able to bridge the gap between the public, the for-profit, and the non-profit sectors and integrate human and financial resources to find solutions to multifaceted problems. Networks have emerged around issues of public health, financial regulation, international crime, and the global environment.

Where networks appear spontaneously around certain problem areas, they should be integrated more consciously into a system of global environmental governance. The effectiveness of less formalized and flexible networks could then point toward a more viable solution to protect the global commons.

FEATURES OF GLOBAL PUBLIC POLICY NETWORKS

Global public policy networks generally form around issues of an international character. They minimize hierarchy through the involvement of multiple stakeholders across many sectors. The network participants bring complementary resources to the process, allowing for synergies and more effective responses:

> A typical network (if there is such a thing) combines the voluntary energy and legitimacy of the civil society sector with the financial muscle and interest of businesses and the enforcement and rule-making power and coordination and capacity-building skills of states and international organizations. Networks create bridges that enable these various participants to exploit the synergies between these resources. They allow for the pooling of know-how and the exchange of experience. Spanning socioeconomic, political, and cultural gaps, networks manage relationships that might otherwise degenerate into counterproductive confrontation. (Reinicke and Deng, 2000)

Several key features characterize successful global public policy networks:

- *Diversity.* The trilateral nature of global public policy networks, involving the public sector, civil society, and business, makes them distinct institutional arrangements. In the context of economic, social, and cultural globalization, the participation of the private sector has become critical to finding effective solutions to international problems. At the same time, political liberalization has led to a rapid growth of transnational advocacy coalitions of non-governmental organizations (NGOs), which need to be involved in policymaking (Gemmill and Bamidele-Izu, this volume; Tamiotti and Finger, 2001; Wapner, 2000).

- *Openness and flexibility.* Global public policy networks offer policy mechanisms adaptive to a constantly changing environment and open to new actors. Different approaches of policymaking and varying cultural perspectives increasingly demand recognition and integration. Networks provide a vehicle for incorporating such diverse perspectives, including local knowledge, and involving affected communities in the problem-solving processes.

- *Speed.* Global public policy networks provide for rapid responses and rapid "activation of reputational effects" (Rischard, 2001). They are well equipped to quickly identify issues, outline a vision, options, and an action plan, and launch a concrete effort for their attainment. Moreover, through the political energy and urgency they generate, networks can put pressure on traditional institutions to respond in a quicker and more efficient manner.

- *Subsidiarity and legitimacy.* Global public policy networks respond effectively to the need for delegating policy processes to the governance levels that can most effectively formulate and implement policy solutions. They provide a means of implementing agreements and policies at various levels of decision-making. Through the open architecture now allowed by the internet, participation in networks at multiple levels is facilitated, leading to greater legitimacy and ultimately to the development of common global norms.

Due to their structure, networks are largely opportunistic, and are most likely to emerge in situations of political deadlock. A stalemate can trigger a special engagement by institutions and individuals who can assume leadership roles in bringing stakeholders together. Global public policy networks can also emerge wherever national policymakers lack the information, knowledge, or means to address complex policy issues, or where responses need to be built on a broad consensus of stakeholders. Finally, networks may arise around treaties, where diverse stakeholders are expected to take a coordinated approach in translating international consensus into action.

FUNCTIONS OF GLOBAL PUBLIC POLICY NETWORKS

There is so much variation among networks that no consistent pattern of network-building under specific circumstances and conditions has yet been observed.[1] However, it is possible to highlight different functions that networks perform even though no simple typology can do justice to the full range of network activities:

- *Agenda-setting.* Global public policy networks can bring new issues to the international agenda and initiate public discourse on the issues at stake. Moreover, they can "increase the prominence of issues that are already on the global agenda by articulating clear

---

1   See Global Public Policy Network Project: Case Studies: http://www.globalpublicpolicy.net/About GPP.htm

and focused goals, often justifying them on incontrovertible moral grounds" (Witte, Reinicke, and Benner, 2000). A handful of individuals with the right leverage and powers of persuasion can create a common vision and convince important actors to throw their weight behind an issue.

- *Standard-setting.* An important role for global public policy networks is the development of soft law guidelines and other non-binding legal instruments. Whereas treaties often provide a framework for international cooperation in a certain policy field, conferences of parties and other fora of international negotiations are not suited to formulating quick policy responses on burning issues. Networks can help affected parties or their representatives reach compromises that can then be poured into soft law agreements or standards.

- *Generating and disseminating knowledge.* The rapid change in the state of knowledge, and in the technological capabilities for its transmission, have often left governments at a disadvantage in comparison with the private sector, and even NGOs. Global public policy networks can serve as tools for gathering existing knowledge in a fast and efficient manner and even for the generation of new knowledge where gaps have been identified. A number of networks – the Roll Back Malaria Initiative of the World Health Organization, the Consultative Group on International Agricultural Research, and the Global Water Partnership – have made the generation and dissemination of knowledge their primary activity.

- *Bolstering institutional effectiveness.* By addressing participatory shortcomings, global public policy networks can facilitate building institutions, increasing their effectiveness and broadening their constituency base. During the institution building stage, multi-sectoral networks can help raise awareness of issues and gather political and financial support. Subsequently, institutionalized multi-stakeholder participation can ensure transparency, encourage flexibility, and allow for adaptability to change.

- *Providing innovative implementation mechanisms.* Some global public policy networks could be formed with the specific purpose of translating the results of intergovernmental negotiations into concrete action.

THE VALUE AND PROMISE OF GLOBAL PUBLIC POLICY NETWORKS

Ultimately, global public policy networks represent a potential strategy for governments, businesses, and NGOs to address the challenges of interdependence and globalization in an effective, participatory, and sustainable manner.

The promise of these networks lies in two central domains. First, through their ability to formulate quick responses to urgent problems, networks offer the opportunity to close the operational gap that characterizes international environmental policy today. Second, through their multisectoral and non-hierarchical structure, networks promise to bridge the participation gap that often is the main reason behind international political deadlocks. Because of these two characteristics, global public policy networks generate benefits that go beyond the sum of their parts.

CASE STUDIES: NETWORK STRUCTURES IN ENVIRONMENTAL POLICY

Global public policy networks in the environmental domain are more prevalent than any other type of public-private network, with the possible exception of public health networks. These networks, however, vary substantially from case to case, and carry out many different functions. The following examples illustrate the range of inter-sectoral cooperation, the variety of functions and operational arrangements, and the respective lessons for global environmental governance.

Standard-Setting Networks
Case Study: The World Commission on Dams

Large dams bring together many of the issues central to conflicts over sustainable development at the local, national, and international levels. The World Commission on Dams (WCD) demonstrates the potential of multi-sectoral networks to contribute to international consensus building and standard-setting.

Origins of the World Commission on Dams

For many years, large dam projects were synonymous with development and economic progress. Costs were underestimated and many environmental and social impacts ignored. Over time, civil society from both the North and the South organized to protest the construction of large dams. A global alliance of NGOs was formed, through which coordinated resistance grew and even escalated into conflicts.

By the early 1990s, opponents and proponents of large dams had reached a stalemate that brought several large dam projects to a halt. The World Commission on Dams was formed in 1998 as a two-year initiative in response to this political deadlock.

Operation of the World Commission on Dams

Inclusiveness, openness, and transparency are the key principles around which the WCD was formed. The mandate of the Commission was broad and comprehensive – to undertake a global review of the effectiveness of large dams for development and to establish internationally acceptable criteria and guidelines for future decisionmaking on dams. Twelve individuals, acting in their personal capacities and chosen to reflect regional diversity, expertise, and stakeholder perspectives, comprised the Commission.

With funding from a variety of public, private, and civil society organizations, the WCD conducted a comprehensive global review of the performance and impacts of large dams. It held public consultations on five continents and was funded through a new model involving contributions from governments, businesses, and NGOs. The Commission operated under the core values of equity, efficiency, participatory decisionmaking, sustainability, and accountability, which provided the essential test to be applied to decisions relating to the construction of large dams. The Commission developed criteria for future large dam projects and formulated a set of guidelines for Good Practice on how to meet these criteria. The final report was published at the end of 2000 (WCD, 2000).[2]

Lessons for Global Environmental Governance

The WCD illustrates the potential of collaborative arrangements to overcome an international stalemate and to formulate a set of soft guidelines that can alter the political landscape around an issue rife with conflict. Several important lessons can be gleaned from the inception and operation of the WCD (Witte, Reinicke, and Benner, 2000):

- Establishing a basic measure of trust is critical for consensus building and standard-setting in a conflict-ridden environment, although it is time consuming and costly.

- A truly trisectoral structure, process, and funding, as well as sourcing of knowledge are key to building consensus and closing the operational and participatory governance gaps.

- Time limitation is an important precondition for effectiveness of concrete initiatives. Time-bound activities ensure the pertinence of the results and preclude degeneration into a "talk shop."

- In highly contentious policy arenas, a participatory and inclusive approach, using open sourcing to pool knowledge, is imperative for producing effective and politically sustainable results.

The completion of the process that the WCD had embarked upon generated a series of reactions. The criticism from some governments, industries, and community-based organizations, together with an unenthusiastic response by the World Bank, showed that the consensus of the Commission did not translate into a broader stakeholder consensus (Dubash et al., 2001). While it was unrealistic to believe that the Commission could solve all of the issues around the construction of large dams, it created a document which initiated a process that could lead to a consensus. Without a doubt, the WCD has created a standard – albeit informal and not legally binding – against which future projects involving the construction of large dams will be measured.

---

2 The 2000 report of the World Commission on Dams is available online at http://www.dams.org/report

Networks and Institutional Flexibility
Case Study: The Global Environment Facility

The Global Environment Facility (GEF) has attempted to operationalize a unique and integrative governing structure which combines structural flexibility with a strong ability to adapt to a changing environment. The Facility answers new challenges of international public policy with a new type of international institution, bridging the traditions of UN and Bretton Woods agencies, like the International Monetary Fund and the World Bank.

Origins of the Global Environment Facility

The Global Environment Facility was established as a three-year pilot program in March 1991. It provides co-financing to developing countries and economies in transition for projects with global environmental benefits. Its grants finance only for the incremental costs of projects – the extra costs incurred in the process of redesigning an activity vis-à-vis a baseline. The Facility's financing is available for investment and technical assistance in five focal areas – global warming, biodiversity, international waters, ozone depletion, and persistent organic pollutants. The operational responsibility is shared among the UNDP, UNEP, and the World Bank as implementing agencies.

Operation of the Global Environment Facility

During its pilot stage, the GEF attracted significant criticism. The dominant role of the World Bank provoked mistrust from developing countries, which saw the GEF as an instrument of conditionality. Non-governmental organizations possessed no formalized rights within its framework. Following the Rio Earth Summit in 1992, however, the role of the GEF as the key financing mechanism for the global environment was recognized and a restructuring for its integration into the UN-driven convention system ensued.

As a result of negotiations around the restructuring, the GEF emerged as a new international entity linking different interests and stakeholder groups. Developing countries, UN agencies, and the majority of NGOs were in favor of a mechanism with a governance structure similar to the UN system and the values of the UN regime, namely, transparency, accountability, democracy, and universality. In addition, NGOs demanded more participation in GEF procedures and projects. The World Bank and OECD countries, on the other hand, preferred the governance structure of the Bretton Woods system and argued in favor of efficiency, cost effectiveness, effective management, and executive abilities. The new governance structure became an amalgamation of traditional features of UN and Bretton Woods institutions. Through the restructuring process, the GEF became more transparent, more democratic (with a double majority voting system), and more detached from the control of the World Bank (Streck, 2001). It built a significant role for NGOs, recognizing the value of institutionalizing alternative perspectives (Esty, 1998).

Lessons for Global Environmental Governance

Although today's GEF is far from ideal, its governance structure shows features of a network that tries to flexibly integrate multiple actors. This network structure has contributed to several key strengths of the GEF:

- *Adaptability.* Comprising actors with divergent and shifting interests, the GEF must adapt in order to survive. Its mandate and overall goal of protecting the global environment requires it to respond to a constantly changing environment both outside and inside the organization.

- *Cooperation.* Despite the differences in resources, ideology, and interests among GEF participants, there is a common understanding among all countries that cooperation is necessary to address global environmental issues. Cooperation between North and South is greater in the GEF than in other fora. The increasing participation of developing countries over the years indicates a generally positive outlook for the GEF.

- *Transparency and participation.* The GEF is among the most transparent of the existing international institutions. NGO representatives are allowed to attend the GEF Council meetings not only as observers, but also as active participants. They have a right to make statements on each topic on the agenda except during the discussion of the GEF budget. NGOs played an important role in the establishment and restructuring of the GEF and continue to facilitate coalition building, to influence the debate, and to serve as partners in implementing GEF projects.

- *Innovation.* The GEF submits itself to internal and external evaluations and is characterized by a strong ability to innovate, evolve, and change. Soft law agreements dominate over legally binding treaties. The renunciation of binding and sometimes narrow legal structures enables the creation of new and innovative mechanisms that comprise the GEF.

NGO ACTIVITIES WITHIN THE GLOBAL ENVIRONMENT FACILITY

- Contribute to consultations prior to each Council meeting;
- Observe at Council meetings;
- Engage in working groups on demand by the GEF Secretariat;
- Generate data, information, and independent analyses;
- Provide inputs to other activities initiated by the Secretariat (monitoring and evaluation activities, programs, and operational strategies)
- Lobby for donor contributions.

However significant, the strengths of the GEF do not disguise important flaws within the institution. Shortcomings include the very limited integration of the private sector, a problem of asymmetry of power, and overall operational complexity.

Implementation Networks of the Kyoto Protocol
Case Study: The "Flexible Mechanisms"

Through the Clean Development Mechanism (CDM) and Joint Implementation (JI), the flexible mechanisms of the Kyoto Protocol, the Parties to the UN Framework Convention on Climate Change established a platform that allows public-private networks to develop, execute, finance, and supervise projects. The different stages of the project cycle involve a broad range of actors from developed and developing countries, as well as from international development and finance institutions. The design of these new institutional mechanisms allows for the emergence of international implementation networks.

Origins of the Flexible Mechanisms in the Kyoto Protocol

Through the so-called "flexible mechanisms" of project-based emission crediting or emission trading,[3] the Kyoto Protocol fosters the creation of markets for greenhouse gas emission reductions. Under JI and CDM, Parties that have agreed to abide by greenhouse gas emission reduction targets may achieve some portion of their targets beyond their own borders. The global climate benefits from emissions reductions regardless of where they occur. The CDM encourages the achievement of emissions reductions in developing countries and the Joint Implementation mechanism in economies in transition. These flexible mechanisms are designed to enhance the cost-effectiveness of greenhouse gas emission reduction policies (Freestone, 2001).

The Prototype Carbon Fund is a multi-donor trust fund established and administered by the World Bank.[4] Launched in 1999, the Carbon Fund brings interested parties from developing and industrialized countries together to implement projects that follow the rules set forth under the Kyoto Protocol. At its second closing in 2000, six countries[5] and seventeen private sector entities[6] had agreed to participate in the Carbon Fund. Public sector participants contributed U.S. $10 million each and private sector participants $5 million each, bringing the size of the fund to $145 million. The Fund's projects are expected to generate emission reductions that, once certified by an accredited independent third party, could be used by industrialized countries toward their compliance with emission reduction obligations under the Kyoto Protocol.

Operation of the Kyoto Flexible Mechanisms

The World Bank launched the Carbon Fund even before the Parties to the Convention on Climate Change had approved the implementation guidelines for the mechanisms. By creating the Fund, the World Bank took the lead in implementing CDM and JI projects and the first step

---

3 Emission trading, established under Article 17 of the Kyoto Protocol, forms part of the flexible mechanisms. However, since it does not involve the execution of projects, it does not promote the creation of implementation networks.

4 Resolution 99-1, authorizing the establishment of the Prototype Carbon Fund, was approved by the Executive Directors of the International Bank of Reconstruction and Development (IBRD).

5 Canada, Finland, Japan, the Netherlands, Norway, and Sweden.

6 These include Tokyo, Chubu, Chugoku, Kyushu, Shikoku, and Tohoku, Mitsubishi and Mitsui (Japan); BP (United Kingdom); Deutsche Bank and RWE (Germany); Electrabel (Belgium); Gaz de France (France); Norsk Hydro and Statoil (Norway); Fortum (Finland) and Rabobank (through Gilde Strategic Situations BV) from the Netherlands.

from talk to action. It created a "prototype" network designed to evolve and provide a platform for discussion for participating governments and companies. The Fund is intended to translate emerging international obligations into the hard law of property rights. By preparing the early market in carbon transactions, it also opened the door to a new source of income for developing countries and economies in transition while promoting a shift toward less environmentally destructive behavior.

The Carbon Fund pays for the emission reductions it purchases on delivery. It bundles projects to reduce transaction costs. Assets are certified and verified by an independent third party. In order to be certified, the projects must lead to real, significant, and long-term climate change mitigation benefits and result in emission reductions additional to any that would occur in the absence of the project. While in the years to come other networks are likely to emerge in this area, the Carbon Fund already shows how various actors can work together to translate the international agreement on project-based activities under the climate change regime into action. The Carbon Fund thus combines some of the features of the "internalization deals" described by Whalley and Zissimos in this volume, as it compels private actors to consider the incremental costs of climate change to others.

Lessons for Global Environmental Governance
A greenhouse gas emission control implementation network is emerging under the framework of the project-based mechanisms of the Kyoto Protocol. The CDM and JI provide examples of incentive-based mechanisms supported by a global public policy network:

- *Dealmaking.* The flexible mechanisms of the Kyoto Protocol open the door for negotiated project arrangements underpinning the broader framework of international law and demonstrate the viability of project-based "dealmaking."

- *Matching interests.* The flexible mechanisms bring together the public and the private sectors.[7] The motivation behind the engagement of different participants varies. Industrialized countries and

---

7   Non-governmental experts are represented in a Technical Advisory Group to the Prototype Carbon Fund. NGOs are also important partners in raising general awareness and in providing a platform for knowledge dissemination. Environmental NGOs also play an important role in developing and implementing projects.

private companies are interested in supporting emission reductions for credit against their reduction targets. Developing countries and development agencies are interested in promoting development. Civil society seeks to foster activities to mitigate global warming and to bring development to local communities. These various interests can be matched through bargains and deals.

- *Matching resources.* Each actor brings different and important resources to the table – funding, projects, opportunities to cut emissions, specialized knowledge, or political leverage. Each participant in the fund in general and in each project in particular has an interest in the success of the fund and its operations. Participants are able to cooperate in order to achieve the common goal – to the benefit of the global environment.

SUPPORTING GLOBAL PUBLIC POLICY NETWORKS

International organizations can play an important role in fostering and supporting global public policy networks. They could perform a convening and a supporting function, providing leadership, a platform for sustained deliberation, and financing. International organizations could also serve as advocates and implementors of the norms developed by global public policy networks (see box on International Organizations and Global Public Policy Networks). Proposals to strengthen global environmental governance should be developed with an eye toward the potential of such cooperative arrangements.

INTERNATIONAL ORGANIZATIONS AND
GLOBAL PUBLIC POLICY NETWORKS

International organizations can help to create and sustain global public policy networks through various roles:

- International organizations may act as *conveners*, bringing all the parties to the table, mobilizing key constituencies and providing a forum to exchange views. United Nations agencies in particular have acted as conveners, successfully making use of their credibility across different sectors.

- International organizations can provide a *platform* or *"safe space"* for people and institutions coming together in a network, by establishing a level playing field for negotiations. In highly contentious policy domains, providing such a haven and bringing together outside parties may also have a catalytic effect on negotiations.

- One of the clear lessons learned from the empirical work on trisectoral networks is that *social entrepreneurship* is of crucial importance for the setup of a network. While there is no reason to believe that such leadership must necessarily emerge from the public sector, *political high-profile leadership* on the part of international organizations in the initiation phase has in some cases proven to be decisive.

- International organizations can *advance norms* developed by public policy networks. Sustainable development and human rights are two realms where the interplay between public policy networks and international bodies has helped to change global understanding and expectations.

- International organizations also serve as *multilevel network managers*. With the dual trends of greater devolution of authority through decentralization and the strengthening of supranational forms of governance, the challenge for international organizations is to develop strategies for simultaneously interacting with the appropriate levels of governance on particular issues at appropriate stages of the public policy cycle. By serving as a hub, international organizations can facilitate multi-tier linkages (local-national-global) in public policymaking.

- Despite often limited budgets, international organizations sometimes act as *financiers*, providing resources for a range of programs related to the implementation of global public policies.

Source: Witte, Reinicke, and Benner. 2000. "Beyond Multilateralism: Global Public Policy Networks." *International Politics and Society*, 2/2000.

CONCLUSION

A sound institutional architecture for global governance must combine features of traditional intergovernmental cooperation, implementation of national legislation, and innovative networked governance approaches. Instruments of international law and intergovernmental cooperation need to be supplemented by structures that can
react faster and promote consensus among stakeholders.

Dynamic in both process and structure, global public policy networks can provide alternative means to finding solutions where traditional policy or lawmaking have not or cannot deliver effective results.
Networks can facilitate international policy processes as well as
encourage and assist effective implementation. Networks, however, are
dependent on existing or future international organizations to provide
a platform through which stakeholders can engage in collaborative
management of global affairs.

Strong environmental governance structures, built on a set of networks, coordinated and initiated by international organizations, may
close current participatory, operational, and institutional gaps in global environmental governance and provide a more successful means of
addressing environmental threats to our planet.

REFERENCES

Dubash, Navroz K., Mairi Dupar, Smitu Kothari, and Tundu Lissu. 2001. *A Watershed in Global Governance? An Independent Assessment of the World Commission on Dams.* Washington, D.C.: World Resources Institute. Available from http://www.wcdassessment.org/report.html

Esty, Daniel C. 1998. "Non-Governmental Organizations at the World Trade Organization: Cooperation, Competition, or Exclusion." *Journal of International Economic Law* 1 (1): 123-148.

Freestone, David. 2001. "The World Bank's Prototype Carbon Fund: Mobilizing New Resources for Sustainable Development." In *Liber Amicorum Ibrahim F. I. Shihata: International Finance and Development Law,* edited by Sabine Schlemmer-Schulte and Ko-Yung Tung. The Hague: Kluwer Law International.

Reinicke, Wolfgang H. 1998. *Global Public Policy: Governing Without Government?* Washington, D.C.: Brookings Institution Press.

Reinicke, Wolfgang H., and Francis Deng. 2000. *Critical Choices: The United Nations, Networks, and the Future of Global Governance.* Ottawa, Canada: International Development Research Council.

Rischard, Jean-Francois. 2001. "High Noon: We Need New Approaches to Global Problem-Solving, Fast." *Journal of International Economic Law* 4 (3): 507-525.

Strange, Susan. 1996. *The Retreat of the State: The Diffusion of Power in the World Economy.* New York: Cambridge University Press.

_____. 1997. "Territory, State, Authority, and Economy." In *The New Realism: Perspectives on Multilateralism and World Order,* edited by Robert Cox. New York: St.-Martin's Press.

Streck, Charlotte. 2001. "The Global Environment Facility – A Role Model for International Governance?" *Global Environmental Politics* 1 (2): 71-94.

Tamiotti, Ludivine, and Matthias Finger. 2001. "Environmental Organizations: Changing Roles and Functions in International Politics." *Global Environmental Politics* 1 (1): 56-76.

Wapner, Paul. 2000. "The Transnational Politics of Environmental NGOs: Governmental, Economic, and Social Activism." *The Global Environment in the Twenty-First Century: Prospects for International Cooperation*, edited by Pamela Chasek. Tokyo, Japan: United Nations University. Available from http://www.ciaonet.org/book/chasek/

WCD. 2000. *Dams and Development: A New Framework for Decision Making: The Report of the World Commission on Dams*. London: Earthscan Publications. Available from http://www.dams.org/report/contents.htm

Witte, Jan Martin, Wolfgang Reinicke, and Thornsten Benner. 2000. "Beyond Multilateralism: Global Public Policy Networks." *International Politics and Society*. Available from http://www.fes.de/IG/ipg2_2000/artwitte.html

Sustaining Global Environmental Governance: Innovation in Environment and Development Finance

Maritta R.v.B. Koch-Weser

SUMMARY

The 1992 Rio Earth Summit established a sustainable development plan of action, Agenda 21, but failed to achieve a global governance and finance system strong enough to implement it. Experience suggests that the additional funding needed for global-scale investments in environment and sustainable development is unlikely to come from the public sector alone. New efforts to fund the necessary initiatives must therefore come from enlightened citizens, social entrepreneurs, and the growing segment of the business community that associates shareholder value with sustainability and corporate social responsibility.

This chapter highlights a series of policy reforms that must underpin any improvements in global environmental governance. It argues, in addition, that funding must be increased significantly, and proposes the creation of 1) a Johannesburg Commission on Sustainable Development Finance, and (2) a new global financing mechanism – a Sustainable Development Exchange Facility.

THE MILLENNIUM GAP

To improve global environmental management, we need a stronger global environmental governance system. Stronger governance requires not only a solid financing system, but, very importantly, environmentally friendly national and international fiscal policies and legislation.

No matter how much the 1992 Rio Earth Summit appears to have galvanized governmental and public support for the environment, recent budget numbers stand in stark contrast to public rhetoric. Accelerated, often irreversible losses of biodiversity, forests, and ocean resources attest to the fact that we are not meeting the Rio targets. Instead, we are witnessing a deepening crisis.

Budget numbers reveal waning international commitment to the environmental cause and broader, overall stagnation in official development assistance. Today's public finance picture for the environment is epitomized by the limited resources of the United Nations Environment Programme. UNEP's core budget of some $44 million annually (UNEP, 2001: 45) falls woefully short of its needs in fulfilling its global mandate.

Overall, trends in development aid allocations show continuous decline. The gap between official development assistance (ODA) pledges by the international community and actual contributions has never been wider.

Despite unprecedented levels of global wealth, the long-standing pledge by governments to contribute 0.7 percent of gross domestic product (GDP) to development assistance has remained largely unfulfilled. Instead, contributions since 1992 have fallen to 0.2-0.1 percent of GDP in many developed countries.

At the same time, the 2000 UN Millennium Summit committed national governments to numerically specific and time-bound targets for sustainable development. The global community has committed itself to halving absolute poverty by the year 2015 (lifting some 750 million people out of poverty over the coming decade). To achieve this goal, the world needs an estimated additional annual amount of $50 billion in official development assistance (ODA).

This wider-than-ever gap – "the Millennium Gap" – between meager ODA pledges, on the one hand, and growing new commitments, on the other, must be narrowed and closed.

The World Summit on Sustainable Development (WSSD) in Johannesburg could continue to chart the course that the 2002 Monterrey Conference on Financing for Development outlined. In the *Monterrey Consensus*, heads of state agreed to mobilize financial resources and to achieve the national and international economic conditions required to fulfill internationally agreed development goals, including those contained in the UN Millennium Declaration.

It remains to be seen whether the Monterrey Conference should be hailed as a major success. So far, all it seems to have produced is a broader feeling of goodwill and promises for timid increases in development finance – many of which have yet to be approved and enacted by national parliaments.

In fact, the Monterrey Consensus provides neither new visions nor grand designs. In addition, a few weeks after the Monterrey Conference, its promises for greater global fairness have been derailed by stepped-up trade distortions in the form of increased agricultural subsidies.

The leaders gathered in Monterrey also failed to come to the rescue of the Global Environment Facility (GEF) – the only true additional line of environmental grant funding made available by the international community since the 1992 Rio Earth Summit. Established in 1991 as an experimental program, the Global Environment Facility was instituted as a permanent body after the 1992 Rio Earth Summit.[1] GEF funding is available for investments and technical assistance to address five major threats to the environment – global warming, biodiversity loss, degradation of international waters, ozone depletion, and persistent organic pollutants. The World Bank, UNDP, and UNEP share the responsibility for operating the GEF. Official pledges to the GEF had

---

1   See Streck, this volume, for an analysis of the GEF.

increased in earlier years – in 1994, thirty-four nations promised $2 billion in support of the GEF's missions and in 1998, thirty-six nations pledged $2.75 billion (GEF, 2002). Recently, however, and in spite of its fine performance, liquidity at the GEF has reached a low point.

It is ironic that at the very time we approach the Johannesburg Summit, funding for the GEF has fallen and stalemate about its future has ensued. Some of the GEF's sponsors are failing to meet their funding obligations. And the majority – who would be willing to continue to contribute and perhaps increase their support – does not wish to bail out those who fail to pay up, and on goes the downward spiral. This is a most depressing spectacle.

THE FIFTY BILLION DOLLAR CHALLENGE

An additional $50 billion per year – the sum stipulated by the international community to close "the Millennium Gap" – is a large sum.

It has become clear that, for the time being, there is no prospect of achieving this goal within the current ODA framework alone. We must therefore chart a second, complementary path to fulfill the commitments our societies have made.

We could meet the "fifty billion dollar challenge" by scaling up a host of already successful innovative strategies and by testing some more recently proposed additional options:

- *Voluntary efforts.* Most require synergies between, on the one hand, civil society voluntarism and private sector social responsibility systems, and, on the other hand, government legislation conducive to voluntary giving.

- *Mobilization of large numbers of small contributions.* In the electronic billing and internet age, billions of tiny contributions can be raised at minimal administrative cost, and aggregated as sizable additional funding sources.

- *Creation of special funds, credit insurance, and lines of socially and environmentally oriented banking.*

- *New paths of government engagement.* Charges for the use of the global commons, voluntary or imposed charges on capital flows or currency transfers,[2] or Special Drawing Rights[3] (SDRs) are among the proposals.

A scaling up of a broad-based approach to innovative sustainable development finance, involving all of the above, would need to be promoted from a suitable institutional base. Thus, institutional reform and a commitment to a stronger environmental policy structure must be advanced in tandem with a new system of finance.

POLICY REFORMS PLUS FINANCE

Before setting out an innovative finance agenda for Johannesburg in more detail, there is a need to address the arguments of policy reform advocates who suggest that the world should firmly hold on to its national purse strings until major policy reforms are put into place. They rightly claim that the lack of finance for sustainable development is of subordinate importance when compared to the importance of policy reforms. They also stress the need to root out poor governance and corruption, and establish new partnerships and alliances.

Some commentators argue that only if structural reforms on a greater scale came along would all be well. Consider, they say, the amounts – hundreds of billions of dollars – that could be mobilized

---

2 Such charges are known as the Tobin tax – a very small tax, a fraction of one percent, on currency transfers across borders. It is intended to discourage speculation, but to remain small enough not to affect trade in products and services. See Patomaki (2001) for the case for a Tobin tax.

3 Special Drawing Rights (SDRs) are a form of financial assistance to developing countries. They are a claim on the freely usable currencies of International Monetary Fund (IMF) members, in that holders of SDRs can exchange them for these currencies (IMF, 2002). When countries exchange their SDRs for hard currency, they have to pay interest on the amount they receive, but not so long as they keep their allocations in the form of SDRs. See Soros (2002) for a detailed analysis of SDRs.

by debt relief, reductions in subsidies and other perverse economic incentives, and the elimination of trade barriers. They are right in many respects. The current global regime is off balance. What can small amounts of ODA achieve in the face of much larger, countervailing currents? This case has already been made convincingly for more than ten years now – starting with the World Bank's 1992 *World Development Report on Environment and Development.* It is addressed under the World Bank's debt initiative for heavily indebted poor countries, and under various proposals advocating the cancellation of debt servicing on old debts and the increase of grants and loans to developing countries (Sachs et al., 1999; Greenhill, 2002). Likewise, there is broad recognition of the fact that a reduction in import barriers in developed countries can positively support poverty alleviation in exporting countries in the developing world (IISD, 1994).

As much as they are needed, policy reforms should not be construed as substitutes for actual finance. They will not trickle down soon as direct sources of finance for urgently needed programs. Nor should they be construed as the precondition for any stepped-up support in line with the UN Millennium Goals.

The "fifty billion dollar challenge" remains: additional cash finance for development is needed now to pay for nature protection, education, sanitation, cleaner production, preventative health, natural disaster mitigation, and many other pressing needs.

Some analysts say that it is not money, but development effectiveness – the efficiency with which available funds are used – that is the real problem. Arguments that the key problems are institutional and that money does not matter are wrong-headed. To the contrary, institutional performance usually improves with adequate finance. In many poor countries, success can only come when institutions are strengthened financially and when public employees receive incomes decent enough to keep them outside the corruption trap.

A related concern is transparency and good governance. Some will say that not a penny should be given to developing countries so long as they fail to root out corruption and poor governance. This view reflects universally held ideals as well as research findings. A report of the United Nations General Assembly states that "transparent and accountable governance" is necessary for "the realization of social and people-centered sustainable development" (UN General Assembly, 1997). Similarly, studies by the World Bank have shown that development effectiveness is closely correlated with good governance (Buckley, 1999; Evans and Battaile, 1998). Transferring scarce resources to corrupt governments with proven records of misusing aid may aggravate poverty among the world's most vulnerable nations (Easterly, 2001). The World Bank and many bilateral donors put their money strategically where they witness better governance and withhold it explicitly from others.

And yet, the "good-governance-or-else" policy can also reflect an alarming lack of sincerity and understanding of institutional complexities. The quest for pure and transparent governance as a precondition for aid serves, at times, as a moral case for inaction – to the detriment of the poor and of urgent, time-bound sustainable development needs. If, for example, an ecosystem or biological species were threatened with extinction, we are obliged to ask whether their eternal fate should really be made so single-mindedly contingent on the quality of a temporary, current local government.

Some people and some threatened ecosystems will need support in spite of governments. And we cannot address the threats in the poorest regions if we insist on corruption being cleared up first. Development finance must not stay away, but try to make a positive difference within the current reality by advancing the good elements and people within bad systems.

In addition to reforms in policies and good governance, emerging public-private partnerships are frequently seen as one of the most effective strategies to address environmental and broader sustainable development issues. Public-private partnerships offer an alternative to privatization "by combining the social responsibility, environmental awareness and public accountability of the public sector, with the finance, technology, managerial efficiency and entrepreneurial spirit of the private sector" (UNDP, 2002). Moreover, government efforts to develop partnerships with the private sector would lower the risks and costs of investments for private firms (Shin, 2001). However, public-private partnerships at times seem to be prematurely hailed as "the solution." For now, many of them remain exceedingly *ad hoc* and small scale. To be considered a major global avenue to sustainable development, these partnerships must mature.

To sum up, efforts to advance policy reforms, development effectiveness, good governance, and public-private partnerships should all be seen as underpinnings, but not as substitutes, for improvements in sustainable development finance. Regardless of what other strategies are undertaken to promote sustainable development, the need for additional finance from new sources remains unchanged.

A JOHANNESBURG COMMISSION ON SUSTAINABLE DEVELOPMENT FINANCE

Two years ago, there were hopes that Johannesburg might become a watershed – overcoming the post-Rio shortcomings in global environmental governance and finance. These hopes have not been realized. The Monterrey conference took a step in the right direction, but did not go far enough. Time has now run out for a serious finance initiative to emerge in Johannesburg. Instead, the best possible WSSD outcome would be to launch a serious, in-depth technical work process, which might lead to tangible reforms over the course of the coming two years. The pre-Johannesburg process has produced an analysis of current shortfalls as well as many good ideas. These ideas now need to be galvanized in a follow-up process. A Johannesburg Commission on Sustainable Development Finance should be launched at the Summit – with terms of reference and the requisite political support and funding.

A Commission on Sustainable Development Finance should be launched to serve as an incubator for new ideas to promote development of funding instruments and institutional options. A technically skilled and multi-disciplinary team should be assigned to work for one to two years on financial, legal, and institutional designs, outside the formal public sector domain. Developing new financing systems requires space for entrepreneurship and innovation outside customary institutional confines.

The proposed Finance Commission should build on the achievements of previous government-focused initiatives, such as the Zedillo Commission. New emphasis should be placed on voluntary contributions by non-government entities, including corporations, NGOs, and citizens. The Johannesburg Commission should also examine the possibilities for encouraging private agents to participate in development finance efforts, and simultaneous ways to involve the public sector. The Finance Commission should develop design options and test concepts in the context of a meaningful consultation and engagement process. Its work should lead to pilot projects and actual start-up engagements.

Members of the Johannesburg Commission on Sustainable Development Finance should come from the world of innovative leaders and entrepreneurs, think tanks, foundations, NGOs, the private sector, and the government sector. Because the requisite thinking "outside the box" will require large degrees of creativity, freedom, and independence, the process of innovation would best be driven by those operating from outside the official family of environmental and development institutions.

THE ZEDILLO COMMISSION

UN Secretary General Kofi Annan appointed the Zedillo Commission, a panel of eleven financial experts under the Chairmanship of former Mexican President Ernesto Zedillo, in December 2000. Members included former U.S. Secretary of the Treasury Robert Rubin and former French Finance Minister and President of the European Commission Jacques Delors. Annan asked panel members to identify practical means of fulfilling international commitments to fight poverty, as set out at the 2000 Millennium Assembly, and building political momentum for the March 2002 Monterrey Conference on Financing for Development.

The report of the Zedillo Commission, *Financing for Development*, was presented in June 2001 at UN Headquarters in New York. The report advanced several reforms, including the creation of an International Tax Organization that would develop national tax policy norms, consideration of a global tax on carbon emissions, and new Special Drawing Rights (SDRs) allocations by the IMF. Unlike several civil society organizations, the Commission expressed skepticism at the idea of an international tax on financial transactions (Tobin tax). The Commission also suggested that the World Trade Organization attempt to fully integrate developing countries into the world trading system and called for the consolidation of the various organizations that share responsibility for environmental issues into a Global Environmental Organization.

http://www.un.org/reports/financing/index.html

A NEW GLOBAL FINANCING MECHANISM: A SUSTAINABLE DEVELOPMENT EXCHANGE FACILITY

The proposed Johannesburg Commission on Sustainable Development Finance should consider setting up a Sustainable Development Exchange Facility. Such a Facility would complement current multilateral and bilateral funding. The existing multilateral institutional system for financing sustainable development relies primarily on the World Bank and the regional development banks in Asia, Africa, Latin America, and Eastern Europe. The United Nations

**STRUCTURE OF THE PROPOSED JOHANNESBURG
FINANCE COMMISSION**

Membership: The Commission Members would be experts drawn primarily from non-governmental organizations and corporations, with some representatives from international organizations and the public sector. They would guide and oversee the work of a technical secretariat.

Secretariat: A small technical secretariat, under the leadership of a director appointed by the Commission, would – in close consultation with innovators, experts and subject matter leaders around the world – carry out the day-to-day work of the Commission.

Mandate: The Commission would be given a mandate to:

- Identify creative ways of raising funds for sustainable development, emphasizing the interconnection between private capital and social capital (non-governmental social entrepreneurship for sustainable development).

- Conceive of a system that would permit the continuous generation of new sources of funding. During its mandate and subsequently through a successor institution, the Commission would permanently seek new sources of funding.

Duration: The Commission's original mandate would extend over two years. It would be succeeded by a more permanent system, perhaps conceived along the lines of the Sustainable Development Exchange Facility outlined below, in order to continue the task of finding new sources of funding for development.

Development Programme also plays a critical role in capacity building, and the Global Environment Facility supports environmental efforts of global significance.

The purpose of a Sustainable Development Exchange Facility would be to achieve genuine financial "additionality." Its quest for funds should not interfere or compete with current fundraising by civil society organizations or public entities. Such an Exchange Facility would succeed the proposed Johannesburg Finance Commission once its mandate expires.

The Exchange would develop several business options in parallel, in response to varying needs. It would:

- Raise and channel funds for loans or credit guarantees among the banking and insurance industries;

- Seek to raise funds for grants among the private sector and civil society;

- Develop financial sources based on international charges and taxes;

- Foster productive interrelationships between civil society and business initiatives and governmental schemes, such as tax breaks and other incentive systems;

- Become a continuous driver for financing deals, continually seeking out new and creative funding modalities;

- Be a trustworthy link for financiers and donors with implementing institutions, which would become eligible for funding on the basis of a certification system.

The Sustainable Development Exchange Facility would need to be incorporated as a cooperative, franchise-type system. It could combine the functions of a foundation and/or trust with services among its certified membership. The Exchange's governing body would comprise representatives predominantly from the private sector and civil society. At the same time, it would need to have strong and structured links to public sector local, national, regional, and international institutions.

The Exchange could start small and grow as "proof of concept" is achieved. To help attain the UN Millennium goals, the Exchange would have to be designed to eventually reach globally significant proportions. Pre-existing Exchange-type facilities (which exist under various social entrepreneurship ventures) could opt to accede to it.

The proposed Exchange would need strong leadership and convincing performance to engage increasing numbers of financiers and donors. It must be designed as a learning institution with continuous innovation functions to develop ever-smarter new instruments and methods. Above all, it must insist on and monitor the integrity and efficiency of the programs and institutions to which it channels funds.

The structure of the Exchange would bring into interaction four elements: financiers and donors, recipients, certification services, and financial services (Figure 1). It would be supported by two external pillars: eminent experts, as a resource for the Exchange's certification services, and public sector development programs and supportive governmental structures.

Figure 1   Exchange Facility Structure

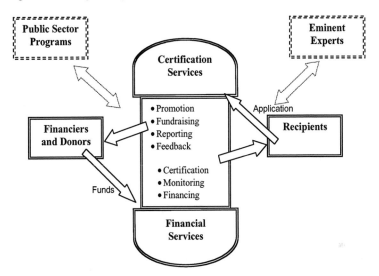

Recipients of the Exchange Facility

The Exchange Facility would function as a results-oriented environment and development resource service for accredited users. Recipients would typically be non-profit organizations focused on sustainable development through programs in environmental protection, poverty alleviation, provision of basic social services, or renewable energy projects. Private companies and public entities in need of compensation for adoption of environmentally superior business practices or technologies could also qualify as users with the Exchange.

For the recipients, the Exchange would facilitate matching proposed projects with financier and donor funds. Against a simple set of eligibility standards, it would apply streamlined project review and approval procedures, relying primarily on the track records and Exchange certification of applicants.

Financiers and Donors to the Exchange Facility

Sources of funding for the Exchange Facility could fall into a series of highly varied categories.

Donations would remain a central category. Some of the funding might come from governments. All funding would be on a voluntary basis, including:

- *Regular voluntary subscriptions.* Very small amounts could have a significant cumulative effect. If given the option, individuals worldwide could choose to contribute through different kinds of payment plans. For example, contributors' utility, telephone or credit card bills could be rounded up to the dollar every month, or an amount of $0.05 could be deducted from their bank accounts after a certain number of transactions as a contribution to the Exchange Facility.

- *Corporate grants.* Corporations could be encouraged to make donations. These could take the form of one-time grants. They could also take the form of a long-term commitment of a very small percentage of revenue from a product line to match an environmental cause that requires continuous funding. Corporate grants of this sort could be publicized, benefiting the corporation's reputation, and advancing the general concept that shareholder value is associated with corporate responsibility and sustainability.

- *Donations by philanthropists.* Affluent individuals could be encouraged to make significant grants to finance projects in their name.

- *International lotteries.* In addition to voluntary donation programs, the Exchange Facility, with the approval of national governments, could organize an international lottery and/or collaborate with existing lottery systems. Given the international nature of the initiative, all citizens would be eligible to participate and potentially win a considerable amount in convertible currency. The proceeds from the lottery would be contributed to and earmarked by the Exchange Facility for projects of global environmental significance.

Private sector finance would be equally important. The Exchange Facility should seek to collaborate with private sector financiers willing to accept below market profit levels for environmentally friendly ventures. The Exchange would, for example, work with:

- *Development financiers* willing to invest in development and environment projects that promised at least a minimum measure of return;

- *Insurance companies or banks* willing to guarantee/provide collateral for meaningful commercially fundable environment and development entrepreneurship ventures.

Public contributions could also become significant. The Exchange Facility could work with governments and international organizations worldwide to set up other international schemes that would not place a burden on national budgets. These could include:

- *International transaction surcharges.* These taxes could involve micro-percentages on capital flows, currency flows, or trade- or labor-related transactions. The Tobin tax on international currency transfers is an example of this kind of surcharge. While the Tobin tax itself has its critics, some of its underlying concepts could inspire alternative schemes suitable for fundraising for development finance.

- *User charges for global public goods.* Very small fees could be imposed on goods that relate to car registrations, international travel or tourism – for instance, in connection with charges on aviation gasoline, flight tickets, or high seas transportation. In aggregate, these could add up to very significant sums.

- *Global energy or carbon tax.* Some scholars have called for a tax on carbon emissions to secure a more appropriate level of global emissions – a proposal that has been endorsed by the Zedillo Commission. By linking the money levied through such a tax with the proposed Sustainable Development Exchange Facility, such a carbon tax could produce a double benefit for the environment.

The Certification System of the Exchange Facility

A certification system would regulate recipient access and participation in the Exchange. For donors and financiers, such a system would provide a guarantee that their money is likely to be well spent, by organizations that have demonstrated their competence in the past. Certification would give financiers a realistic picture of the qualities and risks of applicant recipient institutions.

The certification system would draw on eminent experts worldwide. Some would come from academia and civil society, others from institutions like the World Bank, the UNDP, and the secretariats of various multilateral environmental agreements. A Global Environmental Mechanism and its global environmental information clearinghouse could also play a role in the proposed certification process (see Esty and Ivanova, this volume).

Demonstrable achievement and good past performance would be at the core of applicant certification. Development entrepreneurs and other potential recipients would need to apply to the certification system before receiving any financial (applicant certification) support.

Recipients who participate in the Exchange should also be required to submit to periodic re-certification; that is, to a general review of their achievements and administrative and accounting practices. Poor performers would lose their certification temporarily or permanently depending on the case. In reviewing proposed projects and programs, the Exchange would rely largely on the good judgment of applicants, provided their past record lent them sufficient credibility. Within tight timeframes, criteria, and service standards, a basic review of projects would be carried out.

Institutional reviews in the course of the certification process would also permit the Exchange to attend to rather specific requests and designations made by donors. The Exchange could thus serve as a broker between donors and users, matching particular donor preferences to particular recipient institutional profiles.

A Financial Service Window

A financial service window could also be established to administer and leverage funds received from donors. A financial service window might foster the development of a web of standardized high quality, transparent, and duly audited transactions between participating certified sponsors, financiers, and recipients. The financial service window would support certification services in monitoring the progress of ongoing projects.

While the certification service window would evaluate progress primarily in terms of sustainable development criteria, the financial service window would audit the users and ensure that funds had been used appropriately. The financial service window could also provide feedback to donors through regular financial and other progress reports, and use the results in the overall promotion of the Exchange.

Beyond directly funded projects, funds could be used to leverage limited resources. The monies might be used to stimulate and promote investment by private companies in cleaner production technologies (Deere and Bayon, 2002). Financial incentives could be particularly effective at promoting environmental investment among small and medium-sized enterprises whose characteristics, cost structures, and technical support needs allow them to respond better to promotional strategies than to imposed charges or taxes.

THE BENEFITS OF AN EXCHANGE FACILITY

The proposed Exchange Facility would aim to be an efficient connection between private capital and social capital. It could develop into:

- *An instrument to facilitate the work of those who serve the poor directly.* A fundamental constraint of the current institutional arrangements for financing environment and development is the mandate of the Bretton Woods institutions to provide financing exclusively through national governments. So long as international institutions are obliged to reach the poor through the mandatory intermediation of governments – many of whom who are not committed to the wellbeing of their citizens – many efforts will come to naught. Instead, much like servicing the commercial private sector through the International Finance Corporation (IFC), social entrepreneurs should be treated under the Exchange as direct clients in recognition of their key roles in front-line development work.

- *Just-in-time funding.* Based on its institutional certification system, the Exchange could be designed with the capacity to approve new projects in a short time – from a few weeks to a few months – in contrast to official ODA processes, which often take years.

- *Emergency stand-by funding arrangements.* In some cases, even a response time of a few weeks can be too long. In this regard, the Exchange Facility could establish an emergency oriented stand-by system with the potential to rush with funds to the site of critical problems. This mechanism might be deployed to protect endangered environmental species or resources in times of calamity, war, migrations, fires, floods, and other disasters. To facilitate these operations, an "International League of NGOs" might organize environmental monitoring efforts along the same lines that Amnesty International does for human rights (Susskind and Ozawa, 1992: 159) and might find interested donors through the Exchange.

- *Continuity funding.* More than any of the existing sources of funding for development, the Exchange would prioritize sustained support for long-term programs, recognizing the importance of operation and maintenance beyond project start-up periods. For example, following start-up environmental investments in the 1980s and 1990s, funding is now required for the long-term maintenance of established protected areas and services. Ecosystem conservation requires small, uninterrupted contributions, rather than one-time grants. In linking donors to users, therefore, the Exchange could encourage long-term matching of funds and donor-users relationships.

- *Low transaction costs.* The Exchange would work with a minimum of core staff, and rely otherwise on outside technical experts who would be engaged on a task basis. To the greatest extent possible, the Exchange should remain an (almost) virtual institution, rather than turning into yet another development bureaucracy.

The effectiveness of the Exchange will depend on the degree of convergence between the interests of financiers, donors, and recipients.

Donors and Financiers of the Exchange Would Benefit From:

- The ability to earmark funds in accordance with geographical, thematic, or institutional preferences they might have;

- Transparent information about the project selection process, criteria, and results;

- Feedback on funded projects through internet-based reports from recipient institutions and users, along with periodic monitoring, evaluation, and independent audit reports, as well as the option to visit sites;

- Quality assurance services.

Recipients of Funds From the Exchange Would Benefit From:

- Assistance in matching highly varied needs with the equally diverse interests of the donor community;

- Advice and support for efforts to seek commercial loans for viable sustainable development investments;

- Guarantees and insurance instruments to back up market-based transactions for the environment;

- Advice on the design and development of projects;

- Leveraging and co-financing for cooperative funding schemes;

- Grants for operations not eligible for commercial finance;

- Advice on sound management and reporting practices.

CONCLUSION

The "Millennium Gap" can be narrowed and eventually closed. Multiple financing mechanisms could be mobilized and, in aggregate, provide the required additional funding. Much of the initiative to make this happen will need to come from civil society and the private sector, in close collaboration with governments.

This agenda can only advance with careful technical design – a task the proposed Johannesburg Commission on Sustainable Development Finance should take on. The design of the Finance Commission will need to be tested, implemented, and refined – a task for which the proposed Sustainable Development Exchange Facility would be well suited.

REFERENCES

Buckley, Robert. 1999. *1998 Annual Review of Development Effectiveness.* Washington, D.C.: World Bank. Available from http://wbln0018.worldbank.org/oed/oeddoclib.nsf/htmlmedia/pu bparde.html

Deere, Carolyn, and Ricardo Bayon. 2002. "Investing in the Environment of the Americas." Working paper, on file with author.

Easterly, William. 2001. "Debt Relief." *Foreign Policy,* November/ December 2001: 20-25

Evans, A., and William Battaile. 1998. *1997 Annual Review of Development Effectiveness.* Washington, D.C.: World Bank.

GEF. 2002. *What Is the Global Environment Facility?* Global Environment Facility [cited June 23 2002]. Available from http://www.gefweb.org/What_is_the_GEF/what_is_the_gef.html

Greenhill, Romilly. 2002. *The Unbreakable Link: Debt Relief and the Millennium Development Goals.* London: Jubilee Research, New Economics Foundation.

IISD. 1994. *Principles of Trade and Sustainable Development.* Winnipeg, Manitoba: International Institute for Sustainable Development.

IMF. 2002. *Special Drawing Rights: A Factsheet.* International Monetary Fund [cited June 28 2002]. Available from http://www.imf.org/external/np/exr/facts/sdr.HTM

Patomaki, Heikki. 2001. *Democratising Globalisation: The Leverage of the Tobin Tax.* New York: Zed Books.

Sachs, Jeffrey, Kwesi Botchwey, Maciej Cuchra, and Sara Sievers. 1999. "Implementing Debt Relief for the HIPCs." Cambridge, MA: Center for International Development, Harvard University.

Shin, Myoung-Ho. 2001. "Financing Development Projects: Public-Private Partnerships and a New Perspective on Financing Options." Paper read at OECD/DAC Tidewater Meeting in Penha Longa, Portugal.

Soros, George. 2002. "Special Drawing Rights for the Provision of Public Goods on the Global Scale." Paper read at Roundtable on New Proposals on Financing for Development, in Washington, D.C.

Susskind, Lawrence, and Connie Ozawa. 1992. "Negotiating More Effective International Environmental Agreements." In *The International Politics of the Environment: Actors, Interests, and Institutions*, edited by Andrew Hurrell and Benedict Kingsbury. New York: Oxford University Press.

UN General Assembly. 1997. *Agenda for Development.* New York: United Nations. Available from http://www.un.org/Docs/SG/forward.htm

UNDP. 2002. *What Are Public-Private Partnerships?* United Nations Development Programme [cited June 23 2002]. Available from http://www.undp.org/ppp/about/what.htm

UNEP. 2001. *UNEP 2001 Annual Report.* Nairobi, Kenya: United Nations Environment Programme. Available from http://www.unep.org/Evaluation/AR%202001%20FINAL%20MINUS%20PIS.pdf

Zedillo Commission. 2001. *Report of the High-Level Panel on Financing for Development.* New York: United Nations. Available from http://www.un.org/reports/financing/index.html

Making Environmental Deals: The Economic Case for a World Environmental Organization

John Whalley and Ben Zissimos

SUMMARY

Others in this volume have spelled out *what* the problems are on the global environment front. We discuss *how* these issues might be addressed. We advance a rationale for a new international environmental body – a World Environmental Organization or WEO – whose primary function would be to facilitate bargains on the global environment.

We use, as a point of departure, the international trade regime. The General Agreement on Tariffs and Trade/World Trade Organization (GATT/WTO) tries to liberalize trade in goods and services by removing border impediments through negotiated exchanges of trade policy concessions. We suggest that a World Environmental Organization (WEO) should have a similar principal focus, namely, removing impediments to bargaining (and trades) on the global environment. Exchanges of commitments on forest cover, maintenance of coral reefs, species management, biodiversity protection, and other environmental concessions in return for cash, policy changes (trade policy changes, for instance), and other considerations might fall under the bargaining umbrella of a WEO.

We contend that such bargains would result in improved environmental quality and transfers of resources for developmental purposes to poorer countries, which are the main custodians of these assets.

WHAT WE ARE NOT PROPOSING

Our idea differs from those underpinning other recent proposals for a global environmental body, stemming, in one way or another, from the trade and environment debate now embroiling the World Trade Organization. Calls have come from high levels, including WTO Director-General Supachai Panitchpakdi, for a new body separate from the WTO, where environmental issues could be discussed. According to several academics, such a body would be more qualified than the WTO to resolve conflicts between trade agreements and the environment (Charnovitz, 1993; Runge, 2001; Esty, 2000). Prominent politicians, such as French President Jacques Chirac, former French Prime Minister Lionel Jospin, and former Soviet leader Mikhail Gorbachev, have suggested the need for both a strengthened and consolidated global environmental agency, and an agency to oversee present international environmental treaties and other arrangements now in place.[1]

Our view is that these calls have not really focused on how to address central or substantive environmental policy problems, but instead have dealt with tangential issues, in proposals that are likely to be inconsequential in impact. Even worse are vague proposals to strengthen the United Nations Environment Programme (UNEP), to oversee enforcement of existing environmental treaties (which contain their own enforcement arrangements), or to provide an alternative location in which to discuss trade and environment issues (von Moltke, 2001; Juma, 2000). Neither the restructuring proposals nor the tinkering reforms deal with the central global environmental problem, namely, the relative lack of internalization of cross-border and global externalities.

The issue is not one of seeking out mutually agreed upon statements of principle of what constitutes sound environmental management (in the tradition of sustainability, the Stockholm Declaration, the Brundtland Report, the Rio Declaration, and Agenda 21) or suggesting reorganization of current institutional arrangements, but rather of how we design mechanisms to achieve internalization goals.

---

[1]   For texts of speeches, see Ruggiero (1998), Panitchpakdi (2001), and Jospin (2002).

THE CHALLENGE OF INTERNALIZING CROSS-BORDER EXTERNALITIES

We regard the lack of "internalization of cross-border and global externalities" as the central global environmental problem. An externality is a (usually negative) consequence of the production of a commodity that is not reflected in its price. In other words, society's valuation of the good does not reflect its real social and environmental cost. For example, pollution emitted from an industrial plant that affects residents of the neighboring area is regarded as an externality. When the plant's operating decisions do not take these consequences into consideration (i.e. do not compensate the population, do not alter the price of the products, or the process through which they are manufactured), the externality is not internalized.

"Failure to internalize," means, essentially, the collective failure to pay for the environmental costs associated with having commodities in the marketplace. These costs are often not borne by the producers and are either assumed by governments or never addressed, leaving others to suffer the consequences.

Internalizing *cross-border* externalities entails finding ways to prevent or repair damages that transcend borders or affect global systems like the atmosphere or the oceans. In the case of the industrial plant, if the people who suffer from air pollution could measure the harm done to them and negotiate compensation from the polluters, the externality would be internalized. Facilitating the negotiation of similar deals for transboundary and global concerns would be one of the central tasks of a World Environmental Organization.

CURRENT ARRANGEMENTS DO NOT ADDRESS INTERNALIZATION

We see the present global environmental regime as deficient in attaining the internalization goal we suggest. The principles embodied in the Rio Declaration and a series of approximately 200 largely issue-specific environmental agreements (UNEP, 1996) have, in our view, relatively little to do with solving the problems caused by the environmental consequences of market transactions that are not factored in by parties to the transaction.

Even though a small number of recent treaty arrangements encourage bargaining deals between parties with different interests (for example, the Kyoto Protocol allows countries to buy or sell permits to emit CO_2), we suggest that the patchwork quilt of issue-specific, science-driven global and regional treaties have not achieved full internalization, as might be possible under a World Environmental Organization (WEO). These narrow topic and largely non-side payment negotiations have spawned shallow treaties under which opportunities for achieving more substantial joint gains are not discussed.

Currently, few mechanisms guide and focus efforts to internalize externalities that cause global environmental failure.

A DEALMAKING AGENCY COULD ADDRESS INTERNALIZATION

We suggest that these failures of negotiation can best be corrected through a new agency that aims to account for as many of the social costs of market transactions as possible through innovative and aggressive environmental dealmaking. The World Environmental Organization we propose remedies what we regard as a relative lack of Coasian deals to internalize externalities at the international level.[2] Such a WEO could be designed to cover all externalities, both within and across countries. Our main focus is on cross-border externalities, since within-country externalities can in principle be dealt with by solely domestic initiatives.

---

2 Coase (1960) suggested that those who cause and those who receive damage can (and often do) bargain between themselves so as to internalize externalities. For this to occur, Coase stressed that property rights assignments are needed to clarify who has rights to do what. In the case of a factory that causes air pollution, for instance, a Coasian deal is possible if all parties agree that the factory owners must compensate people who suffer from pollution, or that those who suffer from air pollution should compensate the factory owners for using cleaner but more expensive production technologies.

We see the central objective for a WEO as facilitating cross-country deals on environmental issues with the aim of raising environmental quality. Those who have custody of assets in one country should, through bargained deals, be able to get those abroad who value these assets highly to pay for higher standards of environmental management for the wider benefit.

The result would be improved environmental quality, as well as monetary transfers to custodians of assets, many of whom are in poor countries. We do not claim that such an innovation will fully and immediately achieve complete internalization, but we do think that significant improvement on the current situation is possible through such an approach.

Entities such as a WEO also sometimes evolve out of small beginnings, and slowly grow into full form. Only time will tell whether the institutional structure we outline here emerges from the present global environmental regime, or whether radical response to future external shocks will ultimately prove to be the main driving force.

INITIATING CROSS-COUNTRY INTERNALIZATION DEALS

The central activity of a World Environmental Organization would consist of generating internalization deals between countries (and/or groups of agents within countries) on global environmental issues. Deals would involve verifiable environmental commitments exchanged across countries in return for various forms of compensation, including cash. The deals could be government-to-government deals of various kinds, or also involve private sector agents (companies, representatives of community groups) in various ways.

The deals could have specific environmental goals. For species, for example, the target might be species population levels by a specified target year. For biodiversity, it might be access to undisturbed lands guaranteed over a period of time. For coral/oceans, it might be the portion of unimpaired coral in coastal waters. For carbon emissions, it might be a maximum emission level from the country over a time period, or (as in the Kyoto Protocol) cutbacks from emission levels. With water, where there are international disputes over flow rates through territories and water quality indicators, these could also be bargained for in return for considerations, as above. Toxic waste commitments could be bargained for in terms of annual levels of discharges. All these deals would constitute implementable and verifiable environmental commitments, and could be bargained over in a WEO for considerations in cash or other compensation.

While some of these commitments are currently covered by treaty arrangements in various forms, a WEO would allow deals to go considerably further. As such, there seem to be no conflicts with existing treaties. If new WEO deals go beyond what is in treaties, the treaties simply become redundant. If WEO deals are not up to the terms of treaty arrangements, they will not be concluded.

The effect of these deals would be for agents who were the source of global environmental damage to take into account the costs of that damage to others through their private decisions.

Species and forests would be protected in the interests of foreign consumers, who in turn would pay for environmental quality improvements. Carbon emitters, for example, would take into account the costs that incremental climate change inflicted on others; deforesters would take into account the incremental loss to others in global amenity value and habitat loss. Custodians of assets would be compensated in the case of forest stewardship, or emitters in the case of carbon if they agree to use more expensive but cleaner production technologies. Explicit bargained arrangements involving both governments and non-governmental groups would thus reflect negotiated deals in which property rights dictated the direction of payment for reduced environmental damage.

WEAKENING THE IMPEDIMENTS TO INTERNALIZATION DEALS

Ambiguous property rights, free riding, time inconsistency, and contract enforcement are four central reasons why global externalities go un-internalized. The difficulty of assembling coalitions and the problem of side payments are other related concerns. A central aim of a WEO would thus be to weaken the impediments to internalization deals that currently exist. [3]

Property Rights and Environmental Dealmaking

A key impediment to global environmental dealmaking in a World Environmental Organization will clearly be the ambiguities of property rights both across and within countries.

Across countries, national governments often assert their implicit right to regulate and protect economic activity, involving different claims over environmental assets. OECD countries often argue, for instance, that forests are the lungs of the earth (globally communal property) and thus they have the right to, say, block imports of tropical lumber until improvements in environmental quality (forest cover targets) occur in exporting countries. Developing countries with forest cover argue that this is eco- (or green) imperialism, which forces them to slow their growth and development, and yields environmental benefits mainly to wealthy countries. They argue that they should instead be compensated for showing environmental restraint over the use of their own environmental assets. The issue is whether forests are a global or a national asset.

Within countries, there are also substantial ambiguities as to property rights over environmental assets. Some countries have multi-level government registration of ownership (national and provincial), which produces conflicting claims that courts often do not adequately resolve. Native peoples may have various rights to biological species, even if formal land rights are held elsewhere. Squatters in some countries exert de facto property rights over species, forests, and biodiversity.

---

3 Note that a WEO such as we propose is some distance from the current WTO. While the latter is both a rule and a bargaining framework, it is restrictive, since no cash is allowed in bargaining and the rules of the WTO Charter (via GATT 1994) also constrain allowable bargaining (such as through the Most Favored Nation rule, which prevents pair-wise deals). The WTO Charter's initial focus was more on preventing a reversion to the global trade regime of the 1930s in the postwar years, as well as further liberalizing through negotiated exchanges of concessions, than on internalizing externalities.

EXAMPLES OF BARGAINS

A government in country X with no rainforests might strike a deal on behalf of its citizens with a government of country Y with rainforests. Its effect might be that a specified fraction of land in country Y would remain under forest cover for a specified time period (twenty or forty years, for example). In return for this commitment, the government of country X would pledge to transfer a sum of money to country Y at the end of the period. The commitment would need to be verified in some way and country Y would need to impose this undertaking upon its residents. This could be done through logging bans, export taxes on logs, logging licenses, or other internal arrangements.

Alternatively, a group of concerned citizens in country X could negotiate independently of their national government with a community group that has custody of an environmental resource in country Y. They might again agree to a transfer of financial resources directly to the group at the end of a time period if a particular environmental target is met (again, say, forest cover). Issues of verification and compliance would arise in both cases.

For a WEO, this raises difficult questions of who is to deal with whom to generate environmental quality-enhancing bargaining. Coase (1960) argued that clear assignment of property rights is needed before any environmental dealmaking occurs, and a central task for a WEO would be to help to clarify property rights to facilitate such deals. Property rights related problems partially explain why cross-country deals on environmental issues have been science-based and lowest common denominator in outcome, rather than Coasian in character, and why property rights issues would have to be a part of WEO activity.

This will not be easy, although some aspects may be more straightforward than others. Where multiple land registration schemes operate, a WEO could help simplify and consolidate them. Where non-timber rights to forests arise, for example, a WEO might codify them and bring them in as part of the deal. Across countries, a WEO could accept that de facto rights devolve to the country with assets on its territory.

Because coercion is not a viable solution, bargained compensation would seem to be the only practical way forward, although this involves effectively ceding currently contested property rights over environmental assets in developing countries. The operational principle, in the absence of international courts with clear authority to rule on such rights, would seem to be that custody of assets yields ability to bargain, and that bargaining becomes more satisfactory as an internalization device the more secure the custody is.

Some environmental conflicts at the international level are themselves primarily about property rights. An example of this is water conflicts, where one country controls the headwaters that flow to other countries further down the river. Here, negotiated deals, say, to maintain water flow relative to target levels in return for other concessions, could be brokered by a WEO. Documenting existing overlapping and inconsistent property rights where they occur may help resolve the situation. Suggesting ways to proceed where property rights are contested might also help.

We do not claim that a WEO could definitively resolve all international property rights issues. Coase, in any case, suggested that they lie outside of formal economics and rest on arguments of natural justice. The aim would be both to contribute to the alleviation of some disputes and to work with de facto rights on other cases through existing custody of assets.

The Problem of Free Riding

The problem of free riding can occur when the benefits of pollution control accrue to many different nations regardless of their behavior. By bargaining for environmental protection in another country, country A would assume all the costs of environmental protection, but environmental protection would benefit other countries as much as it would benefit country A. Nations would have an incentive not to enter into a deal, hoping that someone else would do it for them. For example, if countries, or groups within countries, hold existence value over forests abroad, and if bargained environmental deals were bilateral, countries could free ride on each other's deals, since the benefits from a deal committing a country to preserve its forests accrue to countries other than those that are party to it. Free riding greatly undermines the attractiveness of environmental deals at the global level, since the benefits of any pair of bilateral actions are spread much more widely.

Deals made only by subsets of affected parties would therefore be difficult to conclude and would likely span groups of countries with similar interests on both sides of the environmental resource. A strength of a WEO would be its potential ability to orchestrate simultaneous deals across groups of affected parties. This would further raise the degree of internalization of the global externality achieved in the deal through crossovers, and hence would reduce free riding.

As another example, all OECD countries may benefit from a species population target negotiated, say, in Cameroon by Germany (or a German NGO).

A WEO could help countries capture the benefits to others from free riding through multilateral rather than bilateral dealmaking, with packages of environmental deals put together in rounds of negotiation, much as the WTO utilizes crossovers of benefits in one area and costs in others in allowing countries to conclude mutually advantageous deals on trade barrier reduction.

A WEO could even aggressively seek out dealmaking opportunities by proposing a package of deals to consortia of interested parties, and in this way reduce free riding benefits.

The Problem of Time Consistency

Time consistency is a problem because an arrangement entered into by one government might not be honored by a later government that is either unwilling or unable to fulfill the terms of the agreement made to another state. If Brazil, for example, were to promise to restrain deforestation over some number of years in return for financial inflows, then if the funds were paid immediately, Brazil could request more funds after initial receipt. But if funds were to be paid at the end of the period, Brazil would have no assurance that payment would be forthcoming.

Some form of intermediary guarantor, therefore, seems needed by both sides to reduce the risks involved in bargained environmental transactions. A WEO could act as such a guarantor by receiving funds for deals agreed to and holding them in escrow, pending execution of the commitment. If the environmental target were deemed to be met, funds would then be released to the country or group making the commitment, and if not, returned to the country or group pledging the funds.

Problems of Contract Enforcement

Enforcing the environmental deals concluded within a World Environmental Organization would require robust procedural arrangements. Who ensures that a pledged environmental target has actually been met, and what are the remedies if this is not the case? Under a WEO, staff could monitor compliance on environmental commitments, and make determinations of whether or not commitments have been met. A set of agreed upon procedures for verification would be needed to this effect. These, in turn, would require undertakings from parties to deals monitored by the WEO to accept WEO determinations, and a system of dispute resolution and appeal.

Difficulty of Assembling Coalitions

There are difficulties in putting together coalitions for dealmaking aimed at reducing transaction costs. Often it is difficult to determine the benefits from deals, and hence who should be approached with dealmaking proposals. Preferences underlying deals need to be estimated and represented, because revealed "willingness to pay" measures are hard to put together. Parties to deals typically have little information on what deals may be worth to other parties, and hence how to negotiate. Who assesses and acts on behalf of the collective willingness to pay in OECD countries for global environmental improvements? If it is to be national governments, how are they to do this and with what effect? A WEO could play a role by undertaking studies, producing willingness to pay estimates for enhanced global environmental quality, setting out scenarios for deals, and orchestrating and stimulating the process with information.

The Problem of Side Payments

It is often said that side payments do not occur to any significant degree in existing inter-country environmental arrangements, and that financial resource transfers from countries that belong to the OECD where demand for global environmental quality is high, to lower income countries with significant endowments of environmental assets, are small and do not take place on a regular basis. If resource transfers do occur, it is usually as a result of a country's being a signatory to one of the global treaties, such as the United Nations Framework Convention on Climate Change (UNFCCC), rather than as a negotiated environmental deal focused on internalization. Under the current system, negotiations occur for specific Conventions or Protocols, each addressing a major global issue. By encouraging ongoing negotiation and constant dealmaking between countries, a WEO would make side payments much more common.

Overview of the Role of a World Environmental Organization

We envision a World Environmental Organization that could undertake activities underpinning environmental dealmaking on a global scale, aiming at accounting for as many social costs of market transactions as possible. It would not have the power to conclude deals (these would be for national governments to decide on) but proposals for deals, mechanisms to support deals, arrangements to enforce deals – all would be the bailiwick of the WEO.

A WEO could act as an intermediary on deals of the type sketched out in this chapter. It could receive and hold funds until determinations were made as to compliance (with either transfers to the custodian country, or return to the other country). A WEO could provide verification as to whether the terms of deals had been met, and act as a dispute settlement and arbitration vehicle. This would go much further than the Clean Development Mechanism of the Kyoto Protocol, which initiates and oversees North-South transactions on climate change with oversight by the Conference of the Parties (Sebenius, 1994).

A WEO could be proactive in identifying areas and countries between which deals would make sense, even to the point of initiating proposals. It could coordinate single country offers and explicitly seek to internalize free riding in the deals it brokered. It could propose mechanisms to be used in countries to assess and reflect collective willingness to pay.

In setting out our view of a WEO, we see a possible progressive graduation from weaker to stronger forms as the likely evolution. Such an entity in its strong form is unlikely to be implemented quickly, and the demand for it, as much as anything else, will reflect the level of concern for global environmental quality and the global costs stemming from lack of internalization.[4]

DEVELOPING ENVIRONMENTAL/NON-ENVIRONMENTAL POLICY LINKAGE

By bringing global environmental arrangements under a single bargaining umbrella, a WEO should also make it easier for cross-country concessions to be exchanged between environmental and non-environmental areas, potentially leading to both a stronger environmental regime and gains elsewhere. Thus, developing countries might make concessions on their internal environmental management in return not only for cash, but also for improved trade access. A problem in making such concessions is how to do it within the existing patchwork quilt of global environmental arrangements. By systematizing these arrangements, a WEO could better facilitate bargains of this kind.

The WTO involves bargaining concessions on trade barrier reductions, but no cash is exchanged and only national governments may bargain. A WEO could go further. Cash for commitments could be allowed, and bargains would not be restricted to national governments. A WEO can be seen as a parallel and expanded bargaining framework for country and group concessions. Linkage to non-environmental issues, while a second or third step, implies that bargaining

---

4   In a parallel paper (Whalley and Zissimos, 2001), we set out three variants of a possible WEO progressing from weaker to stronger forms, which we suggest could be implemented gradually, moving from one to the next.

need not be restricted to cash compensation for environmental commitments. A wider forum for global bargaining could evolve from the WEO, encompassing both the WTO and various issues on which groups want to exchange concessions.

Developing countries have been cautious over such bargains, arguing that they should be compensated for undertaking environmental restraint of the form sought by OECD countries. They are fearful that a willingness to bargain indicates both a relaxation of this position and, implicitly, a concession on property rights. But the opposite is true.

A World Environmental Organization would give developing countries the opportunity to take advantage of their property rights and obtain resource transfers for environmental restraint. Thus, by providing institutional support for bargaining across issue areas, incentives to cooperate would be multiplied, and the basis for global environmental cooperation significantly broadened.

Underpinning Domestic Environmental Policy

An international environmental entity such as a WEO could also lend support to domestic groups (including NGOs) trying to raise levels of compliance with domestic environmental laws.[5] Governments in countries with such problems, in turn, might be able to use the WEO as a masthead to support domestic policy change in the environmental area.

A WEO might also consolidate the information clearinghouse functions of the Commission on Sustainable Development (CSD), and build a wider range of information sources, again underpinning domestic policy. It could also help build institutional capacity in less developed countries, based on the recognition that, in the past, compliance has been hampered by administrative weakness and poor institutional infrastructure.

---

5   If an NGO vehemently opposed a deal its national government entered into that was brokered by a WEO, it remains to be worked out whether the NGO should be able to appeal the case to the WEO. Our inclination would be to treat these as issues to be resolved within the domestic political process.

POSSIBLE FORM OF A WORLD ENVIRONMENTAL ORGANIZATION

Structure
- Head Office
- Governing Council
  - All WEO members would have a seat *
  - All sign protocol of accession to uphold all WEO decisions
- Chief Officer

Mandate
- To improve global environmental quality through structured environmental deals

Issues Covered
- All issues on which agents wanted to strike deals
- Primarily transboundary issues and global commons issues**

Services Offered
- Facilitation of deals
- Verification of deals
- Property rights verification
- Intermediation of financial arrangements
- Advancement of cross-country negotiations
- Initiation of proposals

Structure of Deals
- No set format for negotiations
- No principles or general rules
- Country-to-country, including non-state parties
- WEO notified once deals are completed

Possible Additional Activities
- Call for negotiating rounds on the environment
- Initiation of negotiations to streamline, codify current treaties
- Exploration of cross-linkage negotiations
- Exploration of whether WEO commitments might underpin domestic environmental policy

*   Whether non-governmental organizations as well as countries would be members needs to be determined.
** Environmental issues within countries could also be dealt with but are more likely to be resolved through a process outside a WEO, since the impediments to successful bargaining are fewer.

POTENTIAL BENEFITS TO DEVELOPING COUNTRIES

While we see a WEO playing a central role in achieving improvements in the areas of global dealmaking, there could be additional potential benefits of the resulting environmental deals for developing countries. These benefits would be an important step in driving forward efforts at global environmental protection, considering that developing countries often see economic development and poverty alleviation as more urgent priorities and have traditionally been reluctant to embrace environmental treaties proposed by the developed world:

- Low-income developing countries may be able to obtain valuable resources for development by making commitments to undertake environmental protection at home;

- Negotiations could be about much more than the environment, since these countries will also be able to bargain collectively on both environmental and non-environmental dimensions of issues in a WEO, substantially enhancing their bargaining power;

- Issue linkage in negotiation between environmental and non-environmental areas would be made easier through a WEO, since these links require a level of coordination across sub-areas and regions in the environmental area that is currently difficult to imagine occurring without agency support;

- Opportunities may exist for countries experiencing difficulties in implementing their own domestic environmental policies to use the political support of an international entity such as a WEO to achieve their objectives;

- A WEO could act as a focal point for developing country coalition formation in negotiation. By formulating joint positions in WEO negotiations, developing countries with similar interests might be able to act together. Resource transfers to developing countries in return for strengthened environmental regimes might be more significant if developing countries were to bargain jointly through a WEO rather than as single countries.

POSSIBLE REASONS FOR CAUTION ON THE PART OF DEVELOPING COUNTRIES

Developing countries may, however, be cautious about such proposals. Their concerns would likely be:

- Whether advantages to them would be large enough to contribute significantly to development;

- Whether any new flow of funds and technology would justify the raised expectations of improved environmental performance;

- Whether an additional global "pressurizing agency" along the lines of the World Bank or the International Monetary Fund (IMF) might result;

- Whether growth and development might be slowed by taking on environmental commitments. The heterogeneity of both interest and circumstance across individual countries may further complicate a developing country reaction to our WEO proposal.

Caution toward a WEO may be a likely initial response, and one that has to be clearly acknowledged, but we would argue that potential gains remain. For now, the catalyst for a possible global environmental body is seen as the trade and environment conflict in the WTO, but we think this may change. If major additional global environmental damage occurs in the next few years and cooperation might have mitigated it, this could prove to be a more powerful catalyst.

CONCLUSION

The central aim of the World Environmental Organization we propose, regardless of the speed at which it evolved, would be to redress international environmental negotiation failures in a way that would move the global economy closer to achieving fuller internalization of global environmental externalities. Its overarching purpose would be to improve environmental quality worldwide. It is our contention that such an organization would provide more concrete benefits to the environment than any arrangement or organization that currently exists, and for that reason, we urge serious consideration of its merits by the international community.

REFERENCES

Charnovitz, Steve. 1993. "The Environment vs. Trade Rules: Defogging the Debate." *Environmental Law* 23 (2): 475-517.

Coase, Ronald H. 1960. "The Problem of Social Costs." *Journal of Law and Economics* 3 (1).

Esty, Daniel C. 2000. "The Value of Creating a Global Environmental Organization." *Environment Matters* 6 (12): 13-15.

Jospin, Lionel. 2002. "French Prime Minister Calls for Creation of New World Environment Organization." *International Environment Reporter* 25 (5): 213.

Juma, Calestous. 2000. "The Perils of Centralizing Global Environmental Governance." *Environment Matters* 6 (12): 13-15.

Panitchpakdi, H.E. Dr. Supachai. 2001. "Keynote Address: The Evolving Multilateral Trade System in the New Millenium." *George Washington International Law Review* 33 (3): 419-449.

Ruggiero, Renato. 1998. *A Global System for the Next Fifty Years, Address to the Royal Institute of International Affairs.* London: Royal Institute of International Affairs.

Runge, C. Ford. 2001. "A Global Environment Organization (GEO) and the World Trading System." *Journal of World Trade* 35 (4): 399-426.

Sebenius, J. 1994. "Towards a Winning Climate Coalition." In *Negotiating Climate Change*, edited by I. Mintzer and J. Leonard. New York: Cambridge University Press.

UNEP. 1996. *Register of International Treaties and Other Agreements in the Field of the Environment.* Nairobi, Kenya: United Nations Environment Programme.

von Moltke, Konrad. 2001. "The Organization of the Impossible." *Global Environmental Politics* 1 (1).

Whalley, John, and Ben Zissimos. 2001. "An Internalization Based World Environment Organization." Centre for the Study of Globalisation and Regionalisation, University of Warwick, Warwick.

Revitalizing Global Environmental Governance: A Function-Driven Approach

Daniel C. Esty and Maria H. Ivanova

SUMMARY

We advance the case for a Global Environmental Mechanism (GEM) on the basis of our analysis of four key questions: Do we need environmental efforts at the global scale? What functions are essential at the global level? Where has the existing system fallen short? What would an effective institutional mechanism for addressing global environmental problems look like?

Our central argument is that there exists today a set of inescapably global environmental threats that require international "collective action." They demand an institutional mechanism at the global level, we argue, but one quite different from traditional international bodies. We propose *not* a new international bureaucracy but rather the creation of a Global Environmental Mechanism that draws on Information Age technologies and networks to promote cooperation in a lighter, faster, more modern, and effective manner than traditional institutions.

We see three core capacities as essential to a GEM: (1) provision of adequate information and analysis to characterize problems, track trends, and identify interests; (2) creation of a policy "space" for environmental negotiation and bargaining; and (3) sustained build-up of capacity for addressing issues of agreed-upon concern and significance. We envision a GEM building on the expertise of existing institutions and creating new mechanisms where key functions are currently not being provided or are inadequate.

A NEED FOR EFFECTIVE ENVIRONMENTAL INSTITUTIONS

Ten years after the Rio Earth Summit, and thirty years after the Stockholm Conference on the Human Environment, the world community lacks effective institutional and legal mechanisms to address global-scale environmental degradation. This deficiency weighs ever more heavily as nation-states come to recognize their inability to address critical problems on a national basis and to appreciate the depth and breadth of their interdependence.

Devised during the infancy of environmental awareness, when problems were perceived as largely local, relatively distinct, and subject to technological fixes, the current international environmental regime is weak, fragmented, lacking in resources, and handicapped by a narrow mandate. There is motion, but there is little progress. More than 500 multilateral environmental treaties are now in existence (UNEP, 2001), more than a dozen international agencies share environmental responsibilities, and yet environmental conditions are not improving across a number of critical dimensions. Problems such as climate change, ocean pollution, fisheries depletion, deforestation, and desertification persist – with trends that are often broadly negative. Moreover, advances in a range of ecological sciences continue to unveil new threats to the global commons – from airborne mercury to disrupted hydrological systems – as well as new interrelationships among issues.

The environmental challenges we now face clearly illustrate the extent of interconnectedness of the earth's ecological as well as economic systems. These problems demand collective action on a global scale, yet there is no established and effective forum where parties can engage in a sustained and focused dialogue, identify priorities, and devise action plans for tackling environmental concerns with worldwide implications. Absent a vibrant international environmental body, many decisions with serious environmental repercussions are taken within the economic, trade, and finance institutions, where short-term economic priorities often trump long-term sustainability.

Some of the current failings can be attributed to a history of management shortcomings and bureaucratic entanglements, but other aspects of the problem are deeper and more structural. Governments have failed to create a functional institutional architecture for the management of ecological interdependence. The fact that other global challenges – international economic affairs, population control, and various world health problems (e.g., eradication of polio and small pox) – have been addressed more successfully is notable.

The disconnect between environmental needs and environmental performance in the current international system is striking. New institutional mechanisms for better global governance are urgently needed.

The haphazard development of international environmental laws and agencies has left three important institutional gaps in the existing global environmental governance system: (1) a jurisdictional gap, (2) an information gap, and (3) an implementation gap.

Jurisdictional Gap

The discrepancy between a globalized world and a set of inescapable transboundary problems on the one hand, and a dominant structure of national policymaking units on the other, has led to a gap in issue coverage. National legislatures often do not see their role in addressing worldwide transboundary harms, while global bodies often do not have the capacity or the authority to address them.

The United Nations lacks a coherent institutional mechanism for dealing effectively with global environmental concerns (Palmer, 1992; Esty, 1994). The UN Charter provides for no environmental body. Responsibilities are instead divided among a suite of agencies, including the Food and Agriculture Organization, the World Meteorological Organization, the International Maritime Organization, the International Oceanographic Commission, the UN Educational, Scientific and Cultural Organization, the Commission on Sustainable Development, the Global Environment Facility, and the UN Development Programme, with a coordinating and catalytic role assigned to the UN Environment Programme (UNEP). Adding to this fragmentation are the independent secretariats to the numerous treaties, all contending for limited governmental time, attention, and resources. The Economic and Social Council of the UN has the gargantuan task of coordinating all of these diffuse efforts and has proven incapable of carrying out its mission (Palmer, 1992).

A mere program in the UN system, UNEP has accomplished more than its limited mandate might seem to make possible and its minute budget might have been expected to allow.[1] UNEP has supported the creation of a large body of international environmental law and has contributed to efforts to generate environmental data, assessments, and reporting. A number of UNEP executive directors have been forceful advocates for change and international environmental cooperation. But UNEP has no executive authority. It has failed to coordinate the various global and regional environmental arrangements around the world and "lacks political clout to serve adequately as the lead international organization for the protection of the global environment" (Dunoff, 1995).

The scattering of environmental activities across many international organizations has greatly compromised participation, especially that of developing countries. Negotiations on a variety of critical pollution control and natural resource management issues often occur simultaneously around the world. Moreover, the costs associated with attending intergovernmental sessions to negotiate international environmental agreements and treaties are high, both in terms of direct economic expenses and opportunity costs of days away from the already understaffed environmental ministries.[2] Countries with limited diplomatic and financial resources have thus been forced to choose which conferences to attend, or whether to attend them at all (Kelly, 1997).

---

[1]   UNEP was created following the Stockholm Conference in 1972 with the mandate "to provide leadership and encourage partnership in caring for the environment by inspiring, informing and enabling nations and peoples to improve their quality of life without compromising that of future generations" (UNEP, 2001): http://www.unep.org/about.asp Its annual budget of $100 million is comparable to that of many environmental non-governmental organizations (NGOs), such as the U.S. National Wildlife Federation (Kelly, 1997).

[2]   Edith Brown Weiss (1995) points out that "A normal negotiation may require four or five intergovernmental negotiating sessions of one to two weeks each during a period of eighteen months to two years. The Climate Convention negotiations required six sessions of two weeks each in less than sixteen months. Despite this very full and expensive schedule of negotiations, the Climate Convention negotiations were only one of more than a half dozen global or regional environmental agreement negotiations occurring more or less at the same time."

Without an effective forum with an action orientation, rule-making and norm development have been inadequate and left to a chosen few, leading to prolonged discussions, lowest-common-denominator outcomes, and poor results.

There is, moreover, no structured system of dispute settlement. Most environmental agreements have no procedures for resolving disputes among parties. A few agreements, notably the UN Convention on the Law of the Sea and the Montreal Protocol, have dispute settlement mechanisms, but these provisions have gone unused. Other treaties, like the Biodiversity Convention and the UN Framework Convention on Climate Change, expressly defer disputes to the International Court of Justice (ICJ). And while the ICJ has set up an "environmental chamber," it has never heard a case. As a result of the weakness of the environmental institutions, the disputes they might have addressed end up being taken to other fora, such as the World Trade Organization. This pattern leaves those with international environmental claims with no institutional mechanism for redress (Kalas, 2001). This lack of institutional capacity has broad implications:

- Individuals harmed by transboundary effects of state or corporate activities have nowhere to turn;

- The existing bodies have jurisdiction only over *states*. Private actors can neither be brought before the court nor do they have standing to request adjudication;

- Jurisdiction is largely "by consent" and remedies are not enforceable.

Information Gap

As the long-standing literature on international cooperation makes clear, the availability of reliable information is critical to policy formation (Hassan and Hutchinson, 1992; Martin, 1999; Esty, 2001, 2002). In the environmental field, where problems are dispersed across space and time, sound decisionmaking hinges on the availability of information regarding (1) environmental problems, trends, and causal relationships, and (2) policy options, results, and compliance with commitments. Data collection, "indicator" development, monitoring and verification, and scientific assessment and analysis thus emerge as central to sound decisionmaking.

High quality data with cross-country comparability is necessary to support an effective approach to problem definition and assessment (Esty, 2002). A suite of international organizations, scientific research centers, national governments, and environmental convention secretariats are responsible for data collection and scientific assessment. UNEP has established an Environment and Natural Resources Information Network to help collate, store, manage, and disseminate environmental information and data in developing countries and to assess environment and development issues for decisionmaking, policy setting, and planning. UNDP has launched a similar initiative with its Capacity 21 program. Numerous other international organizations, NGOs, universities, and think tanks have information initiatives underway. However, significant data gaps remain. There is little coordination among data collection efforts, and comparability across jurisdictions is poor (WEF, 2002).

Compliance monitoring and reporting are even more unsystematic, scattered, and informal. International environmental agreements have, until recently, contained few substantive mechanisms for monitoring and evaluation. Although environmental agreements usually require parties to report their compliance to the respective treaty secretariat, few guidelines exist as to the scope or methodology of the reports. Moreover, the convention secretariats often lack the authority and resources to monitor agreements through verification of reported information or through independent assessments. The analysis and publication of collected data is also severely limited. With the proliferation of agreements, countries have found it increasingly difficult to meet their reporting obligations under the various conventions, and nations' self-reported data are often incomplete, unreliable, and inconsistent (GAO, 1999). UNEP has, in fact, begun to consider the potential of streamlining reporting requirements across similar conventions.

Implementation Gap

The biggest single obstacle to environmental progress at the global scale is the lack of an action orientation. This might be attributable to an implementation gap. Treaty congestion has led to overload at the national level, where the political, administrative, and economic capacity to implement agreements resides. Many international environmental institutions, including the numerous secretariats of international environmental conventions, have some claim on the administrative capacity of national states. Even industrialized states with well-developed regulatory mechanisms and bureaucracies have become overwhelmed (Brown Weiss, 1995; UNEP, 2001).

For developing countries, financial and technology transfer mechanisms are critical. But the efforts to date in these regards are modest and noticeably inadequate.

The existing financial mechanisms are scattered across the Global Environment Facility, UNEP, the World Bank, and separate treaty-based funds such as the Montreal Protocol Finance Mechanism. This dispersion and lack of integration reinforces the perception of a lack of seriousness in the North about the plight of the South. The institutional mechanisms for technology transfer have also been less than effective. Tying technology transfer to official aid and export promotion policies has resulted in the imposition of inappropriate technologies on countries with little capacity to choose, assess, operate, and maintain them.

Moreover, few international environmental agreements contain serious enforcement provisions. In most cases, the only incentive for compliance with treaty obligations comes from peer pressure or the threat of public exposure. However, when performance data are scarce, the "name and shame" strategy provides little traction. Even when agreements do include enforcement provisions, resource or other constraints limit their effectiveness. For example, the Northwest Atlantic Fisheries Convention has the authority to establish and allocate fishing quotas, but allows for the exemption of any member from any enforcement proposal through the lodging of an objection. It also permits members to choose not to be bound by rules already in force. Finally, although members are allowed to board and inspect the vessels of other member nations, only the nation under whose flag the vessel is operating can prosecute and sanction a vessel's owner for violations. Nations are often reluctant to penalize their own fleets. In 1993, for example, out of forty-nine vessels charged with offenses, only six were prosecuted (GAO, 1999).

A multi-pronged agenda of refinements to the existing structure and reforms of UNEP and the other elements of the current international environmental system should be developed to address these glaring gaps in global environmental governance.

The list of problems is so long and the baggage associated with the current regime so heavy that at some point a fundamental restructuring rather than incremental tinkering becomes a better path forward.

In the face of so many difficulties and the existing regime's poor track record, any presumption in favor of working with the status quo cannot be sustained. Moreover, as the analysis above suggests, the nub of the issue is structural. This fact makes a different starting point and a new institutional design desirable if not essential.

RATIONALE FOR GLOBAL ACTION

The need for international cooperation to address environmental problems with transboundary or global implications is clear both in theory and in practice. Some environmental problems (local air pollution and waste disposal, for example) are of limited geographic scope and can be handled at the national or local scale. An increasingly large set of issues, however, from persistent organic pollutants to fisheries depletion to climate change, demand an effective response among several jurisdictions and, sometimes, coordinated action across the globe. Governments around the world are beginning to recognize the limits of their ability to tackle transboundary environmental problems on their own.

Global Public Goods

To understand the need for a new institutional design, it is helpful to understand that the underlying conceptual framework of the environmental problem set central to this framework is the notion of a "public good."[3] Clean air and an intact ozone layer are classic examples of public goods. While markets are the primary producers of private goods, which are delivered to individual buyers, public goods confer benefits that cannot be confined to a single individual or group. Once provided, they can be enjoyed for free.

The challenge public goods pose is that, unless carefully managed, they trigger behavior that is individually rational but collectively suboptimal or even disastrous. Since the very nature of public goods is that individual users cannot be excluded, some individuals may choose to "free ride" on the efforts of others rather than contribute resources to the provision of the good in question. It is rational for a fisherman, for example, to try to maximize his personal gain by catching as many fish as possible as quickly as possible. Collectively, however, such a strategy leads to overexploitation of the resource and can result in a "tragedy of the commons" (Hardin, 1968). The fish stock will be depleted, leaving the entire fishing community worse off than it would have been had it found a cooperative arrangement for controlling the rate at which the resources were extracted.[4]

Similarly, in a world of multiple governing authorities and jurisdictions, optimal pollution reduction is unlikely to occur without some structure to promote collaboration. Fundamentally, public goods – including global public goods – will be underproduced without mechanisms to promote cooperation (Kaul, Grunberg, and Stern, 1999). The problem that public goods (especially global public goods) pose, therefore, is one of *organizing* cooperation to overcome the tendency toward what is called in game theory a "lose-lose" equilibrium. The situation must be converted from one in which decisions are made independently based on narrow self-interest to one in which actors overcome the "collective action" problem and adopt cooperative solutions (Ostrom, 1990).

---

3   Kaul, Grunberg, and Stern (1999) define global public goods as "goods whose benefits reach across borders, generations, and population groups." Among these are equity and justice, market efficiency, environment and cultural heritage, health, knowledge and information, and peace and security.

4   As Hardin put it in his seminal piece in 1968, "Ruin is the destination toward which all men rush, each pursuing his own best interest in a society which believes in the freedom of the commons. Freedom in a commons brings ruin to all."

Super Externalities

In the environmental arena, the problem of collective action is especially acute where shared resources or pollution harms spill across national boundaries, creating "super externalities" (Dua and Esty, 1997). At the national level, a regulatory agency is usually given authority to direct (and coerce if need be) the behavior of private actors so as to ensure cooperation. In the absence of an overarching sovereign at the global level, the incentives to free ride are even stronger (Young, 1999).

Take the example of the fishing community again. Even if local fishermen could reach an agreement to regulate catch, the tragedy of the commons will persevere unless there is oversight and control over *foreign* commercial fleets. Crucial fisheries have indeed collapsed worldwide as heavily subsidized fleets sweep across thousands of kilometers scooping up fish. In the face of such competition, local fishermen behave "rationally" by rushing to catch more fish more quickly. But in doing so, they generate a "lose-lose" outcome in which everyone is worse off than they might have been had they cooperated. In the words of a Mexican fisherman, "The philosophy is: get it now, grab it – if I don't, the next guy will" (Weiner, 2002).

Global collective action is further hampered by the fact that impacts of "externalities" are often hard to grasp. They are often spread out, both spatially and temporally. In the case of climate change, for example, the abatement and adaptation costs can be transferred not only across space – to other countries – but also over time – to future generations. Cooperation is also difficult to obtain when the impact is unidirectional, i.e., when activities in one country cause damage only in another jurisdiction. Upstream users of a shared river, for instance, have little incentive to limit their extraction of water or curb pollution, as the costs they impose will largely be borne by others downstream. As Whalley and Zissimos demonstrate in this volume, internalization of global environmental externalities through bargains involving financial resources or policy changes will be critical to solving collective action problems and improving environmental quality worldwide.

Global Environmental Governance Functions

The nature of current and future environmental problems – spanning jurisdictions and generations – requires new governance mechanisms that alter incentives in favor of environmentally sound choices. We see three major sets of functions as critical to addressing the global collective action problem: (1) provision of adequate information on the problems at hand and on whose behavior is contributing to the problem; (2) creation of a forum for sustained interaction, bargaining, and rulemaking; and (3) establishment of concrete mechanisms for implementation of the deals and rules upon which agreement has been reached.[5] A series of functions falls within each of these categories (Figure 1).

Data collection, indicator development, monitoring and verification, and scientific assessment and analysis emerge as central functions in the information domain. A policy space for continued interaction instills a sense of reciprocity, facilitates adoption of common rules and norms, and assists the "internalization of externalities," tackling potentially contagious phenomena at the source, before they spill across borders. Within the forum function, we thus place issue linkage and bargaining, a mechanism for rulemaking, environmental advocacy within the global regime, a mechanism for inclusive participation, and a dispute settlement framework. Sound and reliable financing mechanisms coupled with appropriate technology transfer would ensure that targets are met. A database of best practices and implementation strategies would further facilitate the implementation of commitments.

A GLOBAL ENVIRONMENTAL MECHANISM

In our view, a Global Environmental Mechanism (GEM) could effectively respond to both the common elements of national problems and the special demands of transboundary issues and global public goods. Conceptually, a GEM fills the need for a mechanism to promote environmental collective action at the international scale. Practically, it offers the chance to build a coherent and integrated environmental

---

5   See also Haas, Keohane, and Levy (1993) for a similar analysis and an assessment of the causes of institutional effectiveness – what they term "the three Cs" – concern, contractual environment, and capacity.

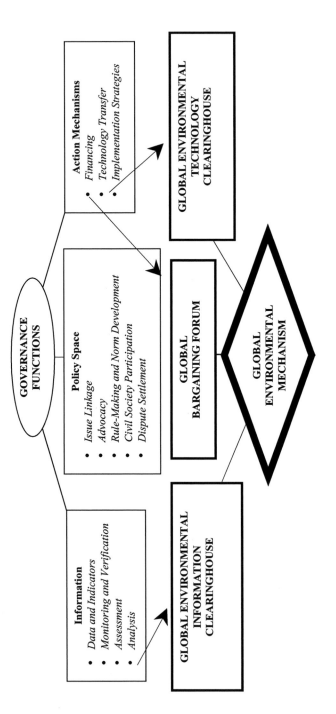

Figure 1   Global Environmental Governance Functions

policymaking and management framework that addresses the challenges of a shared global ecosystem.

We see three core capacities as essential to a Global Environmental Mechanism:

- Provision of adequate information and analysis to characterize problems, track trends, and identify interests;

- Creation of a policy "space" for environmental negotiation and bargaining;

- Expansion of capacities – both global and national – for addressing issues of concern and significance.

We envision a "network-based" GEM that builds on the functioning elements of existing institutions and creates new structures where gaps exist in the current regime. We see a GEM growing organically as consensus develops around issues and needs. A GEM might contain the following elements:

- *A Data Collection Mechanism,* ensuring the availability of reliable data of high quality and comparability, developing indicators and benchmarks, and publishing *State of the Global Environment* reports;

- *A Compliance Monitoring and Reporting Mechanism,* providing a repository for information on compliance with agreements and established norms, and a continuous and transparent reporting effort;

- *A Scientific Assessment and Knowledge Networking Mechanism,* drawing on basic research on environmental processes and trends, long-term forecasting, and early warnings of environmental risks;

- *A Bargaining and Trade-offs Mechanism,* facilitating the internalization of externalities through exchanges of commitments on various environmental issues (forest cover, biodiversity protection, species management, etc.) in return for cash or policy change (market access);

- *A Rulemaking Mechanism for the global commons,* establishing policy guidelines and international norms on protection of shared natural resources such the atmosphere and oceans;

- *A Civil Society Participation Mechanism,* providing a business and NGO forum for direct participation in problem identification and policy analysis;

- *A Financing Mechanism*, for global-scale issues mobilizing both public and private resources to provide structured financial assistance to developing countries and transition economies;

- *A Technology Transfer Mechanism*, promoting the adoption of best options suited to national conditions and encouraging innovative local solutions;

- *A Dispute Settlement Mechanism*, with agreed procedures and rules to promote conflict resolution between environmental agreements and vis-à-vis other global governance regimes in an equitable manner;

- *An Implementation Strategies Mechanism*, ensuring coordination with institutions with primary implementation responsibility (such as national governments, UNDP, World Bank, business, civil society organizations) and providing a database of best practices.

Through these capacities, the GEM would contribute to the closing of the three institutional gaps we describe – the jurisdictional gap, the information gap, and the implementation gap. For real progress to be achieved, an extraordinary mix of political idealism and pragmatism will be required. If global politics require, the GEM could start modestly and grow over time, progressively gaining new responsibilities and enlarging its mandate as its value is demonstrated.

Because scientific activities represent the dimension of the policy realm where economies of scale and other efficiency gains can most quickly be realized from increased cooperation, a *Global Information Clearinghouse* could become the first concrete step toward the establishment of a GEM. The coordination of existing institutional mechanisms for data collection, scientific assessment, and analysis might attract broad-based support. A *Global Technology Clearinghouse* focusing on information sharing and best practices dissemination might also be launched as an early GEM element. With its competence established in these areas, the GEM mandate might then be expanded to include monitoring, rulemaking, and the development of a *Global Bargaining Forum*. Subsequently, the GEM might acquire a dispute settlement mechanism.

Global Environmental Information Clearinghouse

An institutional mechanism is needed to channel relevant scientific and technical expertise to the appropriate policy arena. Better environmental data and information make it easier to identify issues, spot trends, evaluate risks, set priorities, establish policy options, test solutions, and target technology development (Esty, 2002). A global information clearinghouse for relevant, valid, and reliable data on environmental issues and trends could shift assumptions, preferences, and policies. In the case of acid rain in Europe, for example, knowledge of domestic acidification damage triggered emission reductions in several countries (Levy, 1993). Simply put, data can make the invisible visible, the intangible tangible, and the complex manageable.

The availability of information on how others are doing in reducing pollution and improving resource productivity tends to stimulate competition and innovation. Comparative performance analysis across countries – similar to the national PROPER scheme in Indonesia[6] – could provide much greater transparency, reward leaders, and expose laggards (Afsah, Blackman, and Ratunanda, 2000). Just as knowledge that a competitor in the marketplace has higher profits drives executives to redouble their efforts, evidence that others are outperforming one's country on environmental criteria can sharpen the focus on opportunities for improved performance. The attention that the World Economic Forum's Environmental Sustainability Index has generated demonstrates this potential (Seelye, 2002; Yeager, 2002).

While data gathering should primarily be the function of local or national organizations, a central repository for such information and a mechanism for making the information publicly available would represent a significant discipline on slack performance (Chayes and Chayes, 1995). An information clearinghouse will, in reality, not centralize science policy *functions* but create a "centralized source for coordinating information flow between the institutions responsible for performing the different science policy functions" (UN University, 2002).

---

6   PROPER (Program for Pollution Control, Evaluation, and Rating) is Indonesia's innovative program for reducing pollution by rating and publicly disclosing the environmental performance of industrial facilities.

Global Environmental Technology Clearinghouse

Most multilateral environmental agreements contain provisions related to technology transfer as part of the incentive packages for developing countries to meet their obligations under the conventions. The Basel Convention on the Control of Transboundary Movements of Hazardous Wastes and their Disposal, the Montreal Protocol on the Ozone Layer, the Convention on Biological Diversity, and the Framework Convention on Climate Change and its related Kyoto Protocol all cite technology transfer as a critical method for achieving concrete environmental improvements. Agenda 21 also underscores the importance of technology transfer to sustainable development.[7]

However, the process of selecting and operating environmentally sound technologies is not as simple and straightforward a process as is sometimes believed. Selecting a technology that is suitable for local needs, adapting it to local conditions, and maintaining it require substantial skills and information. Yet, the recipients of technology transfers have limited access to information and limited technical capacity, underscoring the need for an information clearinghouse on various abatement technologies (Worrell et al., 2001).

An environmental technology clearinghouse could serve as the repository and disseminator of information on available technologies, their sources, their environmental risks, and the broad terms under which they may be acquired. It could also encompass information on best practices around the world, promoting continuous learning. The clearinghouse would thus be critical to the expansion of technological and innovation capabilities in recipient countries. It could address the need "to work out a collaborative model between the North and the South that can cater to both the soft and the hard aspects of technology transfer, be driven by local needs, adapted to the developing country operational environment and sustained through facilitated private sector participation" (Aslam, 2001). In order to be effective, the clearinghouse would also need to provide referrals to other services, including sources of advice, training, and technology assessment.[8]

---

7   See Agenda 21, Chapter 34, "Transfer of Environmentally-Sound Technology, Cooperation, and Capacity-Building," available at http://www.igc.org/habitat/agenda21/a21-34.htm

8   For a proposal for the creation of international information networks and technology clearinghouses, see Agenda 21, Chapter 34 at http://www.igc.org/habitat/agenda21/a21-34.htm

Global Bargaining Forum

A global bargaining forum could act as a catalyst between countries or private entities to negotiate the transfer of resources in exchange for commitments to agreed-upon policies and behavior. Thus, a government in one country might negotiate a deal to preserve a particular natural resource – part of a rainforest, a set of species, etc. – in another country in return for a sum of money or other policy benefits, as Whalley and Zissimos explain in this volume.

Market access, for example, is an issue of paramount economic importance for developing countries, and has been used as a condition for many concessions on issues of interest to the North. Brazil has made a market access agreement in agriculture a precondition for its involvement in a new trade negotiations round. India has made commitments on intellectual property rights in exchange for expanded market access in agriculture and textiles (Runge, 2001). A global bargaining forum would allow such deals to be negotiated, and ensure that incentives are altered in ways that include commitments to higher environmental quality. Such a forum would also help to stimulate a flow of new resources to developing countries, which often bear the costs of producing many global public goods. The forum would also need to comprise a set of mechanisms for verification, financial transfers, and contract enforcement.

A permanent negotiation forum, moreover, would substantially reduce the costs of diplomatic activity around global issues. Rather than holding a series of international meetings at different locations around the world, a "campus" for international environmental activity could be devised where relevant scientific information is presented and negotiations conducted (Spencer, 2001). This process of continuous interaction, mutual education, and creative trade-offs would encourage increased coherence of rules, revelation of preferences and assumptions, and innovative solutions to cross-cutting issues.

Networked Governance

In proposing a loosely structured GEM, we emphasize the need for form to follow function. We envision a light institutional superstructure, which would provide coordination through a staff comparable in size and expertise to the WTO Secretariat in Geneva that manages the international trading regime. The secretariat would help to promote cooperation and achieve synergies across the disparate multilateral environmental agreements and other international institutions with environmental roles. It would also act as a mediator and buffer between the environment and the Bretton Woods institutions with their economic focus.

The Global Environmental Mechanism would thus *not* add a new layer of international bureaucracy nor create a world government. Quite to the contrary, movement toward a GEM should entail consolidation of the existing panoply of international environmental institutions and a shift toward a more modern, "virtual" organizational structure.

At the center of our proposal for a GEM lies a global public policy network that draws in issue-specific expertise from around the world. Global networks represent an innovative organizational mechanism for responding to an ever more complex international policy environment, taking advantage of Information Age communications and technologies to build new opportunities for cooperation (see Streck, this volume). Engaging an established set of private and public organizations with environmental expertise, these networks operate as a flexible system for advancing international environmental agenda-setting, analysis, negotiation, policy formulation, implementation, and institutional learning.

Two benefits from networked governance are most notable – minimized complexity and hierarchy, and fast boot-up and delivery times (Rischard, 2001). While capitalizing on existing institutions and harnessing the power of governments and civil society alike, networks offer a faster, agile, problem-tailored process, inclusiveness on a merit basis, access to state of the art knowledge, and simultaneous proximity to both the local and the global scale.

CONCLUSION

Global environmental policymaking in the last decade has focused mainly on principles and declarations rather than on mechanisms that alter incentives and produce change. The global environmental management system is clearly falling short of the world community's needs and expectations. It is time to re-engineer the regime, aiming for a new, forward-looking, sleeker, and more efficient architecture that will better promote the environment while also serving governmental, public, and business needs.

The logic of a Global Environmental Mechanism is straightforward: a globalizing world requires better and more modern ways to manage ecological interdependence. A vibrant and focused Global Environmental Mechanism would contribute to improved collective action in response to global-scale challenges by:

- Closing the jurisdictional gap through the provision of an authoritative environmental voice in the international arena and a recognized forum where national officials and other stakeholders can work cooperatively to address global issues;

- Closing the information gap by bringing relevant data and analysis to the appropriate policy arena, elucidating problems, and framing solutions;

- Closing the implementation gap by matching interests and commitments in a global bargaining forum and providing functional, coordinated financing and technology mechanisms. With a global public network at its core, a GEM would contribute to improved legitimacy through greater participation, representation, and fairness in the policy process.

The 2002 World Summit on Sustainable Development presents an opportunity to make real progress.

We suggest launching a Global Information Clearinghouse and a Global Technology Clearinghouse as immediate concrete steps forward and initiating a Commission of eminent people to examine options for more fundamental structural reform.

More broadly, a commitment to revitalize the international environmental regime should be cast as part of a wider "global bargain." Specifically, the launch of a GEM needs to be paired with a major new poverty alleviation initiative, perhaps driven by a rechartered World Bank and UNDP.

In conclusion, we turn to the words of former New Zealand Prime Minister Geoffrey Palmer, who, before the 1992 Rio Earth Summit, observed:

> [T]he methods and techniques now available to fashion new instruments of international law to cope with global environmental problems cannot meet the challenge. The emerging issues are so big and so all-embracing that current ways of doing things will not solve these problems. The institutional mechanisms within the United Nations system are not capable of handling the issues. The time has come for 'something more innovative, for a conceptual leap forward in institutional terms.' (Palmer, 1992)

These words continue to ring true today and underscore the urgency of the task before us.

REFERENCES

Afsah, Shakeb, Allen Blackman, and Damayanti Ratunanda. 2000. *How Do Public Disclosure Pollution Control Programs Work? Evidence from Indonesia.* Washington, D.C.: Resources for the Future. Available from http://www.rff.org/CFDOCS/disc_papers/pdf_files/0044.pdf

Aslam, Malik Amin. 2001. "Technology Transfer under the CDM: Materializing the Myth in the Japanese Context?" *Climate Policy* (1): 451-464.

Brown Weiss, Edith. 1995. "International Environmental Law: Contemporary Issues and the Emergence of a New World Order." *Georgetown Law Journal* 81 (1):675-693.

Chayes, Abram, and Antonia Handler Chayes. 1995. *The New Sovereignty: Compliance with International Regulatory Agreements.* Cambridge, MA: Harvard University Press.

Dua, Andre, and Daniel C. Esty. 1997. *Sustaining the Asian Pacific Miracle: Economic Integration and Environmental Protection.* Washington, D.C.: Institute for International Economics.

Dunoff, Jeffrey L. 1995. "From Green to Global: Toward Transformation of International Environmental Law." *Harvard Environmental Law Review* 19(2): 241-269.

Esty, Daniel C. 1994. "The Case for a Global Environmental Organization." In *Managing the World Economy: Fifty Years After Bretton Woods*, edited by Peter Kenen. Washington, D.C.: Institute for International Economics.

_____. 2001. "Toward Data-Driven Environmentalism: The Environmental Sustainability Index." *The Environmental Law Reporter* 31: 10603-10612.

_____. 2002. "Why Measurement Matters." In *Environmental Performance Measurement: The Global Report 2001-2002*, edited by Daniel C. Esty and Peter R. Cornelius. New York: Oxford University Press.

GAO. 1999. *International Environment: Literature on the Effectiveness of International Environmental Agreements.* Washington, D.C.: United States General Accounting Office. Available from http://www.gao.gov/archive/1999/rc99148.pdf

Haas, Peter M., Robert O. Keohane, and Marc A. Levy. 1993. *Institutions for the Earth: Sources of Effective International Environmental Protection.* Cambridge, MA: MIT Press.

Hardin, Garrett. 1968. "The Tragedy of the Commons." *Science* 162.

Hassan, H. M., and C. Hutchinson. 1992. *Natural Resource and Environmental Information for Decision Making.* Washington, D.C.: World Bank.

Kalas, Peggy Rodgers. 2001. "International Environmental Dispute Resolution and the Need for Access by Non-State Entities." *Colorado Journal of International Environmental Law and Policy* 12(1): 191-244.

Kaul, Inge, Isabelle Grunberg, and Marc A. Stern. 1999. *Global Public Goods: International Cooperation in the 21st Century.* New York: Oxford University Press.

Kelly, Michael J. 1997. "Overcoming Obstacles to the Effective Implementation of International Environmental Agreements." *Georgetown International Environmental Law Review* 9(2): 447-488.

Levy, Marc A. 1993. "European Acid Rain: The Power of Tote-Board Diplomacy." In *Institutions for the Earth: Sources of Effective International Environmental Protection,* edited by Peter M. Haas, Robert O. Keohane, and Marc A. Levy. Cambridge, MA: MIT Press.

Martin, Lisa. 1999. "The Political Economy of International Cooperation." In *Global Public Goods: International Cooperation in the 21st Century,* edited by Inge Kaul, Isabelle Grunberg, and Marc A. Stern. New York: Oxford University Press.

Ostrom, Elinor. 1990. *Governing the Commons: The Evolution of Institutions for Collective Action.* 10th ed. New York: Cambridge University Press.

Palmer, Geoffrey. 1992. "New Ways to Make International Environmental Law." *American Journal of International Law* 86 (2): 259-283.

Rischard, Jean-François. 2001. "High Noon: We Need New Approaches to Global Problem-Solving, Fast." *Journal of International Economic Law* 4(3): 507-525.

Runge, C. Ford. 2001. "A Global Environmental Organization (GEO) and the World Trading System." *Journal of World Trade* 35 (4): 399-426.

Seelye, K.Q. 2002. "Study Puts Finland First, and U.S. 51st, in Environmental Health." *The New York Times International,* February 2, 2002.

Spencer, Thomas. 2001. "Improving Global Environmental Governance: A Paper for Discussion." Unpublished, on file with authors.

UN University. 2002. *International Environmental Governance. The Question of Reform: Key Issues and Proposals. Preliminary Findings.* Tokyo: United Nations University Institute for Advanced Studies. Available from http://www.ias.unu.edu

UNEP. 2001. *International Environmental Governance: Report of the Executive Director.* Nairobi, Kenya: United Nations Environment Programme. Available from http://www.unep.org/IEG/docs/working%20documents/reportfromED/GM_1_2E.doc

WEF. 2002. *Environmental Performance Measurement: The Global Report 2001-2002.* Geneva, Switzerland: World Economic Forum.

Weiner, Tim. 2002. "In Mexico, Greed Kills Fish by the Seaful." *New York Times,* April 10, 2002.

Worrell, Ernst, Rene van Berkel, Zhou Fengqi, Christoph Menke, Roberto Schaeffer, and Robert O. Williams. 2001. "Technology Transfer of Energy Efficient Technologies in Industry: A Review of Trends and Policy Issues." *Energy Policy* 29 (1): 29-43.

Yeager, H. 2002. "Scandinavia Tops World League Table on the Environment." *Financial Times,* February 3, 2002.

Young, Oran R. 1999. *The Effectiveness of International Environmental Regimes: Causal Connections and Behavioral Mechanisms.* Cambridge, MA: MIT Press.

Climate Change: National Interests Or a Global Regime?

Christiana Figueres and Maria H. Ivanova

SUMMARY

This chapter addresses the ultimate global environmental governance challenge: climate change. It explores four key questions: 1) Who is responsible for climate change? 2) Who is affected by its consequences? 3) Who should act in response? and 4) What is to be done?

Climate change is profoundly different from most other environmental problems humanity has faced. The atmosphere's planetary scale and scope make it a "global public good," prone to overexploitation and underregulation. The multiplicity of causes of climate change, the uncertainty of timing and effects, and substantial economic costs make global agreement difficult to attain and maintain. Along with a challenge to material wellbeing, however, the climate change problem poses an ethical dilemma stemming from the large physical, social, and even temporal distances between emitters and victims of climate change.

Climate change requires a global response, encompassing the North and the South, local and global communities, and the public and private sectors. Ranging from global negotiations to individual choices, a diversity of actors with different resource endowments, and diverging values and aspirations, need to be involved.

Success will depend on the substance and equity of national commitments and on the process developed for promoting global-scale cooperation. Four conditions need to be emphasized in building a global climate regime: 1) adequate information, 2) issue linkage and bargaining, 3) technological potential, and 4) a shift in values.

CLIMATE CHANGE AND GLOBAL GOVERNANCE

All social structures humanity has ever built have required some form of management. As societies evolved from tribes to kingdoms and from kingdoms to nation-states, they were governed both at an increasingly larger scale, and with increasing levels of complexity. Tribes were managed as relatively simple top-down structures, where the center of influence was the tribe itself, and the circumference of interdependence was the geographically surrounding tribes. Nation-states developed more complex systems of governance, and pushed the circumference of interdependence beyond neighboring states. In the era of globalization, however, governance issues have moved to a global level in response to a growing recognition of planetary interdependence.

Climate change is one of the first truly global environmental challenges. Several key features distinguish it from other environmental problems:

- The atmosphere is a classic example of a global public good – greenhouse gas emissions in one country affect the entire planet; conversely, emission controls in any country benefit all, encouraging "free riding" on the efforts of others;

- The impact of climate change is not likely to be evenly distributed among regions and countries. Developing countries tend to be more vulnerable and, at the same time, less able to respond and to adapt;

- A multitude of human activities result in greenhouse gas emissions, so that efforts at reducing emissions are needed at many levels – from global to national to local to individual;

- Uncertainties as to the timing, scope, and impacts of climate change reinforce reluctance to alter economic behavior.

The scale of climate change requires global collective action, yet the costs and complexity make many countries hesitant to participate. A functioning climate change regime has thus been difficult to construct. This chapter examines the tension between national interests and the creation of a global climate regime by asking four questions:

- Who is responsible?

- Who is affected?

- Who should act?

- What is to be done?

Were the answers to the first three questions one and the same, devising solutions to the problem of climate change would be a relatively simple task – the countries responsible for climate change would tackle the issue themselves, because it would be in their own interest to do so. The fact that the answers vary takes us into a perplexing ethical arena where many of the countries most affected are least able to act, and many of those most able to act are least willing. We will emerge from this quandary to the degree that countries are able to shift from narrowly defined national interests to an internalized notion of global interdependence. Such a shift will need to encompass both a technological revolution and an ethical evolution supported by a new approach to problem solving at the global scale.

Who Is Responsible?

Major components of our biosphere (including the air, the oceans, the range of animal and plant species, and the climate system itself) have been altered by the intensity of human exploitation of the earth's resources in the twentieth century.[1] Responsibility is lodged in the North as well as in the South and must be understood in terms of two major global trends that lead to increased greenhouse gas emissions and reduced "sinks" for carbon dioxide – population growth and increasing consumption (especially of fossil fuels). Population growth is a problem mainly in developing countries while increasing consumption is a problem mostly in the industrialized world.

Global population has doubled since 1960, reaching 6.1 billion by 2001 (UNFPA, 2001). Increasing population entails increasing pressure on the land. Arable land per capita has been rapidly dwindling since the 1950s. The average then was 1.2 acres per capita. The average today is less than half that. In developing countries, pressure on the land has been "eased" by clearing forests and converting them to (poorly

---

[1] For information and data on changes in climate and other consequences of global warming, see IPCC (2001a) and UNEP (2002).

performing) agricultural land. Deforestation, however, contributes significantly to carbon dioxide emissions (UNEP, 2002).

Twenty-three percent of global greenhouse gas emissions are due to deforestation, and most of this comes from developing countries. In Latin America alone, well over two thirds of total emissions are due to deforestation. There is clear climate change responsibility here.

The second macro trend is increasing consumption. The rate of environmental degradation is affected not simply by population growth but by the pressure people exert on natural systems through consumption, especially of non-renewable resources, most notably coal, oil, and natural gas. While world population has doubled over the past fifty years, total energy consumption has increased fivefold in the same period of time (Energy Information Administration, 2002). We have relied mainly on fossil fuels for that energy generation, and the growth in consumption has brought on parallel increases in greenhouse gas emissions. Carbon dioxide (CO_2) concentrations in the atmosphere have increased from 280 parts per million (ppm), before the industrial revolution to 370 ppm today, reaching a level that has not been exceeded during the past 420,000 years, and in all likelihood, not during the past twenty million years (IPCC, 2001a).

The United States alone accounts for as much as twenty-one percent of total world emissions while being home to only four percent of the world's population. In contrast, 136 developing countries are collectively responsible for twenty-four percent of global emissions (Marland, Boden, and Andres, 2000). This situation, however, will shift in or about the year 2020, when population growth and increased energy consumption in developing countries will contribute half the total world emissions. It is therefore imperative that both developed and developing countries make a substantial commitment to action and that the requisite governance structures are created to facilitate agreement, to allow bargaining and trade-offs, and to assist in the implementation of the necessary measures.

Who Is Affected?

It has been universally accepted that countries have "common but differentiated responsibilities"[2] with regard to environmental degradation. Sophisticated climate models and scenarios point out that countries have also common but differentiated vulnerabilities. The comparative susceptibility to adverse climate impacts lies also along a North-South axis, but in an inverse relation to historical responsibility. Recent studies of the likely impact of climate change on regional agricultural production predict positive impacts for the United States, Japan, and parts of Europe (Mendelsohn and Nordhaus, 1996; Mendelsohn, 2001; Reuters, 2002)[3] and considerable negative consequences to sub-Saharan Africa and the Indian subcontinent (IPCC, 2001b; Fischer et al., 2001).[4] Some of the most significant potential effects for the developing world include:

- Exacerbated desertification in Africa due to reductions in average rainfall, runoff, and soil moisture;

- Significant increases in the geographic incidence of insect-borne diseases, such as malaria and dengue, particularly in the tropics and subtropics, due to rising temperatures;

- Increased risk of hunger and famine for many of the world's poorest people as a result of a change in the volume and distribution of water;

---

2   Principle 7 of the Rio Declaration adopted at the 1992 Earth Summit states that "In view of the different contributions to global environmental degradation, States have common but differentiated responsibilities. The developed countries acknowledge the responsibility that they bear in the international pursuit of sustainable development in view of the pressures their societies place on the global environment and of the technologies and financial resources they command." The full text of the Rio Declaration is available at: http://www.un.org/documents/ga/conf151/aconf15126-1annex1.htm

3   Even within the United States, where some studies forecast positive impacts, there is likely to be significant regional differentiation. Southern states are likely to experience substantial negative consequences from higher temperatures, including decreased agricultural productivity, increased unemployment, and increased energy use for cooling that would far outstrip the savings from heating (Mendelsohn, 2001).

4   A warmer climate is also likely to adversely affect far Northern latitudes where permafrost would melt, leading to the collapse of the topsoil and the loss of large forested areas. This would be particularly devastating for Russia, where large parts of the country (rich in natural resources) are covered in permafrost. The global impacts would also be significant as Siberian forests are currently an important natural sink for excess carbon.

- Undermined food security, human health, and infrastructure, and constrained development due to increases in droughts, floods, and other extreme events;

- Food production losses of as much as twenty-five percent in forty of the world's poorest nations, including India, Bangladesh, Brazil, and many countries in sub-Saharan Africa. These countries have a current combined population of about 2 billion, of which some 450 million are already undernourished;

- Displacement of tens of millions of people in the low-lying coastal areas of Asia due to rising sea levels and increasingly intense tropical cyclones.

These adverse impacts will be most severely felt in the poorest countries where vulnerability is greater due to geographic and climatic conditions, and where the ability to respond is very limited. Successful adaptation depends on technological advances, institutional capacity, knowledge and education, and availability of financing.

Overall, developing countries have less favorable economic circumstances, weaker institutions, more limited access to capital, and more restricted information exchange. The nations most vulnerable to global change are often the ones least prepared to respond or to adapt to it.

Who Should Act?

The divergence between the countries most responsible for, and the countries most affected by, climate change creates a profound ethical dilemma. Developed countries have the capacity to act, yet some of them (notably the United States) are unwilling to do so without the assurance of substantial emission reductions on the part of developing nations. Facing pressing domestic concerns, however, countries in the South resent the imposition of economic costs for the amelioration of what they perceive to be a Northern-caused environmental problem.

Currently, the United States emits twenty metric tons of CO_2 per capita annually, while per capita CO_2 emissions in India are 1.05 metric tons. (World Bank, 2002). One is reminded of the famous cartoon of the tall white man who drives up in his gas-guzzling SUV and asks the bushman to put out his campfire in order to reduce global emissions. It is not surprising that Indian negotiators contend that their people should not be limited to a few "survival emissions" while industrial countries are not even willing to accept modest cutbacks in their "luxury emissions."

Finger pointing about past responsibility for or future contributions to the problem will not help countries reach a solution. Constructing a global climate regime without the United States may be possible, but it is certainly not optimal. The Kyoto Protocol target of a 5.2 percent reduction in CO_2 emissions from 1990 levels by industrialized countries cannot be met without the United States. But even if it could be reached, the estimated sixty to seventy percent decrease required to stabilize greenhouse gas concentrations in the atmosphere (Mapes, 2001; Gelbspan, 2001) demands the participation of *all*.

One-sided measures will not be sufficient. Industrialized countries cannot, by themselves, reduce global carbon emissions to levels likely to fall within relatively harmless concentrations; indeed, even a total ban of fossil fuels by all industrialized nations would not be sufficient if developing countries continue to increase their emissions (Jacoby, Prinn, and Schmalensee, 1998).

Many developing countries have shown a willingness and capability to voluntarily participate in global climate protection. The most recent ratification of the Kyoto Protocol comes from Brazil, which – with a unanimous vote from its Senate on June 18, 2002 – joined seventy-five other countries in committing to a global climate regime.[5] Several developing countries are making significant efforts

---

5 Developing countries, however, are not required to reduce greenhouse gas emissions under the Kyoto Protocol. They can participate in the flexible mechanisms of the Kyoto agreement, such as emissions trading and the Clean Development Mechanism.

to reduce emissions, primarily for economic reasons. China, Brazil, India, and Mexico have cut fossil fuel subsidies, reducing consumption by twenty-five million tons of carbon.[6] South Korea, China, Mexico, and Thailand have adopted efficiency standards as well as tax incentives for energy efficiency. China's efforts at restricting carbon emissions are especially impressive. It has reduced carbon emissions substantially, even while its economy has grown steadily, with the help of subsidy phase-outs for coal,[7] market pricing for fuel, and energy conservation initiatives. The World Bank estimates that

THE UN FRAMEWORK CONVENTION ON CLIMATE CHANGE AND THE KYOTO PROTOCOL

The United Nations Framework Convention on Climate Change (UNFCCC), which was opened for signature during the 1992 United Nations Conference on the Environment and Development in Rio, was designed as a first attempt to deal with the threat of global climate change. The main objective of the Convention is to stabilize atmospheric greenhouse gas concentrations at levels that would prevent dangerous consequences for the climate system (UNFCCC, 1992: Note 1, Article 2). Although the existence of the Convention attests to an international consensus that serious steps must be taken to reduce greenhouse gas emissions, the Convention does not set any specific targets, leaving that step to subsequent protocols.

The Kyoto Protocol differentiates Annex B countries, mainly industrialized countries and countries with economies in transition, from non-Annex B countries, the developing nations. The Kyoto agreement provides legally binding emissions targets for Annex B countries, which will be required, by 2012, to reduce their combined emissions of greenhouse gases to below the levels measured in 1990. Different countries have different targets, which range from an eight percent decrease from the base level for the European Union to a ten percent increase for Iceland (UNFCCC, 1992: Annex B).

---

6 Between 1990-91 and 1995-96, total fossil fuel subsidies in fourteen developing countries that account for twenty-five percent of global carbon emissions from industrial sources declined forty-five percent, from $60 billion to about $33 billion. Reduced subsidies are desirable because they lead to higher fuel prices and reduced taxes of growth in carbon emissions (Reid and Goldemberg, 1997).

7 China has reduced its coal use by forty percent since 1996 (BP, 2001: 33).

further efficiency gains in China have the potential of yielding savings of 1,000 to 1,700 million tons of coal equivalents per year by 2020 – an amount greater than China's total energy consumption in 1990 (Johnson et al., 1996).

So far, developed countries have done little to reduce their emissions. The commitment of the 1992 United Nations Framework Convention on Climate Change has gone largely unfulfilled. Inaction is justified by the presumption of prohibitive economic costs.[8] However, a growing body of data and results from progressive corporate and local government practices tell a different, more encouraging story (Hawken, Lovins, and Lovins, 1999). While national governments have been reluctant to respond to the challenge, innovative solutions have sprung up at the company and local levels across the world.

Aware that – with or without the Kyoto Protocol – the future trend is toward less carbon intensive economies, multinational corporations are putting in place efficient energy systems to reduce emissions. BP, for example, has established a voluntary plan with the target of reducing emissions of greenhouse gases by ten percent from a 1990 baseline by the year 2010 (Browne, 2002). A consortium of corporations led by Shell Hydrogen and DaimlerChrysler reached an agreement in 1999 with the government of Iceland to make that country the world's first hydrogen-powered economy. Shell expects to develop its hydrogen capacity and DaimlerChrysler expects to have the first fuel cell-powered automobile on the market. Shell plans to open its first chain of hydrogen stations in Iceland (Brown, 2001).

In developing countries, where access to a central power utility and an electricity grid is limited, local entrepreneurs are investing in solar cell generating facilities and selling power to village households. By the end of 2000, one million households were receiving their electricity from solar cells. About 700,000 of those households were in villages in developing countries.

Similarly, local governments have responded to new information about environmental realities. In the United States, many state governments and local communities have embarked on new energy ini-

---

8 An intensive advertising campaign in the United States by a coal-led industrial lobby with the environmentally friendly name of "Global Climate Coalition" has contributed significantly to the perception by the press and politicians that any climate-related mitigation measures would be prohibitively costly. The United States has large sources of cheap coal and a transition to less carbon-intensive fuels would adversely affect the powerful coal mining industry.

tiatives encompassing energy efficiency and emission reductions programs as well as a shift toward new generation capacities. Advances in wind turbine technology have lowered the cost of wind power dramatically and wind farms have sprung up in Colorado, Iowa, Minnesota, Oregon, Pennsylvania, Texas, and Wyoming. Lester Brown calls the U.S. Great Plains "the Saudi Arabia of wind power" as the steady breezes in this region have the potential to generate enough electricity to meet a significant portion of U.S. needs. In Europe, wind power covers fifteen percent of the electricity demand of Denmark, nineteen percent of Schleswig-Holstein, the northernmost state of Germany, and twenty-two percent of Spain's industrial state of Navarra. China could double its current generation capacity by wind alone (Brown, 2001).

Corporate and governmental action will be fundamental to ensuring greenhouse reduction. However, unlike other environmental problems where blame is easily assigned to industrial pollution or governmental failure, individual decisions are a critical factor in global climate change. In Bangkok, Thailand, the city government decided that at 9:00 pm on a given weekday evening, all major television stations would show a big dial with the city's use of electricity at the time. Once the dial appeared on the screen, viewers were requested to turn off unnecessary lights and appliances. As people watched, the dial showed a reduction of 735 megawatts, enough to close two coal-fired power plants (Brown, 2001). This experiment served as a reminder of the power of individual decisions to make a collective difference.

At the individual level, seemingly insignificant investment decisions of shareholders could also exercise enormous pressure. The Dow Jones Sustainability Index[9] tracks the performance of leading companies worldwide and addresses increasing investor interest in companies committed to innovative technology, industrial leadership, and social wellbeing. There is mounting evidence that the management of these particular factors is directly related to superior financial performance (EPA, 2000).

Global climate change requires a response encompassing the North and the South, local communities, and the global community of nations. Ranging from global negotiations to individual choices, a diverse set of actors with different resource endowments and diverging values and aspirations would need to be involved. Concerns for

---

9 For information on the Dow Jones Sustainability Index, see http://www.sustainability-index.com

equity and justice, however, are central to effective responses to global climate change (Paterson, 2001; Wiegandt, 2001). Differences in the
perceptions of developed and developing countries as to what is fair
and equitable have presented enormous difficulties in constructing
governance mechanisms for addressing climate change. Developing
countries emphasize the need for a historical view of responsibility as
well as present-day distributive justice. An historical perspective
entails not only the widely accepted "polluter pays" principle but also
the principle of "common but differentiated responsibility." However,
absent a supranational body vested with the requisite judicial authority, the application of these concepts is, at best, difficult. Distributive
justice entails a fair distribution of costs or benefits. Some commentators argue that this translates into equal per capita emissions
(Grubb, 1990; Agarwal and Narain, 1990; Bertram, 1992). Given the
political infeasibility of this approach, its defenders have emphasized
the critical importance of financial resources and technology transfers
to assist developing countries in minimizing their impact while allowing economic growth.[10]

Developed countries have formally acknowledged the need for
fairness, but they have shown little interest in operationalizing this
commitment to equity on a basis that satisfies the South. The absence
of governance structures that allow for matching interests, facilitating
bargains, and overseeing the completion of contracts hampers effective responses to many global issues. In the case of climate change, an
equitable agreement could come about if the genuine interests of all
parties involved are duly considered and accounted for. This would
entail the creation of a more agile and multi-layered institutional
structure.

What Is To Be Done?

Climate is an extraordinarily complex system with many delicately
interrelated components. We lack knowledge about thresholds that
might trigger climatic changes for which we are unprepared.
Estimates of global carrying capacity for CO_2 emissions range from
500 billion tons to two trillion tons (Schelling, 2002). Climate change
modeling continually grows more sophisticated, but the complexity of

---

[10] Grubb (1990: 287) estimates that necessary North-South transfers would amount to $100 bil-
lion per year.

the systems modeled and current limitations in technology leave predictions of future changes in the realm of the hypothetical. And yet, in the face of uncertainty that is likely to continue into the future, policy decisions must be made regarding possible ways to advance human development while diminishing its impact on nature. As illustrated by the analysis thus far, action is necessary at the local and the global levels, by private and public actors, in the North and in the South. To this end, an interest-based approach is critical. Interests are shaped by changes in information on vulnerability or abatement costs. Drawing on the analysis of Esty and Ivanova in this volume, we see functioning governance mechanisms for information and technology as critical and a forum for issue linkage and bargaining as imperative for a successful climate change regime that incorporates yet transcends national interests.

Information Provision

Given the distance, scope, and relatively hard-to-see nature of the problem, and the scientific ambiguity and magnitude of the costs involved, climate change decisions are predicated upon a complex array of data on emissions, likely impacts of human activities on the environment, and costs and benefits of abatement strategies. Measurement and indicators can make obscure phenomena such as greenhouse gas emissions seem more tangible. The "electricity meter on TV" in Bangkok provides a vivid example of this effect.

Data and information can expose uncertainties, reveal risks, and demonstrate alternatives (Esty, 2002). As new information emerges, the utility calculus of countries can shift, leading to an altered perception of interests and more optimal strategies. For example, if countries receive new evidence that their ecological vulnerability is higher or that abatement costs are lower than previously estimated, their propensity to support stronger international commitments may increase (Sprinz and Weiß, 2001).

The climate regime has developed considerable data and information capacity, drawing on research institutes around the world. It has built a sophisticated network of experts through the assessment process of the Intergovernmental Panel on Climate Change (IPCC), demonstrating the value of collaborative research and analysis across a variety of disciplines.[11] The climate data and information initiative is an important building block for a more comprehensive environmental information initiative at the global level.

Comparative cross-country data and benchmarking on energy efficiency indicators could be developed to reveal true economic potential, identify best practices, and increase awareness and peer pressure. Greater information availability could also promote a more effective issue linkage and bargaining strategy and more efficient and equitable technology transfer.

Issue Linkage and Bargaining
Recognizing the importance of institutional incentives and flexible arrangements, the Kyoto Protocol features new mechanisms that seek to facilitate greater participation and alter incentives, including Joint Implementation, emissions trading, and the Clean Development Mechanism. These mechanisms provide flexibility in achieving emission reduction targets through the potential for contracts between countries with high and low abatement costs. As Whalley and Zissimos emphasize in this volume, a bargaining forum that allows linkage among various issues could further develop these mechanisms and provide for matching of interests and "give and take" on a series of issues of global impact and significance.

One way to breach the North-South gap might be to establish a place where environmental bargains could be struck. Many developing countries, for example, still manufacture and use chemicals known as persistent organic pollutants. These substances include pesticides such as DDT, deldrin, and endrin, industrial chemicals such as PCBs, and unintentional byproducts of industrial and combustion processes such as dioxins and furans. Persistent organic pollutants pose a serious threat to human and ecosystem health and their effects may span the globe, since they travel great distances, persist in the environment, and bioaccumulate through the food chain. A global forum for negotiation and bargaining across issues might provide a breakthrough in global

---

[11] The IPCC was established by the World Meteorological Organization (WMO) and the United Nations Environment Programme (UNEP) in 1988 to assess scientific, technical, and socioeconomic information about human-induced climate change.

governance. The United States, for example, could agree to reduce CO_2 emissions in exchange for a phase-out of persistent organic pollutants, more stringent controls for preventing influx of non-native species, forest preservation, or other issues of concern to the United States and its citizens. Developing countries would hold powerful bargaining chips in the form of natural resources of global significance. Biodiversity, tropical forests, coral reefs, and pristine ecosystems could be preserved in exchange for market access, debt relief, or immediate financial transfers.[12]

An issue linkage strategy might provide for a more egalitarian approach than current governance structures.

Emission reductions could be linked with minimizing the costs to the North of meeting reduction targets, and would also facilitate North-South financial and technological transfers based on genuine interest-based contracts rather than altruistic promises. Moreover, a bargaining approach, with a light institutional structure to oversee contract completion, could ensure efficiency in implementing obligations.

Technological Potential for a New Growth Imperative

The economic paradigm of the last hundred years of rapid growth was based on the presumption that the environment should be understood as a subset of the economy rather than the economy being a subset of the ecosystem on which it depends. Further, the supply of natural resources was assumed to be infinite and the capacity to absorb waste unlimited. Environmental services such as the ability of plants to convert carbon dioxide to oxygen, of wetlands to cleanse water, or of forests to stabilize aquifers are not assigned any economic value despite their importance to continued economic growth.[13] It was not until it became obvious that economic development and popula-

---

[12] For a full analysis of the rationale for and the functioning of a global bargaining body, see Whalley and Zissimos, this volume.

[13] Many of the ecosystem services that life on Earth depends upon have no substitute at any price. This was demonstrated memorably in 1991-93 when the scientists operating the $200 million Biosphere 2 experiment in Arizona discovered that it was unable to maintain life-supporting oxygen levels for the eight people living inside. The Earth performs this task daily at no charge for 6 billion people (Hawken, Lovins, and Lovins, 1999).

tion growth were affecting the carrying capacities of natural systems that an alternative was put forward – the vision of sustainable development.

A shift from the traditional fossil fuel-based economy to carbon-free energy systems would be the cornerstone of an environmentally sustainable economy. Indeed, as Seth Dunn of Worldwatch Institute points out, an information-age economy cannot conceivably be powered by a primitive, industrial-age energy system (cited in Brown, 2001). Technological breakthroughs can already be identified. Advanced new technologies such as hydrogen fuel cells, film-thin solar cells applicable to facades and windows, and wind turbines with long-term energy storage capacity are being developed and could dramatically alter energy needs. The transition from fossil fuels to an energy economy based on wind, solar, and hydrogen power is taking hold (see Table 1). Moreover, energy restructuring is not only feasible, it could be economically profitable.[14]

Table 1   Trends in Energy Use, by Source, 1990-2000

Energy Source	Annual Growth Rate (percent)	
	1990–2000	2000
Wind power	25	32
Solar cells	20	43
Geothermal power	4	N/A
Hydroelectric power	2	N/A
Natural gas	2	2
Oil	1	1
Nuclear power	0.8	0.8
Coal	-1	-4

Source: Brown, Lester. 2001. *Eco-Economy: Building an Economy for the Earth*. New York: W. W. Norton, available from http://www.earth-policy.org/Books/Eco_contents.htm

---

[14] The United States, for example, could cut its annual energy bills by $300 billion by using existing, more energy efficient technologies (Hawken, Lovins, and Lovins, 1999: 243).

Technological progress is likely to play a key role in a transition toward sustainability. Technological innovation represents a double opportunity, offering prospects for improvement in both developed and developing countries. In the North, new technologies could be gradually introduced as capital stocks turn over. In the South, new, more energy efficient technologies would allow countries to bypass the carbon intensive growth typical of the North, and advance directly into cleaner energy matrices. However, new technologies often represent incremental costs and take time to develop and disseminate. Financing mechanisms for technology transfer from the North to the South would therefore be critical to meeting the rapidly growing energy needs of developing countries, while also facilitating their participation in global efforts to reduce greenhouse gas emissions.

New Ethical Imperative

The pace of progress will be determined by the most important shift that the international community still needs to make – a shift in values. As Speth argues in the opening chapter of this volume, we now find ourselves in a radically different ethical position, one that demands "active management of the planet." We need to extend our value system over space, relinquish our self-centered attitudes, and think beyond the confines of our immediate surroundings. We need to give up our village behavior as we realize that our wellbeing has become intricately tied to the wellbeing of others. We need to also extend our value system over time and overcome our propensity for short-term thinking. Global environmental challenges require long-term commitment and investment. The effects of today's environmental degradation are likely to be experienced most intensely by future generations. At the end of our lives, we must return to our children the planet we have ultimately borrowed from them.

CONCLUSION

Climate change presents the ultimate challenge to global environmental governance. The inherently global nature of the problem mandates a truly global response. The atmosphere is indivisible and greenhouse gas concentrations have a global effect. However, the multiplicity of causes, uncertainty of timing and effects, and significant economic costs are strong deterrents of collective action. Moreover, vulnerability to climate change varies across regions, with the greatest negative impacts likely to be concentrated in the tropics and sub-tropics. While historical responsibility for climate change is undoubtedly lodged with the North, development trajectories are shifting this burden to the South. Climate change thus brings forth deep-seated North-South divisions that demand resolution. Historical fairness would have the North pay a large share of the initial climate change bill, but the existing international institutional arrangements have no authority to impose such a tab. Distributive justice entails an ability to pay approach, but even this version of fairness seems politically infeasible.

An innovative governance architecture is necessary to facilitate a leap from narrowly defined national interests to a global regime. Accurate, comprehensive, and reliable information can reveal preferences, confer negotiating power, and alter interests. Bargaining across issues holds the promise of reaching otherwise impossible agreements and directly addressing preferences for resource transfer or policy changes. A system of international mechanisms to promote changes in behavior across sectors and jurisdictions in an efficient and equitable manner will be critical to the success of a climate change regime.

Despite all the debate, the confrontations, and the frustration, we have begun to move in the right direction. The issue now is the pace at which we are moving. The longer we wait before taking serious action, the more difficult and costly it will be to mitigate global warming. Global governance, whether for climate change or for any of the myriad issues affecting the world as a whole, can only be built on the recognition of planetary interdependence. Anything short of that will keep us paralyzed while the planet's challenges grow far beyond our reach.

REFERENCES

Agarwal, Anil, and Sunita Narain. 1990. *Global Warming in an Unequal World: A Case of Environmental Colonialism.* New Delhi: Centre for Science and Environment.

Bertram, Geoff. 1992. "Tradeable Emission Permits and the Control of Greenhouse Gases." *Journal of Development Studies* 28 (3): 423-446.

BP. 2001. *BP Statistical Review of World Energy 2001.* London: Group Media & Publications. Available from http://www.bp.com/ downloads/702/BPwebglobal.pdf

Brown, Lester. 2001. *Eco-economy: Building an Economy for the Earth.* New York: W. W. Norton. Available from http://www.earth-policy.org/Books/Eco_contents.htm

Browne, John. 2002. *Beyond Petroleum. Business and the Environment in the 21st Century.* [cited June 4 2002]. Available from http://www.bp.com/centres/press/stanford/highlights/index.asp

Energy Information Administration. 2002. *International Energy Outlook 2002.* Washington, D.C.: United States Department of Energy. Available from http://www.eia.doe.gov/oiaf/ieo/index.html

EPA. 2000. *Green Dividends? The Relationship Between Firms' Environmental Performance and their Financial Performance.* Washington, D.C.: United States Environmental Protection Agency. Available from http://www.epa.gov/ocempage/nacept/green_dividends.pdf

Esty, Daniel C. 2002. "Why Measurement Matters." *In Environmental Performance Measurement: The Global Report 2001-2002.* edited by Daniel C. Esty and Peter R. Cornelius. New York: Oxford University Press.

Fischer, Gunther, Mahendra Shah, Harrij van Velthuizen, and Freddy O. Nachtergaele. 2001. *Global Agro-ecological Assessment for Agriculture in the 21st Century.* Laxenburg, Austria: International Institute for Applied Systems Analysis and Food and Agriculture Organization. Available from http://www.iiasa.ac.at/Research/ LUC/Papers/gaea.pdf

Gelbspan, Ross. 2001. "A Modest Proposal to Stop Global Warming." *Sierra Magazine,* May/June 2001: 62-67. Available from http://www.sierraclub.org/sierra/200105/globalwarm.asp

Grubb, Michael. 1990. *Energy Policies and the Greenhouse Effects: Volume 1*. London: Royal Institute of International Affairs.

Hawken, Paul, Amory Lovins, and Hunter Lovins. 1999. *Natural Capitalism: Creating the Next Industrial Revolution*. Boston: Little, Brown and Co.

IPCC. 2001a. *Climate Change 2001: The Scientific Basis*. Geneva, Switzerland: Intergovernmental Panel on Climate Change. Available from http://www.ipcc.ch/pub/tar/wg1/

_____. 2001b. *Climate Change 2001: Impacts, Adaptation and Vulnerability*. Geneva, Switzerland: Intergovernmental Panel on Climate Change. Available from http://www.ipcc.ch/pub/tar/wg2/

Jacoby, Henry D., Ronald G. Prinn, and Richard Schmalensee. 1998. "Kyoto's Unfinished Business." *Foreign Affairs* 77 (4): 54-66.

Johnson, T. M., J. Li, Z. Jiang, and R. P. Taylor. 1996. *China: Issues and Options in Greenhouse Gas Emissions Control*. Washington, D.C.: World Bank.

Mapes, Jennifer. 2001. "U.N. Scientists Warn of Catastrophic Climate Changes." *National Geographic News*, February 6, 2001. Available from http://news.nationalgeographic.com/news/2001/02/0206_climate1.html

Marland, G., T. A. Boden, and R. J. Andres. 2000. "Global, Regional, and National Fossil Fuel CO_2 Emissions." In *Trends: A Compendium of Data on Global Change*. Oak Ridge, TN: Oak Ridge National Laboratory, United States Department of Energy. Available from http://cdiac.esd.ornl.gov/trends/emis/em_cont.htm

Mendelsohn, Robert. 2001. *Global Warming and the American Economy: A Regional Assessment of Climate Change Impacts*. Northampton, MA: Edward Elgar.

Mendelsohn, Robert, and William Nordhaus. 1996. "The Impact of Global Warming on Agriculture: Reply." *The American Economic Review* 86 (5): 1312-1315.

Paterson, Matthew. 2001. "Principles of Justice in the Context of Global Climate Change." In *International Relations and Global Climate Change*, edited by Urs Luterbacher and Detlef F. Sprinz. Cambridge, MA: MIT Press.

Reid, Walter V., and Jose Goldemberg. 1997. *Are Developing Countries Already Doing as Much as Industrialized Countries to Slow Climate Change?* Washington, D.C.: World Resources Institute Climate Protection Initiative. Available from http://www.wri.org/wri/ cpi/notes/devcntry.html

Reuters. 2002. "Global Warming Would Help Many U.S. Crops – EPA Report." *Reuters,* June 3, 2002.

Schelling, Thomas C. 2002. "What Makes Greenhouse Sense?" *Foreign Affairs* 81 (3): 2-9.

Sprinz, Detlef F., and Martin Weiß. 2001. "Domestic Politics and Global Climate Policy." In *International Relations and Global Climate Change,* edited by Urs Luterbacher and Detlef F. Sprinz. Cambridge, MA: MIT Press.

UNEP. 2002. *Global Environment Outlook 3.* Nairobi, Kenya: United Nations Environment Programme. Available from http://www.grid. unep.ch/geo/geo3/index.htm

UNFCCC. 1992. *United Nations Framework Convention on Climate Change.* New York: United Nations. Available from http://unfccc.int/resource/conv/index.html

UNFPA. 2001. *The State of World Population 2001.* New York: United Nations Population Fund. Available from http://www.unfpa. org/swp/swpmain.htm

Wiegandt, Ellen. 2001. "Climate Change, Equity, and International Negotiations." *In International Relations and Global Climate Change,* edited by Urs Luterbacher and Detlef F. Sprinz. Cambridge, MA: MIT Press.

World Bank. 2002. *World Development Indicators 2002.* Washington, D.C.: World Bank.

The Road Ahead:
Conclusions and Action Agenda

Daniel C. Esty and Maria H. Ivanova

We live in a time of contrasts. Ours is an era of fast-paced change and yet persistent problems. More people are wealthier than ever before in history – and yet billions remain desperately poor. News travels in an instant across the planet – and yet old beliefs, values, and prejudices only slowly change. New actors from multinational corporations to non-governmental organizations are playing an increasingly central role on the global stage – and yet, nation-states continue to be the dominant mode of political organization. Transformative technologies, such as the internet, bind us together ever more tightly – and yet old divides remain deep, and new ones seem to be emerging. On one level, the lines between "us" and "them" appear to be more sharply etched than ever. But on other levels, past distinctions have blurred. What is clear is that success in achieving old goals – such as providing opportunities for lives of peace and prosperity, liberty and happiness – will require fresh thinking, refined strategies, and new mechanisms for cooperation.

Recent events have clearly revealed the interdependence of the nations and peoples of the world. Security issues have been in focus but interdependence extends beyond these concerns. Economic integration has demonstrated that some global-scale forces are beyond the capacity of national governments to regulate and control. Simultaneously, we are becoming ever more aware of our ecological interdependence. From shared natural resources such as fisheries and biological diversity to the potential for transboundary pollution spillovers across the land, over water, and through the air, we now understand that the traditional notion of national territorial sovereignty cannot protect us from global-scale environmental threats.

This volume seeks to address the environmental dimension of interdependence. It highlights a set of issues that make the present different from the past and promise to make the future dramatically more dissimilar. The environmental challenges and other problems of sustainability we now face are not all new, but the scope and scale of the threat they pose are unprecedented.

The need to coordinate pollution control and natural resource management policies – across the diversity of countries and peoples, political perspectives and traditions, levels of wealth and development, beliefs and priorities – may seem awkward. But, however uncomfortable, there really is no choice. Ecological interdependence is now an inescapable fact. Moreover, the rapid pace of economic integration has led to interlinked world markets and economies, demanding synchronization of national policies on a number of issues. One dimension of this coordination concerns the environment.

Given the global-scale issues and linkages highlighted in this volume, it is imperative that we manage our ecological interdependence and related economic relationships thoughtfully, explicitly, and effectively. Four basic "governance" options can be distinguished:

- Do nothing;

- Refine the status quo governance structure;

- Launch a new Global Environmental Organization;

- Develop a new governance approach: a Global Environmental Mechanism.

Do Nothing

If the harms that a global environmental regime would address were not serious, there would be a logic to a "do nothing" approach. As economists (Demsetz, 1967; Libecap, 1989), lawyers (Krier, 1974; Rose, 1991), political scientists (Haas, Keohane, and Levy, 1993) and environmental analysts (Esty and Mendelsohn, 1998) have demonstrated, unless the benefits of action justify the costs, the investment in coordination and governance cannot be justified. Organizing a response to a problem demands resources. "Collective action" at the global scale is especially complicated and expensive. Thus, simply put, if the costs of organizing for action are greater than the benefits anticipated, doing nothing makes sense.

Cost-benefit calculations represent an essential starting point in deciding whether to have a global environmental regime and what sort of governance structure to create. But undergirding this analysis must be good data on the environmental problem set and the costs and benefits of taking action. All too often, however, economic costs have been easier to measure and benefits difficult to quantify, leading to "justified" inaction. We thus need refined economic models that more fully account for the ecological services on which the economy – and humanity's existence – depend (see Hales and Prescott-Allen, and Figueres and Ivanova, this volume, calling for a more rigorous approach to environmental valuation). Carefully gathered, rigorously scrutinized, and thoroughly peer-reviewed information on the types of threats to which we are exposed, the risks they pose, the degree of harm threatened, and the value of the damage that might be inflicted must therefore underpin any governance debate.

As demonstrated by Speth and others throughout this volume, and elsewhere in the literature (Haas, Keohane, and Levy, 1993; Hempel, 1996; Vogler, 2000; Vig and Kraft, 2000), the evidence suggests both that investment in global scale environmental protection makes sense and that the current approach is not delivering good results. The question is not *whether* to design a structure of global environmental governance, but *how*. Therefore, we turn to a set of reform options.

Refine the Status Quo

A number of commentators (Juma, 2000; von Moltke, 2001a; Najam, 2002, forthcoming) believe that the most feasible way to improve global environmental results is to revitalize the existing regime centered on the UN Environment Programme (UNEP). They argue that what is missing is political will and claim that we have never tried to make the current system work. Thus, their reform package focuses on giving UNEP a sharper mandate, bolstering its funding, and developing better coordination across UN bodies.

On a practical level, those who favor a refined status quo generally fear that any broader gauge reform effort will fall flat politically. They emphasize the difficulty of carrying out fundamental changes within the UN system and point to the likely bureaucratic obstruction and fierce turf battles that would be triggered by any program of wholesale restructuring. Others say that energies put into revolutionizing the global environmental regime are misplaced. The priority, they suggest, should be strengthening national level environmental capacity.

Some proponents of a refine-the-status-quo strategy also argue that proposals to consolidate global-scale environmental responsibilities might diminish the effectiveness of the system. They note that the range of problems that must be addressed is diverse, making a decentralized structure of multiple international organizations and individual treaty secretariats a virtue. Other reformers have argued for a "clustering" of the various pieces of the existing environmental regime so as to improve policy coherence, tighten potential cross-issue linkages, and avoid the duplication of effort that comes from full decentralization (von Moltke, 2001b; UNEP, 2001a, 2001b).

Launch a Global Environmental Organization

Proposals for major structural reform derive from the conclusion that the existing global-scale environmental architecture is deeply dysfunctional and structurally flawed, making a fresh start easier than reform along the margins. A number of leading politicians (Ruggiero, 1998; Chirac, 2001; Gorbachev, 2001; Panitchpakdi, 2001), academics (Runge, 1994, 2001; Esty, 1994a, 1994b; Biermann, 2000; Schellnhuber et al., 2000; Whalley and Zissimos, 2001) and others (Charnovitz, 2002; Zedillo Commission, 2001) have come to this conclusion. Beyond the difficulties of trying to fix a failed structure, those arguing for a new approach often note that the existing regime was designed for a pre-globalization era, before the full spectrum of worldwide environmental problems was understood and the depth of current economic integration was achieved.

The substantive case for a major overhaul of the environmental regime builds on a number of arguments: (1) the "public goods" logic, which suggests that collective action must be organized at the scale of the problem to be addressed (Olson, 1971), combined with the recognition that some problems arise at a worldwide scale, making national level responses inadequate; (2) the potential to overcome the fragmentation of the current structure, to obtain synergies in addressing problems, and to take advantage of opportunities for better issue prioritization, budget rationalization, and bureaucratic coordination; (3) the benefit of having a body that could serve as a counterpoint and a counterweight to the World Trade Organization, the World Bank, and the other international economic institutions, thus ensuring that environmental sensitivities are systematically built into the international economic regime; and (4) the practical value of having an authoritative international body with a first-rate staff, a reputation for analytic rigor, and the capacity to take on tasks such as dispute resolution.

Develop a New Governance Approach: A Global Environmental Mechanism

Another option for strengthening global environmental governance focuses on creating a structure that can deliver the *functions* needed at the global level. Such an approach acknowledges the diversity and dynamism of environmental problems and recognizes the need for specialized responses. Proponents of a Global Environmental Mechanism (GEM) argue that no bureaucratic structure can build an internal organization with the requisite knowledge and expertise to address the wide-ranging, dynamic, and interconnected problems we now face (GEM PAG, 2002; Esty and Ivanova, this volume). The issues demanding immediate attention arise on various geographic scales, requiring a multi-tier response structure (Esty, 1999). They demand capacities in multiple areas, including ecological sciences, public health, risk assessment, cost-benefit analysis, performance measurement, and policy evaluation. What is necessary is not only a multi-tier but also a multi-dimensional governance structure (Esty, 2003, forthcoming). Today's global environmental governance challenge thus requires a more virtual structure with a multi-institutional foundation capable of drawing in a wide array of underlying disciplines through governments, the private sector, NGOs, and global public policy networks.

As we argue in this volume, a Global Environmental Mechanism could emerge in various ways, driven by functional needs. Its core capacities might include: (1) provision of adequate information and analysis to characterize problems, track trends, and identify interests; (2) creation of a "policy space" for environmental negotiation and bargaining; and (3) sustained build up of capacity for addressing issues of agreed-upon concern and significance. A Global Environmental Mechanism could build upon the expertise of existing institutions and create new mechanisms where key functions were deemed to be nonexistent or inadequate. Initial elements might comprise a global information clearinghouse with mechanisms for data collection, assessment, monitoring, and analysis; a global technology clearinghouse with mechanisms for technology transfer and identification and dissemination of best practices; and a bargaining forum, along the lines proposed by Whalley and Zissimos in this volume, to facilitate deals that improve environmental quality and reconcile the interests of different parties.

While it would take time to weave the dense fabric of relationships across actors and institutions that is required for successful global environmental governance, the concept of a Global Environmental Mechanism would allow for the progressive growth of the regime. It could begin with "the art of the possible" and gradually assemble the elements of an effective institutional structure as issues and mechanisms are identified and developed, building on a core set of functions such as information provision and a mechanism for dissemination of policy and technology strategies. A Global Environmental Mechanism could expand into more ambitious domains such as bargaining, trade-offs, norm development, and dispute settlement as (and only if) the value of those activities is demonstrated. A Global Environmental Mechanism offers a new model of governance that is light, more virtual and networked, and potentially more entrepreneurial and efficient.

TOWARD EFFECTIVE ACTION

In deciding what route to take, careful thinking is needed about what is required from the international environmental regime. The chapters in this volume identify a number of critical roles and functions in a global environmental governance system:

- Problem identification and definition;

- Analysis and option evaluation;

- Policy discussion and coordination;

- Financing and support for action;

- Outreach and legitimacy.

Problem Identification and Definition

Understanding the range of pollution control and natural resource management issues the world community faces requires good data and information. As Hales and Prescott-Allen demonstrate in their chapter, the foundations for effective decisionmaking in the international environmental and sustainable development realm do not exist. With a better picture of the problem set and issue trends, the logic of collective action at the global scale would be clearer and the specific institutional needs might come into sharper focus. Such clarity would help to define the challenge, furnish us with a compass and a roadmap, and make it easier to identify the best path forward.

Analysis and Option Evaluation

Progress depends on more than data. Once a problem is identified, it must be studied so that the risks it poses are understood and the costs and benefits of action or inaction can be calculated. Given the range of issues that must be addressed and the variety of circumstances under which these issues arise, those responding to international environmental challenges need access to significant analytic capacity. Without a global-scale policymaking apparatus, however, critical transboundary issues will likely be neglected (Dua and Esty, 1997). And as Karlsson argues in this volume, the high degree of uncertainty that exists in the environmental domain and the diversity of underlying values and assumptions means that the analytic process needs to draw on a wide range of perspectives.

Managing interdependence in the context of great diversity seems to call for an "open architecture" of decisionmaking that encourages data, information, risk assessments, cost-benefit analysis, policy options, and evaluations to be brought forward not just by governments, but by the business community, environmental groups, and others in civil society who can enrich the foundation on which decisions are made. In their chapter, Gemmill and Bamidele-Izu highlight some of the benefits of a more open and inclusive governance process. Streck's analysis in this volume explains, moreover, how global public policy networks can forge effective working arrangements across sectors and could be part of the answer to the complexity of international environmental problems and the diversity of perspectives that need to be considered.

Policy Discussion and Coordination

Successful intervention to address environmental challenges requires more than analysis; a course of policy action must be agreed upon and executed. Getting all of the relevant parties on board an action plan is never easy. Coordinating effective policies in the international sphere is especially difficult. There is, of course, no global legislature. Thus, one of the critical functions that a global environmental regime must serve is as a forum for dialogue. As Koh and Robinson stress in their analysis in this volume, the current consensus-driven approach to internalize problem solving has resulted in multiple political agreements, but has failed in implementation. What is needed is a mechanism for generating on-the-ground progress. Whalley and Zissimos, in their chapter, suggest a novel option: a "policy space" for sustained environmental interaction, negotiation, and bargaining. Such a forum might engage not only governments in trying to forge multi-country "deals" to address particular issues, but could also draw in the business community and other potential parties.

Financing and Support for Action

Real progress cannot be achieved without resources – and to date the commitments made in this regard have generally been regarded as inadequate. Another aspect of the global environmental regime that therefore demands attention is funding. The financial support required for action could come from a variety of sources: (1) increased government funding and development assistance; (2) a redirection of existing funding, perhaps through a "rechartering" of the World Bank and the UN Development Programme (UNDP); (3) increased economic growth and better channeling of private capital flows (including foreign direct investment (FDI) and national private sector investments); and (4) new commitments of resources from foundations, enlightened citizens, and social entrepreneurs. Given the magnitude of the challenge it seems likely that all of these strategies will need to be pursued. In this volume, Koch-Weser offers an innovative strategy for jump-starting this process through a Johannesburg Commission on Sustainable Development Finance.

Outreach and Legitimacy

A further challenge in the global governance arena emerges from the need for legitimacy. At the national level, governments are usually elected and thus derive authority and legitimacy from their "popular sovereignty." International decisionmaking inevitably involves officials whose claim to power does not derive directly from having won elections. Because they are somewhat removed from the majority-vote-based popular sovereignty, international organizations must make special efforts to ensure their legitimacy (Esty, 2002). They must build bridges to publics around the world, and explain their decision processes, drawing in views and guidance from the citizens of the world community on whose behalf they are meant to act. NGOs can play a useful role in this give-and-take. As Gemmill and Bamidele-Izu explain in their chapter, international organizations must also demonstrate their effectiveness and thus the value of their role as coordinators of worldwide action.

International bodies in general, and any global environmental regime in particular, must also be perceived as fair and equitable. Fairness encompasses both procedural and substantive elements. Procedural fairness requires access to decisionmaking on an equitable basis, with both a horizontal dimension – across governments and bridging the North-South divide – and a vertical dimension – providing individuals and groups as well as governments a chance to be heard. As Figueres and Ivanova suggest in this volume, substantive fairness demands that the polluter pays principle be enforced and the "ability to pay" be recognized in setting the course of international action and in deciding how the costs of intervention will be borne.

THE JOHANNESBURG OPPORTUNITY

As we hope this volume has demonstrated, there are many paths to progress in global environmental governance. The creation of a functioning and effective environmental regime will require years of work and refinement. But windows of opportunity to define the agenda and take major steps do not come around all that often. One exists in 2002: the World Summit on Sustainable Development in Johannesburg.

We urge the countries participating in the Johannesburg process to seize the opportunity and demonstrate a commitment to action with four concrete initiatives, addressing:

- Global environmental data and information;

- Financing for sustainable development;

- Technology promotion;

- Exploration of options for strengthening global environmental governance.

Global Environmental Data and Information

The weak foundations for global-scale environmental decisionmaking could be shored up with a modest commitment of resources to a new coordinated program of global environmental data gathering and information sharing. Building on existing efforts, such an initiative might focus on ensuring that a core set of baseline environmental indicators (covering air, water, and land) were tracked in every country in the world on a methodologically consistent and rigorous basis that would permit cross-country comparisons. Furthermore, individual countries or regional groupings might supplement the global data set with additional metrics addressing local priorities.

Information systems could reveal new policy options and lead to better decisionmaking, improved performance, and greater efficiency through reduced uncertainty, enhanced comparative analysis, and greater ability to define points of policy leverage. Data that are comparable across countries also facilitate benchmarking and the identification of best practices, creating both a spur to lagging jurisdictions and a guide for all. A more "measured" approach to environmental problem solving would not only enhance analysis and decisionmaking, it would make it easier to evaluate policy and program performance, track on-the-ground progress in addressing pollution control and natural resource management challenges, and identify successful (and unsuccessful) efforts and approaches.

Financing for Sustainable Development

Any commitment to enhanced global environmental efforts must come in the context of a "global bargain" that commits the world community to a more aggressive program of poverty alleviation. The Johannesburg process creates an opportunity for such a dual commitment with a major initiative to promote economic progress across the developing world. Such an initiative might include several elements: (1) an expanded emphasis on phasing out trade barriers and broader commitments toward progress in the Doha Development Round; (2) a rechartering of the World Bank and UNDP to redouble their efforts to promote development in the poorest countries and to finance global public goods, including environmental programs; and (3) a new mechanism (or, at least, the launching of a process to create a new mechanism) to promote financing for sustainable development harnessing government, business, foundation, and individual resources.

Technology Promotion

"Technology transfer" has become a buzzword. But too little has been done to translate the concept into action. A step forward could be taken by launching a technology initiative that would seek to make use of Information Age breakthroughs to resolve international environmental challenges. Beginning perhaps as a technology clearinghouse, such a facility might ultimately provide a mechanism for North-South cooperation and for creating incentives for the private sector to develop technologies in response to needs in both developing and developed countries. Engaging leading information technology companies in this initiative would be useful – and could be seen as part of a strategy to bridge the "digital divide."

Exploration of Options for Strengthening Global Environmental Governance

To give momentum to the process of exploring options for strengthened global environmental governance within the context of the Johannesburg process, a Commission could be launched to identify and evaluate the world community's needs in the international environmental realm and various ways of addressing these needs. Comprised of eminent persons from the North and the

South, including a number of environmental ministers as well as distinguished business leaders, academics, and non-governmental organization officials, the Commission could be given a mandate to report back within eighteen months with an evaluation of the options and a recommended blueprint for action.

THE ROAD AHEAD

We have entered a new era of public policy, defined by a growing number of concerns that straddle national borders and transcend national interests. Global environmental challenges represent an issue set on which collective action is critical and through which experience could be gained on how best to build broader mechanisms for international cooperation. Narrow, unstructured government-to-government approaches are no longer sufficient. The global problems we currently face will yield only to a carefully targeted, sustained, and coordinated effort involving novel coalitions of actors and innovative institutional arrangements.

As Speth emphasizes in the opening chapter of this volume, the goals and principles of global environmental governance have been elaborated over the past two decades, and "it is clearly time to launch a second phase moving us from talk to action." With this volume, we hope to contribute to the unfolding debate on concrete options and opportunities for strengthening global environmental governance.

REFERENCES

Biermann, Frank. 2000. "The Case for a World Environment Organization." *Environment* 42 (9): 22.

Charnovitz, Steve. 2002. "A World Environment Organization." *Columbia Journal of Environmental Law*, forthcoming.

Chirac, Jacques. 2001. "Jacques Chirac s'empare de l'écologie." *Le Monde*, May 5, 2001: 6.

Demsetz, Harold. 1967. "Toward a Theory of Property Rights." *American Economic Review* 57 (2): 347-359.

Dua, Andre, and Daniel C. Esty. 1997. *Sustaining the Asian Pacific Miracle: Economic Integration and Environmental Protection.* Washington, D.C.: Institute for International Economics.

Esty, Daniel C. 1994a. *Greening the GATT: Trade, Environment, and the Future.* Washington, D.C.: Institute for International Economics.

_____. 1994b. "The Case for a Global Environmental Organization." In *Managing the World Economy: Fifty Years After Bretton Woods.* Edited by Peter Kenen. Washington, D.C.: Institute for International Economics.

_____. 1999. "Toward Optional Environmental Governance." *New York University Law Review* 74(6): 1495-1574.

_____. 2002. "The World Trade Organization's Legitimacy Crisis." *World Trade Review* 1 (1): 7-22.

_____. 2003, forthcoming. "Strenghtening the International Environmental Regime: A Transatlantic Perspective." In *Dispute Prevention and Dispute Settlement in the Transatlantic Partnership*, edited by E. U. Petersmann and Mark Pollack. New York: Oxford University Press.

Esty, Daniel C., and Robert Mendelsohn. 1998. "Moving from National to International Environmental Policy." *Policy Sciences* 31 (3): 225-235.

GEM PAG. 2002. *In Search of Global Fairness: The Promise of a Revitilized Global Environmental Governance System.* Global Environmental Mechanism Policy Action Group (GEM PAG) of the Yale Center for Environmental Law and Policy, Globus – Institute for Globalization and Sustainable Development, and the Commission on Globalization. Available from http://www.yale.edu/gegdialogue

Gorbachev, Mikhail. 2001. "The American and Russian People Don't Want a New Confrontation." *Newsweek,* April 27.

Haas, Peter M., Robert O. Keohane, and Marc A. Levy. 1993. *Institutions for the Earth: Sources of Effective International Environmental Protection.* Cambridge, MA: MIT Press.

Hempel, Lamont. 1996. *Environmental Governance: The Global Challenge.* Washington, D.C.: Island Press.

Juma, Calestous. 2000. "The Perils of Centralizing Global Environmental Governance." *Environment Matters* 6 (12): 13-15.

Krier, James. 1974. "Commentary: The Irrational National Air Quality Standards: Macro and Micro Mistakes." *UCLA Law Review* 22.

Libecap, Gary D. 1989. *Contracting for Property Rights.* New York: Cambridge University Press.

Najam, Adil. 2002, forthcoming. "The Case Against GEO, WEO, or Whatever-else-EO." In *Global Environmental Institutions: Perspectives on Reform.* Edited by Duncan Brack and Joy Hyvarinen. London: Royal Institute of International Affairs.

Olson, Mancur. 1971. *The Logic of Collective Action, Public Goods and the Theory of Groups.* Cambridge, MA: Harvard University Press.

Panitchpakdi, H.E. Dr. Supachai, and Dean Michael Young. 2001. "Keynote Address: The Evolving Multilateral Trade System in the New Millennium." *George Washington International Law Review* 33(3): 419-443.

Rose, Carol M. 1991. "Rethinking Environmental Controls: Management Strategies for Common Resources." *Duke Law Journal* 1991 (1): 1-38.

Ruggiero, Renato. 1998. *A Global System for the Next Fifty Years, Address to the Royal Institute of International Affairs.* London: Royal Institute of International Affairs.

Runge, C. Ford. 1994. *Freer Trade, Protected Environment: Balancing Trade Liberalization and Environmental Interests.* New York: Council on Foreign Relations Press.

_____. 2001. "A Global Environmental Organization (GEO) and the World Trading System." *Journal of World Trade* 35 (4): 399-426.

Schellnhuber, H.-J., J. Kokott, F. O. Beese, K. Fraedrich, P. Klemmer, L. Kruse-Grauman, C. Neumann, O. Renn, E.-D. Schulze, M. Tilzer, P. Velsinger, and H. Zimmermann. 2000. *World in Transition 2: New Structures for Global Environment Policy.* Bremerhaven, Germany: German Advisory Council on Global Change (WBGU). Available from http://www.wbgu.de/wbgu_jg2000_engl.pdf

UNEP. 2001a. *Improving International Environmental Governance Among Multilareral Environmental Agreements: Negotiable Terms for Further Discussion: A Policy Paper.* UNEP/IGM/2/4. Nairobi, Kenya: United Nations Environment Programme. Available from http://www.unep.org/ieg/docs/K0135338.doc

_____. 2001b. *Proposal for a Systematic Approach to Coordination of Multilateral Environmental Agreements.* UNEP/IGM/2/5. Nairobi, Kenya: United Nations Environment Programme. Available from http://www.unep.org/ieg/docs/K0135344.doc

Vig, Norman J., and Michael E. Kraft. 2000. *Environmental Policy: New Directions for the Twenty-First Century.* Washington, D.C.: CQ Press.

Vogler, John. 2000. *The Global Commons: Environmental and Technological Governance.* New York: J. Wiley & Sons.

von Moltke, Konrad. 2001a. "The Organization of the Impossible." *Global Environmental Politics* 1 (1).

_____. 2001b. *Whither MEAs? The Role of International Environmental Management in the Trade and the Environment Agenda.* Winnipeg, Canada: International Institute for Sustainable Development. Available from http://www.iisd.org/pdf/trade_ whither_meas.pdf

Whalley, John, and Ben Zissimos. 2001. "What Could a World Environmental Organization Do?" *Global Environmental Politics* 1 (1): 29-34.

Zedillo Commission. 2001. *Report of the High-Level Panel on Financing for Development on Financing for Development.* New York: United Nations. Available from http://www.un.org/reports/financing/index.html

Contributors

Abimbola Bamidele-Izu is a partner in the law firm of Balogun, Bamidele & Co. in Lagos, Nigeria. She has consulted for the Nigerian government and corporate firms on policy development, evaluation, and implementation related to trade, environment, and intellectual property. She is an associate and fellow of Leadership for Environment and Development International (LEAD) and has received awards from the International Federation of Women Lawyers and the Foreign and Commonwealth Office of the UK.

bamidele@hyperia.com
http://www.balogunbamidele.com/

Daniel C. Esty holds faculty appointments at both the School of Forestry & Environmental Studies and the Law School at Yale University. He is also the Director of the Yale Center for Environmental Law and Policy and of the recently launched Yale World Fellows Program. He is the author or editor of eight books and numerous articles on environmental policy issues and the relationships between the environment and trade, security, competitiveness, international institutions, and development. He has served in a variety of positions at the U.S. Environmental Protection Agency, including Special Assistant to the EPA Administrator, Deputy Chief of Staff of the Agency and Deputy Assistant Administrator for Policy. Prior to moving to Yale, he was a senior fellow at the Institute for International Economics in Washington.

daniel.esty@yale.edu
http://www.yale.edu/envirocenter/

Christiana Figueres is the founder and Executive Director of the Center for Sustainable Development in the Americas. A native of Costa Rica, she is active in global environmental policy and in efforts to build in-country capacity to mitigate global climate change in Latin America. Since 1995 she has been an official negotiator of the UN Framework Convention on Climate Change. In recognition of her international leadership, National Geographic and the Ford Motor Company named her Hero for the Planet in March 2001. She has served as Director of the Latin American and Caribbean Region for the United States Export Council on Renewable Energy and has over twenty years experience with the Costa Rican government, the United Nations Development Programme, and as an independent consultant in organizational development.

christiana@csdanet.org
http://www.csdanet.org/

Barbara Gemmill is the Executive Director of Environment Liaison Centre International (ELCI), an international non-governmental organization established in 1974 as a civil society link to the United Nations Environment Programme. She is also Honorary Senior Lecturer on the Faculty of Botany at the University of Nairobi. Through her work at ELCI, she has been involved in several projects related to international environmental conventions, such as developing a guide incorporating agrobiodiversity concerns into national planning for the Convention on Biological Diversity. ELCI is presently one of three organizations coordinating NGO input into the World Summit on Sustainable Development in Johannesburg.

barbarag@elci.org
http://www.elci.org/

David Hales is President of DFH Global, an independent consulting firm. From 1994 to 2001, he served as Deputy Assistant Administrator and Director of the Global Environmental Center at USAID, where he led the development and implementation of climate change, biodiversity, environment and natural resource, and urban programs for more than 80 countries. He also led U.S. delegations to the World Water Summit and to the City Summit, and represented the United States at Conferences of Parties of the Framework Convention on Climate Change and the Convention on Biological Diversity. He served as Deputy Assistant Secretary of Interior for Fish and Wildlife and National Parks during the Carter administration, and was Director of the Michigan Department of Natural Resources.

DFHales@aol.com

Maria H. Ivanova is the Director of the Global Environmental Governance Project at the Yale Center for Environmental Law and Policy. Her work focuses on international institutions and organizations, environmental policy at the national and global levels, and equity concerns. A Bulgarian national, she is currently a doctoral candidate at the Yale School of Forestry & Environmental Studies. She has worked at the Environment Directorate of the Organisation for Economic Co-operation and Development (OECD) and the Swedish Environmental Protection Agency on environmental regulatory reform and water quality standards in the New Independent States of the Former Soviet Union.

maria.ivanova@yale.edu
http://www.yale.edu/gegdialogue/

Sylvia Karlsson is an International Science Project Coordinator at the International Human Dimensions Programme on Global Environmental Change (IHDP) in Bonn, Germany. She has worked at the Economic Development Institute of the World Bank and UNEP Chemicals Unit. Her research has focused on cross-level environmental governance, and resulted in her published Ph.D. thesis, Multilayered Governance – Pesticides in the South – Environmental Concerns in a Globalised World (2000). She participated in the NGO-Forum of the Rio Conference, served in the Danish Task Force for the Baha'i participation in the World Summit for Social Development (1994-95), and is following the Rio+10 process for the International Environment Forum.

skarlsson@giub.uni-bonn.de
http://www.ihdp.uni-bonn.de/
http://www.bcca.org/ief

Maritta R.v.B. Koch-Weser is founder and President of Earth3000, a non-profit organization promoting environmental security and long term systemic improvements in local, national, and global environmental governance. She is also head of the Centennial Group's Social and Environmental practice. Prior to founding Earth3000, she was Director General of IUCN – The World Conservation Union. Previously, she worked at the World Bank as Director for Environmentally and Socially Sustainable Development for the Latin

America and Caribbean region, Chief of the Asia Environment and Natural Resources Management Division, and Chief of the Environmental Assessments & Programs Division of the Environment Department.

mkochweser@earth3000.org
mkochweser@centennial-group.com
http://www.earth3000.org/
http://www.centennial-group.com

Koh Kheng Lian is a director and founding member of the Asia-Pacific Centre for Environmental Law at the National University of Singapore. She is Vice Chair for South and East Asia of the IUCN Commission on Environmental Law, and a member of its Steering Committee. She has co-chaired several World Bank Institute/ Singapore Ministry of Foreign Affairs seminars on Urban Industrial Environmental Management in Asia, and was a consultant for the Asian Development Bank. She is one of three editors of Capacity Building for Environmental Law in the Asia-Pacific Region: Approaches and Resources (Craig, Robinson and Koh, eds., ADB:2002), and has written articles on environmental law.

lawkohkl@nus.edu.sg
http://law.nus.edu.sg/

Robert Prescott-Allen has been a consultant on sustainable development for twenty years. He is the author of The Wellbeing of Nations (2001) and coauthor of Caring for the Earth: a Strategy for Sustainable Living (1991), The First Resource: Wild Species in the North American Economy (1986), World Conservation Strategy (1980), and Blueprint for Survival (1972). He is the inventor of the Barometer of Sustainability and principal developer of the Wellbeing Assessment method. Since 1993 he has designed and advised on sustainability assessments and provided assessment training in the Americas, Africa, and Asia, working with the United Nations, governments, environment and development organizations, communities, and industry. He is currently Executive Director of British Columbia's Coast Information Team and a coordinating lead author on indicators for the Millennium Ecosystem Assessment.

rpa@padata.com

Nicholas A. Robinson is the Gilbert & Sarah Kerlin Distinguished Professor of Environmental Law and Co-Director of the Center for Environmental Legal Studies at the Pace University School of Law. He has practiced environmental law in law firms, for municipalities, and as general counsel of the New York State Department of Environmental Conservation. He served as the first chairman of the statutory Freshwater Wetlands Appeals Board and Greenway Heritage Conservancy for the Hudson River Valley in New York. He is currently legal advisor and chairman of IUCN's Commission on Environmental Law. He founded Pace University's environmental law program, edited the proceedings of the 1992 United Nations Earth Summit in Rio de Janeiro, and is author of several books and numerous articles.

nrobinson@GENESIS.Law.Pace.Edu
http://www.law.pace.edu/

James Gustave Speth is Dean of the Yale School of Forestry & Environmental Studies. Most recently, he served as Administrator of the United Nations Development Programme and chair of the UN Development Group. He was founder and President of the World Resources Institute, professor of law at Georgetown University, chairman of the U.S. Council on Environmental Quality, and senior attorney and cofounder of the Natural Resources Defense Council. Throughout his career, he has provided leadership and entrepreneurial initiatives to many environmental task forces and committees, including the President's Task Force on Global Resources and Environment and the Western Hemisphere Dialogue on Environment and Development. In 2002, he was awarded the Blue Planet Prize for major contributions to global environmental conservation.

gus.speth@yale.edu
http://www.yale.edu/environment

Charlotte Streck is Counsel for International and Environmental Law with the World Bank. Before she joined the World Bank in 2000, she cooperated with the Global Public Policy Project, which provided strategic advice for the Secretary-General of the United Nations. For six years, she was a legal consultant for German state and federal administrations on compliance and enforcement issues. She has also collaborated with universities, private companies, law firms, and non-governmental organizations on research projects on international, European, and German environmental law and policy. She is a founding member of the Global Public Policy Institute and has authored and co-authored two books and several articles on environmental law and policy.

cstreck@worldbank.org
http://www.worldbank.org/

Strobe Talbott was the first Director of the Yale Center for the Study of Globalization (2001-02). He served in the U.S. State Department from 1993 to 2001, including seven years as Deputy Secretary of State. Prior to this, he was a journalist for Time magazine for 21 years. His most recent books include The Russia Hand: A Memoir of Presidential Diplomacy and The Age of Terror: America & the World after September 11 (co-edited with Nayan Chanda). He has served as a fellow of the Yale Corporation, a trustee of the Hotchkiss School, a director of the Carnegie Endowment for International Peace and the Council on Foreign Relations, and a member of the Aspen Strategy Group and the Trilateral Commission. Since leaving government, he has rejoined the Carnegie Board and the Trilateral Commission. He became President of the Brookings Institution in July 2002.

stalbott@brookings.org

John Whalley is Professor of Economics at both the University of Warwick, UK and the University of Western Ontario, Canada. At Warwick, he is Co-Director of the Centre for the Study of Globalisation and Regionalisation and at Western Ontario, he is Co-Director of the Centre for the Study of International Economic Relations. He is a Fellow of the Royal Society of Canada and of the Econometric Society, a Research Associate of the National Bureau of Economic Research, in Cambridge, Massachusetts, and the joint managing editor of the journal The World Economy. He has published widely, and is best known for his contributions to applied general equilibrium analysis, and trade and tax policy. In recent years he has worked on environmental issues, producing one of the earliest and most widely cited studies (jointly with Randy Wigle) on carbon taxes.

J.Whalley@warwick.ac.uk
http://www.warwick.ac.uk/
http://www.uwo.ca/

Ben Zissimos is a Research Officer in the Warwick Centre for Public Economics and an Associate of the Centre for the Study of Globalisation and Regionalisation at the University of Warwick. His research interests cover questions of international policy conflict and cooperation, examining the implications of tax competition and issues related to the formation of environmental and trade agreements. He has published on the strategy and efficiency implications of tax competition, permit trading under environmental agreements, a possible role for a World Environmental Organization, and trade block formation under the World Trade Organization.

b.c.zissimos@warwick.ac.uk
http://www.warwick.ac.uk/~ecsfg/

Index

Aarhus Convention, 82, 95
Access to markets. *See* Market Access
Accountability, 32, 38, 48-49, 85, 93, 128, 130, 147-148
Accounts, 38-39. *See also* System of National Accounts
Africa, 33-34, 54, 150, 209-210
Aid. *See* Development Assistance
Air pollution. *See* Pollution, Air
Agarwal, Anil, 58
Agenda 21, 32, 36, 79-80, 82, 92, 111, 141, 164, 196
Agenda-setting, 58, 77, 82, 90-91, 125, 198
Agriculture, 26, 56, 59-60, 69, 105, 107-108, 197, 209
Amnesty International, 158
Annan, Kofi, 150
Anti-globalization protests. *See* Globalization, Anti-globalization protests
Argentina, 33
ASEAN. *See* Association of Southeast Asian Nations
ASEAN Agreement on Transboundary Haze Pollution, 109
ASEAN Coordinating Centre for Transboundary Haze Pollution Control, 110
ASEAN Regional Centre for Biodiversity Conservation, 105, 107-108, 110
Asia, 34, 104, 210
Assessment, 31, 37, 45, 47-49, 55, 57, 60-62, 77-78, 83, 87, 93-95, 109, 184, 192, 196, 216
    Ecosystem assessment, 87, 89
    Environmental impact assessment, 112
    Performance assessment, 93
    Risk assessment, 229, 231
    Scientific assessment, 186, 191, 193-194
    See also Wellbeing Assessment
Association of Southeast Asian Nations (ASEAN), 101-118
    "ASEAN Way," 104, 107, 111, 113, 115, 117
    Organizational framework, 104-106
    Sustainability framework, 110
    History of, 102-103
    Limitations, 111, 113
    Strengths, 110-111
Atmosphere, 19, 165, 193, 205-206, 208, 211, 220
Axworthy, Lloyd, 91

Bargaining. *See* Dealmaking
Barriers to trade. *See* Trade, Barriers
Basel Convention on the Transboundary Movement of Hazardous Wastes and their Disposal, 106, 196
Belgium, 133

Bellagio Principles for Assessing Sustainable Development, 41
Best practices, 38, 63, 93, 115-116, 191, 194, 196, 217, 230, 234
Biodiversity. *See* Biological diversity
Biological diversity, 22, 32, 57, 86, 89, 101, 105-111, 115, 122, 130, 142-143, 163, 167, 169, 185, 193, 196, 218, 225, 242-243
Biotechnology, 85
BP, 24, 133, 213
Bratton, Michael, 79
Brazil, 172, 197, 210-212
Bretton Woods, 130-131, 157, 198
    See also World Bank; International Monetary Fund
British Petroleum. See BP
Brown, Lester, 18, 214, 219
Brundtland Commission/Brundtland Report, 18, 164
Brunei Darussalam, 103
Burma. *See* Myanmar (Burma)
Business community. *See* Private sector

Cairo Plan of Action. *See* United Nations Cairo Plan of Action
Caldwell, Keith, 19
Cambodia, 103, 110
Canada, 133
Capacity building, 49, 57, 64-65, 81, 93, 102, 106, 108, 110, 113, 117, 124, 151, 181, 196, 229
Carbon, 134, 213, 219-220. *See also* Climate change
    Carbon concentrations, 208, 212
    Carbon emissions, 61, 150, 167-168, 208, 211-212, 215, 218
    Emission trading, 133, 136
    Global carbon tax, 150, 155
    Sinks, 207, 209
Carson, Rachel, 16
Central Asia, 33
Certification, 25, 133-134, 152-153, 156-158
CFCs, 17, 19
China, 62, 106, 212
Chirac, Jacques, 164, 228
CITES. *See* Convention on International Trade in Endangered Species of Wild Flora and Fauna
Civil society, 32, 57, 67, 77-96, 121, 123-124, 128, 135, 144, 150-152, 156, 160, 193-194, 198, 231
    Definition, 79-80
    Major groups, 80
    Role in global governance, 78-83
    See also Non-governmental organizations
Clean Development Mechanism, 132-134, 174, 211, 217

Climate change, 18-19, 22, 37, 61, 105-106, 122, 134, 168, 174, 182, 188, 190, 205-221
  Abatement, 190, 196, 216-217
  Consequences, 56, 206, 209
  Responsibility for, 207-208, 221
  Vulnerability to, 209-210, 222
Coase, Ronald H., 166, 170-171
  Coasian deals, 166, 170
Collective action, 181-182, 189-191, 206, 221, 226, 228, 231, 236. *See also* Free riding
Commission on Sustainable Development (CSD), 23, 32, 48, 66, 80, 176, 183, 232
Community-based organizations, 92, 129
Compass of Sustainability, 40, 43
Compliance. *See* Enforcement
Consumption, 26, 35, 42, 47, 207-208, 212-213
Convention on Biodiversity. *See* Convention on Biological Diversity
Convention on Biological Diversity, 32, 86, 89, 108, 196
Convention to Combat Desertification, 32, 70
Convention on International Trade in Endangered Species of Wild Flora and Fauna, 84, 88. *See also* TRAFFIC
Convention on the Law of the Sea, 185
Convention on the Prior Informed Consent Procedure for Certain Hazardous Chemicals and Pesticides in International Trade, 59
Cooperation, 64, 78-79, 83, 101-106, 108-113, 115-118, 122, 126-127, 131, 137, 176, 179, 181, 184-185, 188-190, 196, 198, 205, 225, 235-236
Corporate responsibility, 154
Cost-benefit analysis, 229, 231
Crucible Group, 77, 85-86
CSD. *See* Commission on Sustainable Development

DaimlerChrysler, 213
Dashboard of Sustainability, 40, 43
Data. *See* Information
Dealmaking, 134, 163, 166, 169, 170-172, 174-178, 181, 191-194, 197, 199, 205, 208, 216-218, 221, 229, 230, 232
Debt relief, 146, 218
Decisionmaking, 31, 41, 45, 55, 60, 62, 67-71, 77, 82-83, 85, 87, 91, 95, 105, 107, 112-113, 125, 128, 185-186, 231, 233-234
Deforestation, 20, 35, 114, 172, 182, 208
Delors, Jacques, 150
Democracy, 34, 81, 130
Denmark, 26, 214
Desertification, 18, 20, 22, 209

Developing countries, 25, 34-35, 42, 54-57, 59-65, 71, 77, 92, 112, 130-135, 145-146, 169, 171, 175-179, 184, 186-186, 194-196, 206-208, 210-213, 217-218, 220
  Participation, 62-63, 96, 131-132, 150, 178, 187, 197, 215
  Priorities, 60, 94, 135, 178, 187, 197, 215
Development/underdevelopment, 11-12, 26, 36-38, 41, 44, 49, 54, 65, 67, 71, 82, 85, 103-106, 135, 141-142, 145-148, 151, 153, 158, 163, 169, 178-179, 186, 196, 209-210, 216, 218-219, 221, 226, 231, 234-235. *See also* Sustainable development
  Development assistance/aid, 22, 26, 57, 64, 142-143, 147, 187, 232
  Development indicators, 43
Dispute settlement, 95, 113, 115-117, 174, 185, 191, 194, 230
Dow Jones Sustainability Index, 214
Dunn, Seth, 219
DuPont, 24

Earth Day, 14-15, 19
Earth Summit. *See* United Nations Conference on Environment and Development
Eastern Europe, 33, 150
Eco-labeling, 114
Ecological Footprint, 40, 42
Economic growth, 26, 36, 215, 218, 232
Ecosystems, 35, 42, 44, 54-55, 60, 71, 102, 112, 147, 218
ECOSOC. *See* United Nations Economic and Social Council
Education, 12, 36, 38, 42-45, 64, 66, 108, 112-113, 146, 158, 193, 197, 210, 217
Effectiveness, 49, 78, 105, 111, 123, 126, 128-129, 131, 133, 146-148, 159, 187, 191, 228, 233
Emissions. *See* Carbon emissions
Energy, 38, 42, 105, 208, 212-214, 217, 219-220
  Renewable energy, 24, 26, 153
  Energy consumption, 208-209, 213-214
Enforcement, 23, 108, 110, 124, 164, 187
  Contract enforcement, 169, 173, 197
Environment and Natural Resources Information Network, 186
Environmental Defense Fund, 14
Environmental degradation/damage/deterioration, 10-11, 25, 27, 39, 58, 63, 113, 168, 179, 182, 208-209, 220
Environmental disputes. *See* Dispute settlement
Environmental institutions, 8-9, 24, 115, 176, 182, 185, 187, 198
Environmental groups, 231. *See also* Civil society; Non-governmental organizations
Environmental justice, 77-78, 95, 114, 144

Environmental law, 11, 13, 23, 176, 183-184
Environmental movement, 11, 14-16, 19
Environmental protection, 40, 79, 114, 121,
    153, 171, 178, 227
Environmental Protection Agency. *See*
    U.S. Environmental Protection Agency
Environmental standards, 105-106
Environmental Sustainability Index, 40,
    42, 55, 195
Environmental technologies. *See*
    Technology
Europe, 19, 33, 54, 107, 118, 150, 195, 209, 214
European Union, 106, 108, 212
Equity. *See* Justice
Exchange Facility. *See* Finance, Exchange
    Facility
Externalities, 164-166, 169, 179
    Internalization of externalities, 134, 164-
    167, 169, 171-172, 174-175, 179, 190-191, 193
    Super externalities, 190

Finance, 105, 141-160, 187, 235
    Commission on Sustainable
    Development Finance, 141, 148-150, 160,
    232
    Exchange Facility, 141, 150-158, 160
    Financial assistance (*see* Development
    assistance/aid)
    Financial institutions, 13, 82, 157, 182
    Financing mechanisms, 130, 141, 150,
    160, 187, 191, 194, 220
Finland, 133
First Raise Our Growth. *See* FROG
Fisheries, 19, 106, 116, 182, 187-188, 190, 225
Food, 58, 61, 217
    Food production, 34, 210
    Food security, 35, 106, 210
Food and Agriculture Organization
    (FAO), 183
Foreign direct investment, 232
Forests, 14, 18, 19, 23, 25, 32, 35, 38, 42, 60,
    105, 107-108, 142, 163, 168-171, 193, 207,
    209, 218. *See also* Deforestation
    Tropical forests, 18, 218
Forum, 81-82, 86, 136, 182, 185, 193, 199
    Negotiating and bargaining, for, 176,
    191-192, 194, 197, 216-217, 230, 232
Framework Convention on Climate
    Change. *See* United Nations Framework
    Convention on Climate Change
Free riding, 169, 171-172, 175, 206
FROG, 23-24

GATT. *See* General Agreement on Tariffs
    and Trade
GEOPolity, 23-24

General Motors, 24
Genetic engineering, 85
Genetic resources, 18, 85-86, 111, 143
Germany, 133, 172, 214
Gibbons, Jack, 27
Global commons. *See* Global public goods
Global Environment Facility (GEF), 65,
    121, 130-132, 143-144, 151, 183, 187
Global Environmental Governance
    Project, 5-8
Global Environmental Mechanism
    (GEM), 6, 8, 156, 181, 191-199, 226, 229-230
Global Environmental Organization, 24,
    150, 226, 228. *See also* World
    Environmental Organization
Global Environment Outlook, 87, 89
Globalization, 10, 71, 78, 124, 127, 206, 228
    Anti-globalization protests, 27
    Management of, 10
Global public goods, 155, 189, 191, 197, 205-
    206, 228, 235
Global Public Policy Networks, 121, 123-
    127, 134-137, 198, 229, 231
Global Water Partnership, 126
GM. *See* General Motors
Gorbachev, Mikhail, 164, 228
Governance, 9-10, 12, 36, 45, 78, 85-86, 123,
    125, 130-131, 137, 145, 215-218, 221, 226-
    227, 229
    Economic governance, 13 (*see also*
    Bretton Woods institutions)
    Environmental governance, 8-9, 11-14,
    23, 53, 56-57, 63-72, 77-79, 83, 87-89, 92-
    93, 95-96, 101-118, 121, 127, 129, 131, 134-
    135, 137, 141-142, 148, 181, 183, 188, 205,
    229-230, 233-236
    Functions, 191-192
    Global governance, 53, 57-58, 61-62, 77,
    80, 122-123, 206, 221, 233
    Good governance, 34, 49, 146-148
    Networked governance, 121, 197-198
    Role of non-state actors in global gov-
    ernance (*See* civil society)
Government sector. *See* Public sector
Green Power Market Development Group,
    24
Group of Seven (G-7), 81

Hanoi Plan of Action, 103
Hazardous waste. *See* Waste
Haze, 105-106, 109-110, 114-115
Home Depot, 24
Hong Kong, 33
Human Development Report, 40, 42
Human health, 19, 34, 55, 210
Human rights, 79, 81, 90, 136, 158

IBM, 24
Iceland, 212-213
Implementation. *See* Policy implementation
Index/indices, 38-40, 42-43, 45-46, 55, 195, 214
Indian Methane Campaign, 61
Indicators, 37, 45, 47-48, 63-64, 115, 168, 186, 191-193, 216-217, 234. *See also* Information
Indigenous peoples, 70, 80
Indonesia, 33, 102, 108, 114-115, 117, 195
Industrialized countries/OECD countries, 25, 54-55, 59, 131, 133-134, 169, 172-174, 176, 187, 207, 211-212
Industry, 15, 59, 80, 112, 129, 165, 195, 213-214, 217
Information, 23, 37-38, 40-49, 55, 60, 69, 83, 87, 102, 107, 109-110, 113, 115-116, 125, 132, 156, 159, 173, 176, 181, 191-193, 196-197, 205, 213, 216-217, 224, 227, 229-231, 234-235
    Access to/dissemination, 70, 78, 82, 85, 89, 116, 210
    Collection, 77-78, 116, 189-195
    Comparability, 217
    Gap, 183, 185-186, 194, 199
    Information clearinghouse, 195, 200, 229
    Information technology, 81, 181, 198, 235
Infrastructure, 55, 64, 66, 176, 210
Innovation. *See* Technological innovation
Intellectual property, 85-86, 197
Interdependence, 5, 9, 40, 81, 122, 127, 182, 199, 206-207, 221, 225-226, 231
Intergovernmental Panel on Climate Change (IPCC), 48, 56-57, 61-62, 207-209, 216-217
International Court of Justice (ICJ), 185
International Environmental Agreements. *See* Multilateral Environmental Agreements
International Finance Corporation (IFC), 158
International institutions, 23, 32, 43, 48, 53, 57, 62, 68-69, 77, 115, 122, 125-126, 130-132, 136, 146, 149-150, 152, 158, 181, 193, 198, 221, 228
International Labor Organization (ILO), 84, 91
International Maritime Organization (IMO), 183
International Monetary Fund (IMF), 81, 130, 145, 150, 179
International Union for the Conservation of Nature (IUCN). *See* IUCN-The World Conservation Union
Internet, 68, 125, 144, 159, 225
Investment, 31, 37, 47-49, 64, 68, 90, 95, 114, 130, 141, 143, 148, 157-159, 214, 220, 226-227, 232

IPCC. *See* Intergovernmental Panel on Climate Change
IUCN-The World Conservation Union, 17, 18, 20, 43, 84, 87-88, 109
Issue linkage, 178, 191, 205, 216-218, 228

Japan, 26, 38, 54, 106, 133, 209
Jazz, 23-25
Johannesburg Summit. *See* World Summit on Sustainable Development
Joint Implementation (JI), 132-134, 217
Jospin, Lionel, 164
Justice, 25, 35, 171, 189, 215, 221. *See also* Environmental justice

Knowledge, 9, 39, 44-45, 90, 93, 107-108, 113, 122, 124-126, 129, 135
    Knowledge divide, 53-72, 94
    Traditional knowledge, 70
Koh, Tommy Thong Bee, 114, 117
Kyoto Protocol, 32, 166, 168, 174, 196, 211-213
    Developing countries, and, 133, 211-212
    Flexible mechanisms, 121, 132-135, 217
    (*see also* Clean Development Mechanism, Joint Implementation, Prototype Carbon Fund)
    Targets, 211

Laos, 103
Legitimacy, 77, 83, 95-96, 124-125, 199, 230, 233
Leopold, Aldo, 12
Living Planet Index, 40, 42
Lose-lose outcome, 189-190
Lowes, 24

Malaysia, 102, 105, 116-117
Market access, 175, 193, 197, 218
Market signals, 26
Mexico, 36, 212
Millennium Declaration, 36, 48, 143
Millennium Ecosystem Assessment, 87, 89
Millennium Goals, 36, 146, 152
Molina, Mario, 17
Monitoring, 55, 66-67, 77-78, 81, 83, 88, 92-95, 106, 109, 112-113, 132, 153, 157-159, 186, 191-194, 230
Monterrey Conference, 143, 148, 150
Monterrey Consensus, 36, 48, 143
Montreal Protocol, 106, 185, 187, 196
Most favored nation treatment, 169
Multilateral Environmental Agreements (MEAs), 48, 59, 65, 89, 156, 196, 198
Myanmar (Burma), 103

Nader, Ralph, 16
National Academy of Sciences. *See* U.S.
    National Academy of Sciences
National Environmental Policy Act. *See*
    U.S. National Environmental Policy Act
National sovereignty. *See* Sovereignty
Natural disasters, 35, 146
Natural resources, 70, 92, 101, 107-109, 112,
    115, 186, 193, 209, 218, 225
Natural Resources Defense Council, 14
Negotiation, 13, 22, 25, 57, 62, 81-84, 89, 95,
    113, 115, 126-127, 130, 136, 165-166, 172,
    174, 177-179, 181, 184, 193, 197-198, 205,
    214, 217, 229, 232
Nelson, Gaylord, 15
The Netherlands, 133
Networks. *See* Global Public Policy
    Networks
New Zealand, 200
NGOs. *See* Non-governmental organiza-
    tions
Non-governmental organizations, 8-9, 13,
    32, 66, 70, 78-82, 85, 92, 116, 124, 151, 177,
    184, 225, 236
    Role in global governance, 13, 177, 225
    See also Civil society
Non-tariff barriers to trade. *See* Trade,
    barriers
North-South
    Axis, 209
    Divide, 53-54, 57, 62-64, 217, 221, 233
    Transactions, 174, 215
Northwest Atlantic Fisheries Convention,
    187
Norway, 133

ODA. *See* Development assistance
OECD. *See* Organisation for Economic
    Co-operation and Development
OECD countries. *See* Industrialized coun-
    tries
Official Development Assistance. *See*
    Development assistance
Organisation for Economic Co-operation
    and Development (OECD), 32, 174.
Ozone layer, 16, 189
    Depletion, 16, 17, 19, 122
    See also Montreal Protocol

Palmer, Geoffrey, 200
Panitchpakdi, Supachai, 164
Participation, 31, 34, 41, 47, 62-63, 69-70,
    77-87, 89, 91-92, 95-96, 105, 124-127, 130-
    131, 156, 184, 191-193, 196, 199, 211, 217, 220
Persistent organic pollutants (POPs), 19,
    130, 143, 188, 217-218
Pesticides, 19, 55, 59-60, 217

Philanthropists, 154
Philippines, 102, 105, 114
Pitsuwan, Surin, 114
Policy
    Implementation, 78, 95
    Reform, 141, 145-146, 148
Polluter pays principle. *See* Principles,
    Polluter pays principle
Pollution, 21, 26, 55, 105, 165, 171, 184, 189-
    190, 195, 214, 226, 231, 234
    Air, 14-15, 101, 107-110, 115, 165-166, 188, 225
    Water, 14, 19, 35, 37, 102, 112, 122, 182,
    190, 225
Population, 11-12, 15-16, 19, 25-26, 33-35, 41-
    42, 44, 55, 67, 84, 94, 165, 167, 172, 183,
    189, 207-208, 210
    See also Cairo Plan of Action
Poverty, 11, 25-26, 33-34, 36, 42, 48, 58, 63,
    79, 105, 142-143, 146-147, 150, 153, 178,
    200, 235
Precautionary principle. *See* Principles,
    Precautionary principle
Presidential Council on Environmental
    Quality, 14, 18
Principles
    Common but differentiated responsi-
    bilities, 104, 209, 215
    Polluter pays principle, 215, 233
    Precautionary principle, 68
    Principle 1 of the Rio Declaration, 33
    Principle 7 of the Rio Declaration, 209
    Principle 21 of the Stockholm
    Declaration, 114
Private sector, 14-16, 44, 67, 88, 95, 121, 124,
    126, 132-134, 141, 144, 148-149, 152, 155,
    158, 160, 167, 196, 205, 229, 231-232, 235
Production, 34, 54, 67, 87, 146, 157, 165-166,
    168-69, 209-210
PROPER disclosure scheme, 195
Property rights, 134, 166, 170-171, 176, 197
Prototype Carbon Fund, 133-134
Public participation. *See* Participation
Public sector, 123-124, 133, 136, 141, 148-149,
    151-153
Public-Private Partnerships, 147-148

Quotas, 187

Regulation, 59, 123, 205
    Regulatory means, 22
Religious community, 27, 79
Representation, 41, 83, 122, 199
Rio Conference/Rio Earth Summit. *See*
    United Nations Conference on
    Environment and Development
Rio Declaration, 33, 164-165, 209

Rotterdam Convention. *See* Convention on the Prior Informed Consent Procedure for Certain Hazardous Chemicals and Pesticides in International Trade
Rowland, Sherwood, 17
Rubin, Robert, 150
Ruggiero, Renato, 164, 228
Russia, 209

Sanctions, 48, 114, 188
Shareholder value, 141, 154
Special Drawing Rights (SDRs), 145, 150
Sanitary and Phytosanitary Agreement, 59
Santa Barbara oil spill, 16
Science, 16, 20-21, 54, 63-64, 67, 69-71, 90, 105, 166, 170, 182, 195, 229
    In agenda-setting, 56-58, 61-62
    Scientific uncertainty, 53, 68, 71, 205, 116, 221, 231, 234
    See also Knowledge
Shell, 24, 213
Shrimp-turtle case, 116
Sierra Club, 16
Singapore, 33, 102
South Africa, 31, 48
Southeast Asia, 104, 107-108
South Korea, 33, 212
Sovereignty, 21, 95, 113, 225, 233
Spain, 214
Status quo, 23, 188, 226-228
Stockholm Conference on the Human Environment. *See* United Nations Conference on the Human Environment
Stockholm Declaration, 114, 164
Strong, Maurice, 19
Subsidiarity, 125
Subsidies, 26, 143, 146, 212
Sustainability, 23, 25, 27, 31-33, 36, 40, 42-43, 45, 47-49, 55, 128, 141, 154, 164, 182, 195, 220, 226. *See also* Dow Jones Sustainability Index
Sustainable development, 25, 31, 33, 69, 79, 83, 102, 111-112, 128, 136
    Definition, 32, 67
    Goals, 37, 41, 82, 141-142
    Measurement, 38, 41, 43-44, 63
Sweden, 133
System of National Accounts, 38

Taiwan, 33
Tariffs, 163

Technology, 8-9, 26, 47, 54, 71, 81, 105, 148, 194-196, 199-200, 214, 216, 230, 234-235
    Clean technologies, 146, 157, 166, 168
    Technological innovation, 220
    Technology transfer, 32, 94, 112, 179, 187, 191-192, 194, 196, 215, 217, 220, 230, 235
Thailand, 33, 102, 114, 212, 214
Tobin tax, 145, 150, 155
Trade, 26, 39, 59, 85, 88, 89, 111, 143, 145, 155, 163, 169, 175, 182
    Barriers, 146, 172, 175, 235
    In toxic substances, 122
    In wildlife, 88
    Trade and environment debate, 106, 164, 179
    Trade liberalization, 113, 116-117, 163, 169
Tragedy of the commons, 189-190
Transparency, 38, 126, 128, 130-131, 146, 195
TRAFFIC, 77, 88-89, 92, 94
Type I Outcomes, 49

UNFCCC. *See* United Nations Framework Convention on Climate Change
United Kingdom, 62, 133
United Nations, 13, 38, 60, 79-82, 88, 104, 136, 183, 200
United Nations Cairo Plan of Action, 25, 84
United Nations Conference on Environment and Development (UNCED), 14, 32-33, 79, 81-82, 84, 113, 117, 130, 141-143, 182, 200, 209
United Nations Conference on the Human Environment (UNCHE), 14, 19-20, 81, 104, 182, 184
United Nations Development Programme (UNDP), 42, 130, 143, 150-151, 156, 183, 186, 194, 200, 232, 235
    Capacity 21 Program, 186
United Nations Economic Commission for Europe (UNECE), 82
United Nations Economic and Social Council (ECOSOC), 23, 84
United Nations Environment Programme (UNEP), 17-18, 20, 23, 65, 87, 130, 142-143, 164, 183-184, 186-188, 217, 227
United Nations Framework Convention on Climate Change (UNFCCC), 32, 48, 89, 132-133, 174, 185, 196, 212-213
United Nations General Assembly, 32, 147
United States, 19, 21, 54, 62, 116, 208-211, 213, 218-219
U.S. Environmental Protection Agency, 14, 61

Values, 38-39, 45, 47, 62-63, 68, 117, 128, 130, 205, 214, 220, 225, 231
Vietnam, 102-103, 110
Vietnam War, 15
Vitousek, Peter, 12

Waste, 112, 218
　Hazardous waste, 14, 16, 109, 112, 122, 168, 196
　Waste disposal, 188
Water, 35, 44, 130, 143, 167-168, 171, 190, 209, 225, 234
　Freshwater, 19-20, 42
　Pollution (see Pollution, Water)
　Resources, 19
Wellbeing Assessment, 40, 44-45
WHO. See World Health Organization
Women, 34-36, 80
World Bank, 33, 54, 129-131, 133, 143, 146-147, 150, 156, 179, 187, 194, 200, 211-212, 228, 232, 235
World Business Council for Sustainable Development (WBCSD), 23
World Commission on Dams, 90, 121, 128-129
World Conservation Union (IUCN). See IUCN-The World Conservation Union
World Court, 117
World Economic Forum, 32, 42, 195
World Environmental Organization (WEO), 24, 150, 163-179. See also Global Environmental Organization

World Health Organization (WHO), 126
　Roll Back Malaria Initiative of the World Health Organization, 126
World Meteorological Organization (WMO), 20, 183, 217
World Resources Institute (WRI), 20, 34, 87
World Summit on Sustainable Development (WSSD)/Johannesburg Summit, 5, 14, 31-32, 48-49, 84, 143-145, 148, 199, 233-235
World Trade Organization (WTO), 24, 59, 81, 91, 116, 150, 163-164, 169, 172, 175-176, 179, 185, 197, 228
World Wide Fund For Nature (WWF), 42, 88
Worldwatch Institute, 18, 219
WSSD. See World Summit on Sustainable Development

Yale Center for Environmental Law and Policy, 5-6, 8, 42
Yale Center for the Study of Globalization, 6, 9
Yale School of Forestry & Environmental Studies, 5, 7, 9

Zedillo Commission, 149-150, 155
Zedillo, Ernesto, 15

YCELP
YALE CENTER FOR ENVIRONMENTAL LAW & POLICY

Established in 1994 as a joint program of the Yale Law School and the Yale School of Forestry and Environmental Studies, the Yale Center for Environmental Law and Policy (YCELP) undertakes research, analysis, and policy development on a range of critical environmental topics. Drawing on the expertise of both Yale faculty and students, often in partnership with other environmental organizations, YCELP addresses issues at the local, regional, national, and global scales. Current YCELP priorities include projects on trade and environment in conjunction with the Global Environment and Trade Study (GETS), global environmental governance, environmental performance measurement, Information Age environmental protection, and Next Generation Environmental Policy.

http://www.yale.edu/envirocenter

Yale School of Forestry
& Environmental Studies

PUBLICATIONS

The Yale School of Forestry & Environmental Studies publishes books, monographs, conference proceedings, discussion papers, and other work by Yale faculty and students arising out of events of special environmental interest on the Yale campus, Yale courses, individual faculty projects, or in collaboration with other institutions. Recent publications include *Climate Change and Development*, a collaborative project with the UNDP Regional Bureau for Latin America and the Caribbean, and *Human Population and Freshwater Resources: U.S. Cases and International Perspectives*, a cooperative effort of the Center for Environment and Population, the National Wildlife Federation, the Population Resource Center, the Yale School of Forestry & Environmental Studies, and the Yale Institution for Social and Policy Studies. For a complete list of recent publications and order forms, please go to http://www.yale.edu/environment/publications. Copies of most publications are also available in downloadable PDF format for no charge at the website. Send orders to the following address or call 203.432.8980 for further information:

Yale F&ES Publications
205 Prospect Street
New Haven, CT 06511   USA